"*Winning Sounds Like This* is as charming as it is urgent and sometimes even heartbreaking. The Lady Bison occupy a whine-free space in which challenges are opportunities, miracles occur on a routine basis, and the routine is its own miracle. If I knew how to sign, this is what I would say: 'Read, cherish, and cheer.'"
—MADELEINE BLAIS, AUTHOR OF
IN THESE GIRLS, HOPE IS A MUSCLE

"Wayne Coffey has written a wonderful book. It's about hopes, dreams, basketball, winning, losing, deaf culture. Most of all it's about language. The language of the deaf. The language of basketball. The language of the heart. Read it, and you'll never forget it."
—BILL REYNOLDS, AUTHOR OF *FALL RIVER DREAMS*

"Rare is the sports journalist who hears his subjects, whether they speak or sign, as Wayne Coffey does. In *Winning Sounds Like This*, he takes us into the extraordinary environment in which Gallaudet's basketball team competes, and the result is a powerful human story. Coffey makes you wish Gallaudet's games were on ESPN."
—HARVEY ARATON, *NEW YORK TIMES* COLUMNIST
AND AUTHOR OF *ALIVE AND KICKING*

"In *Winning Sounds Like This*, Wayne Coffey tells the fascinating story of a special group of young women. He makes us root for their success on the court and truly care about what happens to them off of it. This is a unique book about a very unique team."
—REBECCA LOBO, NEW YORK LIBERTY

"Wayne Coffey has few peers when it comes to writing about basketball. That his subjects are female and deaf only adds to the beauty of this special book. Winning not only sounds like this, it reads like this."
—PETER GOLENBOCK, AUTHOR OF *THE LAST LAP* AND *AMAZIN'*

"*Winning Sounds Like This* is much more than a book about basketball. Coffey shows deep appreciation for deaf culture and its critical role in the lives of so many—especially the players about whom he writes. For deaf and hearing readers alike, this is a book that inspires from start to finish."
—I. KING JORDAN, PRESIDENT, GALLAUDET UNIVERSITY

WINNING SOUNDS LIKE THIS

A SEASON WITH THE WOMEN'S BASKETBALL TEAM

AT GALLAUDET, THE WORLD'S ONLY UNIVERSITY FOR THE DEAF

WINNING SOUNDS LIKE THIS

WAYNE COFFEY

THREE RIVERS PRESS
NEW YORK

Author's Note

All interviews with the players were conducted in American Sign Language
with the help of an interpreter. The quotations from these interviews are
italicized in the book.
A portion of the proceeds from this book will be donated to
The Laurent Clerc Center for Deaf Education at Gallaudet University.

Published by Three Rivers Press, New York, New York.
Member of the Crown Publishing Group, a division of Random House, Inc.

www.randomhouse.com

THREE RIVERS PRESS and the Tugboat design are
registered trademarks of Random House, Inc.

Originally published in hardcover by Crown Publishers,
a division of Random House, Inc., in 2002.

Printed in the United States of America

Library of Congress Control Number: 2002283485

ISBN 1-4000-4678-5

10 9 8 7 6 5 4 3 2 1

First Revised Paperback Edition

For Alexandra, Sean, and Samantha, and for
Denise Willi, who delivered them

WINNING SOUNDS LIKE THIS

PROLOGUE

Nanette Virnig wasn't the first sign language teacher I had, but she was one of the best. Her patience was unending. She would show me a sign, I would try to repeat it, and then she would show me again. This is how it went all year in my season with the Gallaudet University women's basketball team. I wasn't fluent by season's end, but I could at least sign "Good morning," "How are you?," and "Great rebound" without provoking overt laughter. Well, that's not quite true. One time I was trying to tell a player that I understood what she was saying. I wound up making an observation about sexual appetite.

Most of my sign lessons in that 1999–2000 season took place on the Gallaudet team bus, traveling to road games. It was a perfect setting. My teachers were captive, and I had a lot of time to correct my mistakes. The bus was a white rectangle on wheels, sort of like the kind rental-car companies use to pick people up at the airport. It had Gallaudet University printed in block letters on the sides. There were big boxy windows and padded blue seats and interior lights that were always left on at night. I didn't understand why the lights stayed on the first trip or two, until Ronda Jo Miller, Gallaudet's All-America center and the greatest basketball player in school history, clued me in.

"How can we talk if we can't see?"

As the bus rolled out of Washington, D.C., through the bare brown hills of the George Washington Parkway in Virginia one Saturday, Nanette and I sat together in a blue seat in the middle. She was a senior cocaptain, an undersized forward who didn't score much, rarely dazzled people with her skills, and never did anything to draw attention to herself. But she played with such passion that it always felt reassuring to see her out there, with her No. 25 jersey and a little knob of a ponytail on top of her head. I was scribbling notes on my pad, and she was scribbling back. The pad was a vital communication tool for me when I was without my interpreter, Mary Thumann, but it was a crutch, too, and not fair besides. It made it too easy for me to retreat to the comfort of English. It forced the players to converse in a cumbersome way, in a language most of them struggle with, instead of in their native American Sign Language (ASL).

So for the rest of the trip, I retired the pad. Nanette taught and I followed. I learned how to sign *"I am hungry"* and *"When are we leaving?"* and worked up to *"I like riding the train"* and *"Gallaudet is a good team."* When I got stuck, I would fingerspell, a skill I was developing, albeit slowly, thanks to Paulina Wlostowski, the team's student manager. Paulina, a Swede of relentlessly sunny disposition, had given me an order a week earlier: *"You need to learn the ASL alphabet."* The next time she saw me, she would be expecting me to be able to fingerspell my name. On the Amtrak trip back to New York, I studied *The Joy of Signing,* a wonderful book I brought with me everywhere during the season. We came into Philadelphia, and I worked on my P's and H's and I's.

When we hit Trenton, I practiced my T's and R's. In Newark, I liked that K's were really P's turned upside down and that you could make a Z by tracing it in the air, like Zorro.

As the Gallaudet bus pulled up to the gymnasium at Marymount University in Arlington, Virginia, the players grabbed their blue-and-yellow equipment bags and filed off the bus. I signed to Nanette, *"Thanks, teacher."* She wants to go into elementary education, and she has a future. She made a fist with her index finger to her chin and flicked it outward. It's the sign for *"Sure."*

In my seat at the end of the bench, I rooted a little harder for Nanette that day. Her assignment was to guard a woman named Rachel Taylor, a diminutive Marymount backcourt player with a placid face and a deadly jump shot. Taylor had destroyed Gallaudet the first time the teams met, scoring thirty-seven points. Gallaudet coach Kitty Baldridge called for a box-and-one defense to contain Taylor, an alignment in which two players are stationed underneath the basket, two are at the free throw line, and one guards the opponent's star player. Nanette was the one, and her job was to follow Taylor everywhere. Nanette was in a mild panic before the game because she couldn't find something to tie her hair up *("I should just shave my head, then I wouldn't have to worry")*. She finally found a rubber band and then played the greatest defensive game of her life. She stuck to Rachel Taylor like tape. When Taylor tried to get free by running Nanette into a screen, Nanette just fought her way through it and stayed in her face. Gallaudet led by fifteen points, 71–56, with four and a half minutes to play. The lead was still eleven after Nanette hit a tough baseline jump shot. Marymount made a couple of quick baskets and started pressing all over the court, and suddenly Gallaudet tightened up and began throwing the ball all over. Marymount closed to within five, then three, then one, 74–73. Touria Ouahid, Gallaudet's standout guard, had a pair of turnovers and looked stricken during a time-out. Nanette put a firm hand on each of Touria's

shoulders and said, *"Don't take yourself out of the game. We need you."*
Touria hit the clinching free throw in the final minute, and Gallaudet
hung on to win, 75–73. It was a needlessly nerve-racking finish to a
contest that proved an old coaching bromide: Offense gets headlines,
but defense wins games.

In a tiny blue locker room, players hugged and high-fived and jostled
one another as they dressed. Kitty saluted Nanette for her defense.
Nanette smiled, her face still red and sweaty. Ronda Johnson, a junior
from Deer River, Minnesota, sat hunched in front of her locker and
covered her ears with her hands. Nobody knew why, but that was often
the case with Ronda. Kitty tapped her on the arm.

"What's the matter, are you afraid of going deaf?"

"No, I'm afraid of going hearing," Ronda said. Everybody laughed.
There was a lot of laughter around this team, and Ronda was usually in
the middle of it, whether by consuming a half-bottle of ketchup with a
single order of french fries or bending her body in unique directions,
as if it were a pipe cleaner.

On the ride home, the lights were on and Ernie Young, the team's
longtime driver, was behind the wheel, his red leather Bible on the
dashboard in front of him. A few minutes into the trip, Kitty stood up,
waved her hand to get people's attention and asked what the fast-food
place du jour was going to be. Roy Rogers won out over Wendy's in a
close ballot. Ten players plus a few managers and statisticians piled in,
a snaking line of wet heads and empty stomachs. Kitty stood at the
counter and, one by one, took each player's order in sign language,
then translated it into English for the counterperson. There are some
things you have to do when you are a hearing coach with deaf players.
Signing the pregame introductions so your players know when they're
supposed to run out on the floor is another. Kitty has been coaching
deaf players for close to thirty years. It's been nearly that long since
she's given any of this a thought.

When the players sat down to eat, they got the usual treatment: a bunch of stares from people who pretended not to be staring. An estimated 20 million people are deaf and hard-of-hearing in the United States, and about 2 million are profoundly deaf. The orbit of most hearing people's lives includes none of them, which is why the sight of young women communicating in sign language is so arresting. Deafness is an invisible condition. It comes with no telltale markers or disfigurement. You can't tell if someone's deaf if you pass him on the street, or post her up on the basketball court. By its very nature, profound deafness leaves those who have it cut off from the hearing mainstream, isolated from the hum of communication that so effortlessly connects those who hear. "The most desperate of human calamities," Dr. Samuel Johnson, the English writer and critic, called it. For most people in the hearing world, deafness is a deep and awful mystery, the parameters of their knowledge beginning with Helen Keller and ending with the airport pencil peddler. Helen Keller herself said that if she had had the choice of regaining her vision or hearing, she would've chosen hearing, for while blindness cut her off from the world around her, deafness cut her off from other human beings. Most of us look at the deaf with a combination of pity and perverse gratitude: "There but for the grace of God . . ." If there was one thing I learned in my time at Gallaudet, it's that the sympathy is neither wanted nor needed.

The 1998–99 women's basketball team at Gallaudet had the greatest season in the one hundred five years the sport has been played at the school. The team finished with a record of 24–6, winning twenty out of twenty-one games in one stretch. Qualifying for the National Collegiate Athletic Association Tournament for only the second time in school history, Gallaudet went on the road to Trenton, New Jersey, and defeated the No. 2 team in the country, The College of New Jersey. Ronda Jo Miller had thirty-eight points, four rebounds, and eleven blocked shots in the victory, as dominant a postseason performance as any player in the country would produce that March. The season ended just two games short of the Final Four.

Gallaudet is not just the only liberal-arts university for the deaf in the world; it is the center of Deaf culture in the United States. Twelve years ago, it was the site of a historic uprising that changed the way deaf people view themselves, the deaf world's equivalent of Martin Luther King's March on Selma. Suddenly, with the success of its high-scoring, fast-breaking women's basketball team, the university had a new source of renown.

I first became aware of how good the Gallaudet team was a short time after that College of New Jersey game, a triumph that Division III basketball followers considered one of the biggest upsets of the season. The extent of my knowledge about Gallaudet then was that it was a college for the deaf and hard-of-hearing, and that it was in Washington, D.C. The total of my experience with deafness consisted of my own low-level hearing loss, the result of chronic ear infections as a small child. I didn't even know how the players felt about their deafness—or whether they were comfortable talking about it—until I heard of the reporter who delicately asked several Gallaudet players how they were able to deal with their "hearing impairment."

"We're not hearing impaired. We're deaf," Nanette Virnig said. Her teammates were flanking her, echoing the sentiment. Among them were a Minnesota farm girl who grew up riding horses and now leads the nation in scoring; a Moroccan-born point guard who was beaten as a child because of her desire to play basketball, but kept playing anyway; a reserve center and team English expert who wants to own a bookstore and loves Gallaudet so much she often cries when she returns to campus.

The more I learned about the team, the more curious I became. Basketball is a game that requires constant communication among teammates. How do they know when to switch on defense? How do they alert each other to an impending double-team? How do they function without being able to hear a horn or whistle? I wondered who Gallaudet played against, how they communicated with game officials. I wondered what it was like to be a student at Gallaudet, what it was like to be a deaf person in the United States, and about how the players were treated by the hearing world.

I met with Kitty Baldridge and told her I was interested in writing a book about her team. She was enthusiastic but wanted to find out how the players felt. She invited me to the annual team barbecue in her turn-of-the-century row house, across the street from campus. The players had questions about the genesis of my interest, and about what I knew about deafness and Deaf culture. They weren't put off at all when I said I knew almost nothing, nor when I told them I wanted to go not only to every game but also to practice, class, their dorms and apartments, everywhere, because the book was going to be about their lives and their feelings, their struggles and insecurities, not just their wins, losses, and free throw percentages. Their only concern was my approach. If I was going to focus everything on their pathology, on the one thing they cannot do rather than the full scope of their lives, then they were going to count themselves out. Like most students at Gallaudet, the players on the team are sick of having their lives reduced to a plight: *Isn't it a shame they can't hear? Can't we do something to help them be like us?*

I asked the players what they felt was the biggest misconception the hearing world has of the deaf. Shanada Johnson, Ronda's sister, said, *"People don't think we can do anything. They're surprised that we can drive a car, go to college, travel around the country, or even take care of ourselves. That's what bothers me. We're not helpless. We just can't hear. Otherwise we're no different from you."* The understanding we reached that day was that they would open up their lives and their season to me, as long as I promised that the book wouldn't be pitying and patronizing, a narrative handwringing over their inability to hear. By the time I left for the Amtrak station that night, bound for my home in New York's lower Hudson Valley, I had an idea of what the biggest challenge of the book would be: to write about heroic people, without making them out to be heroes.

The first time I visited the campus of Gallaudet University was the spring of 1999. It was a brilliant cloudless day and the cherry blossoms hung from the trees like pom-poms. I walked through a black iron gate, up a small hill, and followed the road to the right. A cluster of students were gathered around a statue of a bison, the school symbol. The students were carrying backpacks and attired in baggy jeans, T-shirts, and tank tops, the unkempt uniform of youth. A few wore Gallaudet baseball caps, in school colors (buff and blue or yellow and blue, depending on where you look), with a big G in front. They were engaged in animated discourse, their hands and arms moving vigorously, their fingers furling and unfurling at what struck me as a furious pace. It was a scene I saw everywhere I went that day: outside the Merrill Learning Center, a circular library that sits in the center of campus; in the Ely Center, the two-tiered student union and unofficial hub of campus activity; beneath the Tower Clock, the historic Victorian spire that rises over the front of campus. I wondered what the conversations were about. I felt vaguely uneasy and didn't know why until it hit me: I was on the quietest college campus in America. I was at the only university you will find where you can walk through the student center at noontime and hear no more noise than you do at a prayer meeting. Though some students use their voices at Gallaudet, and guttural shouts and exclamations are not uncommon, most students speak with their hands and listen with their eyes. Their language of choice is American Sign.

The quiet never stopped being surreal to me, even as I found out that it had its exceptions. The night before the start of the season, I spent the first of my many nights in a Gallaudet dormitory. I was on the second floor of Benson Hall, a six-story brick box that was built in the 1960s and has not aged gracefully. Like every dorm on campus, Benson is named after an important figure in school or deaf history; Elizabeth Benson was a longtime interpreter and dorm supervisor at Gallaudet. It took one night in Elizabeth Benson's dorm to discover that even though Gallaudet students cannot hear, that doesn't mean they don't like music, the preferred volume and bass settings being full blast, the better to take in the vibrations of the sound waves. "We don't listen to music," one student would later explain, "we feel it." At one-thirty in the morning, the feeling began. I felt hip-hop vibrations in my mattress. The toilet handle rattled and the medicine chest shook. The show ended about four-thirty, right around the time I was mulling the irony of a hearing person getting aurally assaulted by a dorm full of deaf kids. Still, I had no grounds for complaint; Kitty warned me the day before: "You're a brave man if you stay in the dorms." The nights were more restful after that, thanks to a move next door to more sedate Clerc Hall, and to the kindhearted resident adviser who put the word out that I was going to be a regular visitor. The students didn't have a hard time spotting me. I was the only one who used the handset instead of the Teletype writer (TTY) machine when ordering pizza from the lobby pay phone. It gave me my own distinct status. At halftime of one road game, a skinny kid with tousled hair introduced himself and said, "Aren't you the hearing guy from the third floor?" The players welcomed me, too. It became official one Friday afternoon, on the Field House floor. Kitty needed an extra body to run fullcourt during practice, and I was recruited. I was guarding Touria Ouahid, the point guard. She pulled up to take a jumper. I blocked it. She let out a high-pitched yelp, her all-purpose sound of chagrin. The next time she got the ball, she started near the baseline, faked a shot. I went for it. She drove by me for a layup. As Touria ran back on defense, she gave me a playful shove on the shoulder. She didn't have to sign, "I schooled you." We both knew.

I've been playing or coaching basketball most of my life. I had a good idea of the extent of my fanaticism when I asked Bill Bradley to autograph my left Converse sneaker, while I was wearing it, thirty-five years ago in the Pocono Mountains of Pennsylvania. I was a summer camper. Bradley was a visiting deity, a man whose fame at the time derived solely from his status as a Princeton All-American. I steadied myself against a big oak tree as he signed, my preadolescent body quivering over my good fortune.

For a young basketball player, Converse sneakers were the way you marked membership in the club of players. My first pair was a gift from my older brother, Frank. He and a couple of friends went to the Holiday Festival college basketball tournament at Madison Square Garden a few days after Christmas. My brother took me everywhere with him, but there was no extra ticket this time. I went to sleep feeling sad and left out. When I woke up, there was a red box at the foot of my bed. Inside was the most lovely pair of Chuck Taylor All-Stars (the official name) I'd ever seen. I was nine, and the sneakers were size three. I drank up the fresh-canvas smell and ran my hands over the shiny blue star on the side. With each sniff, I got a rubber rush of legitimacy. No longer was I some interloper in P.F. Flyers, flat-bottomed recess sneakers. I was a ballplayer. I laced them up and headed for the hoop over the garage and swished my first shot. I was sure it was because of the Cons.

As a kid growing up in Huntington, New York, I could not get enough of basketball. I would keep score of games on TV. I would send away for camp brochures, because I liked getting basketball mail. Mostly, though, I played, in all weather, and at all hours. I created an entire eight-team league, complete with star players and story lines, all straight out of my head, all top secret. Nobody—not my brother, my sister, or my best friends—knew about my fictional league. My favorite player was Jim Bradovich. He wore No. 44. I could tell you about his hair (shiny and brown and combed to the side), his walk (athletic and jaunty, but not cocky), and the rotation on his jump shot (a flawless, feathery backspin). Jim Bradovich was handsome, humble, and fearless when the pressure was on. He was who I wanted to be in life. The only moment that may have been better than the day Jim scored forty-two points to win his first league title was when I beat the center of the high school team in a real-life game of H-O-R-S-E. His name was Larry Hill. He had two feet and one hundred fifty pounds on me. Larry was from Oklahoma or Kansas or someplace, and he liked to use the word *mighty*. It came out sounding like MAAA-tee.

"Boy," he said, "you got a MAAA-tee purty shot." Larry was there one holiday when my brother and his buddies snuck into an elementary school gym. They passed me through an open window, and I ran around and opened the door. The lights slowly sizzled on. I felt like the current was surging through me, too.

Gyms have never lost their allure for me. For four years, I was an assistant coach of a junior-varsity girls' team in the Bronx. Each day as I walked in the place for practice, the sight of the honey-colored floor and the orange rims and the shellacked smell of the wood floor made me feel good. Our team wound up winning a bunch of games (forty-three out of forty-seven), and I wound up teaming with a college coach next door to write a basketball instructional book for girls. My picture—circa 1985—is on the back. When Jenny Cooper, a forward for Gallaudet, took a look at the photo—showing me with a dark beard and long hair—she came up next to me and stared at my current salt-and-pepper self. "*What happened to all the black hair?"* We were in the lobby of the Field House, waiting to board the bus. It was not the time for an exploration of the ravages of aging. "You'll find out," I said.

A few weeks after Gallaudet concluded the 1998–99 season with a loss in the NCAA Tournament to Salem State College of Massachusetts, Kitty Baldridge had a series of individual meetings with her players. The game had gone abysmally, and not just because they had lost. Ronda Jo got into early foul trouble and never really recovered. Touria and Ronda Johnson, the next best players, struggled against the Salem State defense and made frequent turnovers. The Bison of Gallaudet fell behind in the first half, and though the players fought back, the deficit was too big to overcome. It was doubly disappointing because to a player, the Gallaudet team felt it was a game they could've, and should've, won.

Kitty wanted to feel out her players about what they thought happened in the game. Even after twenty-two years coaching at Gallaudet, she was thoroughly unprepared for what she heard. Touria and a couple of others told her that they lost because they didn't think they could beat a hearing team in such a big game. They did not feel as though they belonged, that they really could compete for a national title. Nobody expressed the feelings beforehand. Nobody really was conscious of them, but they were there nonetheless, an unseen soft spot in the players' competitive armor. Kitty was stunned. Gallaudet had just beaten the second-ranked team in the country on its home court—a team that heard just fine. The Bison play against hearing teams all year long. Kitty's teams, especially this one, have always been almost defiant about their deafness, wanting no special allowances, no excuses, no coddling. *Don't call us hearing-impaired. Call us deaf.* In the course of my time with the team, I asked each player if she wished she could hear—if she ever thought that life would be better if she could. Not a single player expressed any interest in hearing. As close as I got to a dissenting opinion was from Nanette, who said she was curious about what birds and music sounded like. Nanette said she'd like to try it for an afternoon, then go back to being deaf.

"I think I'd get frustrated and distracted, having all those noises in my ears all the time. I'm better off not hearing at all."

The players on the team—indeed, nearly every deaf person I met at Gallaudet—do not see themselves as needing to be fixed. It's hard to imagine a quadriplegic saying, "No thanks, I'll stay in my chair," or a blind man saying, "I think I'll stay blind." But for many deaf people, their inability to hear is not a problem; it is a way of life. As one Gallaudet professor said, "For most people on this campus, deafness is nothing but an alternate hearing style."

Said Touria, *"You can't compare us to people who are sick or who have other conditions. Our identity is wrapped up in being deaf. It's who we are."* The deaf have their own language, history, Olympics, social clubs, and schools: their own culture. It runs so deep that the preferred grammatical style is to capitalize it: Deaf culture. And while not all deaf people embrace Deaf culture, most at Gallaudet do. To the players on the team, deaf people who eschew sign language and try to learn to lipread and speak and do everything possible to fit into the regular world are nothing but hearing wanna-bes. *"I think they're pretending to be something they're not,"* Touria said.

For students at Gallaudet, a profound sense of community exists, particularly among those who have been deaf since birth and are from families in which deafness goes back generations. Shut out from the information flow of the hearing world, shunted to the sidelines of society, unable to acquire language the way everyone else does—from the spoken word—they turn to each other in a way that those who do not belong to a minority could never fully understand, for sustenance, for affirmation, for belonging. Their deafness becomes so much a part of themselves and their lives that to hope to be something other than that is almost an act of self-denial.

"I call myself deaf," Ronda Jo said as we sat at a table outside the Bison Eatery, the cafeteria in the Ely Center, one morning. *"I have everything I need. Why should I want to change anything?"*

So it was highly curious that, as they prepared for the biggest game of the season, a number of Gallaudet players suddenly and subconsciously were afflicted, not with a sense of their essential differentness, but a riptide of inferiority. *"I think for a lot of us there was this attitude, a little voice in there saying, 'Deaf people tend to lose. Deaf people can't beat a hearing team,'"* Ronda Johnson said. *"I don't think we realized that we were that good."*

Once she had time to think about it, Kitty's shock dissipated. She is the hearing daughter of two deaf parents—a CODA, or Child of Deaf Adults, in Deaf culture's parlance. Her first language was American Sign, and some of her most vivid memories were of seeing how deaf people were, in word and deed, demeaned by the hearing world. "You don't just turn a lifetime of messages off," Kitty said. Touria, a ferocious competitor, the type of player who believes she can drive by anybody, was disgusted that she let such feelings infiltrate her psyche. *"I can't believe I was thinking that way. I don't want to let it happen again."*

Weeks passed. The disappointment eased. As spring bloomed and a campus that Gallaudetians call Kendall Green really did turn green again, thoughts turned hopefully to the 1999–2000 season. Ronda Jo said she wanted to have her best season yet, step up her defense, and get a chance to make a team in the Women's National Basketball Association. Stacy Nowak, the backup center, said she wanted to lose the weight she gained after a serious auto accident during her freshman year and become a major contributor. Ronda Johnson, in phenomenal shape and just back from Cuba, where she played with the U.S. Deaf National Team, was ready to become a star. Another year removed from the horrible knee injury she suffered early in the 1997–98 season, Touria relished the idea of going at people with a strong and fully able body. Forward Jenny Cooper, an intense player who loves the body-banging mayhem underneath the basket, had dreams of champion-ships and glory. Nobody knew how the freshmen players would be, how the pieces of the new team would fit together, but the players were primed. They even put it in writing on the floor of Kitty's kitchen. A row of tiles had peeled up. Kitty scraped off the gunk and painted the underlying plywood white. When the players came over for the barbecue, Kitty asked them to sign it. Touria's message summed it all up:

I'll never forget this season. My next goal is to enter Final Four. Love, Touria #14

Even as her players allowed themselves to muse about a national cham-pionship and Gallaudet fans dreamed along with them, Kitty Baldridge was wary. She is someone who hopes for good things to happen but never expects them. She kept reminding the players, "Everything changes. There are no guarantees. You don't know what kind of player you will be in six months. You don't know who will get hurt, who will be healthy, who will get better and who won't. The team we are today is not necessarily the team we will be next season. The best thing we can do is think about what happened and learn from it and work hard and be ready to play."

Championships are not won by writing on your coach's floor. There is no extra credit applied from one season to the next. The Gallaudet University women's basketball team would start to find out what kind of team it would become in November, when Ernie Young would switch on the light in his bus and the Bison would begin their ambitious chase, looking not just for victories but validation, a chance to show the wider world what they already knew to be true: that deaf people can do anything but hear.

STARTING
OVER

THE ELY CENTER is a rambling, unremarkable place, a low-slung brick building that meanders this way and that, with corridors that seem as haphazardly located as tree branches. It has a rec area (bowling alleys and pool tables), a travel agent and bookstore in the basement, and two places to eat, the Bison Eatery and the Abbey, upstairs. In the center of the center is a soaring atrium with a twenty-five-foot rubber tree and wide-open sight lines between the lower and upper floors. When you can't hear, you want to be able to see, and that's the idea behind the design. It makes for a great gathering room, a place that lets you see a friend's sign-language greeting from two or three stories away, the same way you can in Gallaudet's main classroom center, Hall Memorial Building, which was likewise constructed with an open core. Gallaudet isn't a university without walls; it's just particular about where it places them.

Near the corner of the atrium, across from the campus post office, a messy stack of copies of the school paper, the *Buff and Blue,* spills out of a wire rack. In the back of the paper is a piece by sports editor Alexander Long. It is a mid-November preview of the forthcoming basketball season and captures a buzz that is running through campus like a rush-hour Metro. The 1999–2000 Gallaudet women's basketball team is favored to win the Capital Athletic Conference. It has a pre-season ranking of No. 7 in the nation, as judged by the coaches of NCAA Division III. It has most of the key players back from the greatest season in school history. For decades, Gallaudet athletic programs have done their competing in almost absolute obscurity, getting the barest of mention beyond the spired, iron fence that separates Kendall Green from northeast Washington. The school's principal claim to sporting fame heretofore was probably the invention of the football huddle in the late nineteenth century—a means of preventing other deaf teams from seeing their sign language.

Now Ronda Jo Miller and her Bison teammates are turning up on ESPN, in *USA Today,* the *Baltimore Sun,* the *New York Daily News.* There is a two-page spread in *Sports Illustrated for Kids.* A producer from HBO's Real Sports calls. The Associated Press puts a feature out on the wire. Nobody's calling the Bison household names yet, but quite suddenly the nation is hearing more than ever before about the team that can't hear. The players know some people probably think they play a low-rent schedule, against some manner of "impaired" opponents, by a gerrymandered set of rules. That's okay. They'll learn. It wouldn't be the first time hearing folks underestimated the deaf. It happened when Donalda Ammons played for Gallaudet in the 1960s, and it is happening still.

Ammons is a professor in Gallaudet's Foreign Studies Department and general secretary of Comité International des Sports des Sourds (CISS), the international governing body for deaf sports and the organization that presides over the Deaflympics every four years. Her playing days date to the six-a-side era of women's basketball, which allowed for limited dribbling and was founded on the same dubious premise that kept female distance running events out of the Olympics until recently: Girls shouldn't get too sweaty. As Ammons sits behind the desk of her book-lined office on the first floor of Hall Memorial Building, it's difficult to say what she finds more incredulous: the change in the prevailing mind-set toward women's sports in America, or toward deaf people.

"I think one of the greatest benefits of the team doing well is the way it has impacted the attitude that hearing people have. I think some people looked at them as a curiosity at first: 'Let's go see the deaf girls play.' After awhile you forget that they're deaf and you come away saying, 'They're pretty good basketball players.'"

Deafness runs in a good number of Gallaudet families, and Donalda Ammons's family is one of them. It is a trait that is passed on the same way that blue eyes or turned-up noses are passed on. Both of Ammons's parents are deaf. So are both of her sisters, and her two basketball-playing nieces, who adore Ronda Jo Miller and actually had her as their counselor when they came to Kitty Baldridge's annual Gallaudet summer basketball camp. Counting the farthest reaches of the Ammons family tree, there are some two hundred fifty deaf people. All have seen more progress in the treatment and attitude toward deafness in the last two decades than in the two centuries that went before, a shift that has begun to draw deaf people out of the shadowed margins of American society.

Not even a quarter century ago, as a Gallaudet undergraduate, university president King Jordan would go to Washington Redskins games or to restaurants and feel ashamed to be seen signing in public. *"There was a stigma attached to it, a sense not just of having a different means of communicating, but of being inferior,"* Jordan said. Assistant basketball coach Ben Baylor, who grew up in Washington, recalls seeing Gallaudet students on city buses, stiff and uncomfortable, their hands and bodies frozen, looking as if they were venturing into a place where maybe they shouldn't be. Their faces usually looked tight and sad.

The stigma loosened as the prevailing image of deafness gradually began to change. Nobody did more to accelerate the change than Marlee Matlin in her Oscar-winning role in *Children of a Lesser God.* Linda Bove's signing on Sesame Street became almost as much of a PBS staple as Elmo or Big Bird. American Sign Language began to be recognized by linguistics scholars as a fully developed language with its own syntax, nuances, and vocabulary, no different than Chinese or Swahili or Spanish, and increasingly started to be offered as a language option at numerous colleges and universities. Technological forces were at work, too. Closed captioning became much more prevalent. Teletype telephones (TTYs) got less expensive and less clunky, enabling deaf people to communicate by phone by typing in words, rather than speaking them. The emergence of the Internet, pagers, and e-mail brought down additional barriers, allowing information-gathering and communication to be readily available at the click of a mouse and a send button.

But the most powerful engine of change was fueled by deaf people themselves, in a historic week on the Gallaudet campus in the late winter of 1988. The event became known as Deaf President Now, or DPN, the brevity belying the epic nature of what unfolded beginning on Monday, March 7, the day Gallaudet students seized control of campus. It was a sixties-style rebellion, a quest for respect and self-determination that drew worldwide media coverage. The students didn't let go until the university had its first deaf president in its 124-year history. The man elected was Irving King Jordan, who now is the most recognizable and respected advocate for the deaf community in the world.

"In one week, Gallaudet and the deaf community got more attention than we had in one hundred twenty-five years," Jordan said.

For most of history, deaf people have been viewed as either dullards or misfits, and King Jordan doesn't think one needs to write a dissertation to know why. Dating to the time of Aristotle, the hearing world has almost reflexively linked speech to intelligence; the better you speak, the more verbal dexterity you have, the greater brain you must have. Conversely, if you cannot speak well (and it's almost impossible to if you can't hear your own voice), you are looked at with wariness and pity, or, as Stacy Nowak put it, *"as if you were some form of drooling mutant."*

It would be seriously myopic to suggest that a student revolt and an Academy Award would be capable of wiping away this legacy. Perceptions die hard. Deaf people continue to face huge obstacles, educationally and vocationally. A minute percentage of the deaf population has a college degree, or what would be considered management-level employment. The typical Gallaudet freshman comes in reading at about a fourth-grade level, a fact that inclines many to believe that deaf people really are not very smart. It seems a reasonable deduction, but it's wrong. English is not the first language for most deaf people in America. It is a second language, or even a third, one that is often painfully difficult to pick up, since they do not hear it, cannot acquire it by osmosis as young hearing children do, and thus develop no discernible sense of its syntax or vocabulary at an early age. All over campus, there is evidence that English remains a somewhat foreign language. When workers are in the Field House treating the gym floor, the sign on the blue door reads: "Not Enter." A perfectly intelligent freshman writes to a friend, "I have not go home for 4 weeks." Another otherwise gifted student, writing about why she cherishes ASL and loathes Signed English (a sign system that is structurally and grammatically equivalent to the spoken version), "I had a hard time to understanding what everyone tries to tell me or something like that." When a student enters the library, one of the first things she sees near the circulation desk is a wide selection of young-adult novels. During a camping-equipment sale downstairs in the Ely Center, a poster lists items for sale: tent, ice chest, lantern, cook kit. The epochal event known as DPN did not provide any sort of panacea, any more than it unlocked the mystery of English. What it did do, however, was not tell the world, but show it, that the deaf are tired of being patronized. So hold the pats on the head. A dozen years later, DPN remains a cherished historical marker, dearly held proof that things can change for the better.

A revolution had taken place in northeast Washington, and its impact was felt all over the deaf world.

As sunlight pours through the big arched windows of his corner office in College Hall, King Jordan still seems humbled by the history he was involved in, and the emancipation of the deaf that took place on campus thirteen years before.

"We will no longer accept limits on what we can achieve," Jordon told an overjoyed throng on the night of his appointment. "I am confident we will walk boldly into a future without artificial limits. It is a historic moment for deaf people around the world. . . . You made me president and the deaf world will never be the same."

"The heightened awareness people have now has helped people see us more as a linguistic minority, instead of obsessing about our physical disability," Donalda Ammons said.

It is a few minutes past four on a November afternoon, the sky is the color of slate, and Kathryn Adelle (Kitty) Baldridge is not happy. She is standing on the honey-colored boards of the Field House gym, wearing a blue-and-gold Gallaudet warm-up suit with her name stitched just over the heart. She has a clipboard on the floor and a purple key ring with a big brass K hooked to the ball rack, her customary props in their customary places. There is no whistle in sight. She thinks she might have one somewhere but has never blown one in more than twenty-five years of running practices. "What would be the point?" Kitty said.

She is five feet tall, not much over one hundred pounds, with a slender, athletic physique more befitting a twelve-year-old junior-high girl than a fifty-two-year-old coach and professor. She looks even smaller as she walks briskly crosscourt, a brown-haired speck inside the big, boxy Field House, beneath a flat roof with long stripes of yellow ducts. Kitty has a pleasant face, with a midwestern warmth about it. Sternness and edginess do not come naturally to her, but she's having no trouble summoning them at the moment. Not even ten days earlier, she assembled the players in the team meeting room, Classroom 142, on the south side of the Field House. Climbing on a desk so she could get high enough on the board for the players to see her words, she wrote, "The Time Is Now." Kitty likes slogans and sayings. On her office door is a sign that says, "A woman's place is in the House, Senate and White House." Alongside it is another, from Eleanor Roosevelt: "No One Can Make You Feel Inferior Without Your Consent." Before the season is out, Kitty will write and sign "The Time Is Now" scores of times. She will have the words printed on T-shirts and handouts, reminding the kids at every turn about the ephemeral nature of opportunity, about the special chance they have this year, with the team's mix of skill and experience, and with three straight seasons of improvement (19–9, 19–7, and 24–6) behind them. The players supposedly share her urgency. At least that's what they say. So why isn't Kitty seeing it? Why are players running through drills at three-quarters speed, behaving like a bunch of preadolescents, tickling each other, telling jokes? What could possibly have been going through their minds when Nanette, one of the cocaptains, came to her one Friday afternoon and asked her to cancel practice for the night? The team had been practicing with only five players, because of a few injuries and because volleyball season hadn't ended yet, meaning that Ronda Jo Miller, Stacy Nowak, and Shanada Johnson were all still playing that sport. Kitty was used to starting the year with a skeleton squad, but *five* players? And now here's Nanette telling her they need a night off just a few weeks into the season, promising an extra-good practice Saturday morning, when the volleyball players would rejoin the team. Kitty reluctantly said okay, only to discover later that a fraternity was sponsoring a hayride in the country that night, and a bunch of the players wanted to go. Kitty was furious when she found out. She felt betrayed. As she sat in the basement of her row house later that night, watching her beloved Indiana Hoosiers on television, the sting stayed with her.

"They tell me something, and in my heart, I believe it," Kitty said. "I want to believe it. Sometimes there's this huge gap between what they say and do, and it hurts me." She watched Bob Knight fire off the bench and rip into an official, his belly bulging out of his famous red sweater. "Sometimes I wonder why I even bother coaching," Kitty said. Her body recoiled after she said the words, stiffening from their hardness. She doesn't wonder at all about coaching; she loves it, loves the bond with the players, the intimacy, and the growth. That's the best part, by far, seeing a young woman grow, not so much by learning how to shoot a left-handed hook shot or execute a crossover dribble, but by acquiring a more enduring set of skills: learning about perseverance and accountability, finding the courage to look at her own behavior instead of criticizing somebody else.

Before practice the next morning, Kitty summoned Nanette into the little copier room off the side of the physical education office. Nanette was wearing her dark blue No. 25 practice uniform. Kitty closed the door. No sound came out of the room. Nanette is a dutiful and mature young woman, a senior who takes her cocaptaincy seriously. She craves precision and order; she's always figured it's probably because she is an architect's daughter. Her sock drawer is arranged by color, her clothes so neatly folded they look as if they're in formation. In her sixth-floor dorm room in Clerc Hall, she's almost always the one with the bucket and bottle of Pine Sol, quick to scrub the bathroom, getting a weird sort of hygienic high out of the piney-smelling porcelain. Nanette hates messes of any sort. She knows she screwed up by deceiving Kitty about the hayride.

"I'm sorry about asking you to cancel practice," Nanette said. Kitty told her she's not interested in words, but actions. She told her she was considering pulling her captaincy.

"You have to show me you're committed, show me that you are going to be a leader of this team." Nanette walked out of the office ashen-faced. Kitty followed, not looking much better. Kitty grew up sitting on the bench and serving as towel and water girl for her father, Paul Baldridge, a long-time coach of the deaf and a Gallaudet legend, one of the so-called Five Ironmen—the Gallaudet team from 1943 that won the prestigious Mason-Dixon tournament without a single bench player. There is a picture of the Five Ironmen in the Hall of Fame room, an oblong gathering place in the corner of the Field House lobby.

"If I learned anything from my father, it's that you can yell with your hands," Kitty said. She smiled faintly and headed for the gym, leaning forward, walking as if she were late for an appointment. It was time for practice. "A hayride," Kitty muttered again.

One by one, players begin to fill the floor, plucking balls from the rack and shooting and dribbling in formless clusters, the gym quickly filling with the staccato rhythms of balls bouncing against wood, and sneakers squeaking against it, and the occasional whoop of Stacy, the Bison player who uses her voice the most. Once or twice a season, you can count on opposing fans to mock Stacy's whoop, an evenly pitched noise that sounds like a cross between a train whistle and an owl. Kitty has learned that the best reply to ignorance is to ignore it. Same thing with the people who mimic the Gallaudet coaches' and players' sign language, flapping and flailing their arms like sick ducks. This happens a lot less than it used to, something Kitty likes to take as a hopeful sign, a sprout of tolerance.

When Kitty is ready to start drills, she walks toward the big yellow G in the center of the floor and extends her right arm, fluttering her hand as if she were tapping someone on the shoulder. It is the way she gets her players' attention, the Gallaudet version of "All right, listen up." Her other method—stomping a foot on the floor, creating vibrations players can feel all the way across the court—she prefers to reserve for more urgent occasions, such as the final minute of a tie game, or the third time she has to remind somebody to not give up the baseline on defense.

Kitty gets all eyes turned toward her after a few seconds. She tells the players she wants to run a three-on-two fast-break drill and retreats to the sideline. A few moments later, she is back on the floor, waving her hand again, making a few adjustments to the mechanics of the drill. Kitty muses about what it would be like to be able to stop practice with a single toot of a whistle, about how marvelously efficient that would be. For most coaches, a whistle is not merely a shrill symbol of who's boss, but a vital keeper of order, a time-management tool on a string. "It's not like I think using a whistle would change my life, but when you think about how much time we waste over a season just getting players' attention, making sure everyone can see me, it's mind-boggling," Kitty said, more in observation than complaint.

The players never give the whistle a thought. For them, it is just another one of those strange audio cues that hearing people react to, like a police siren or a popped balloon. Occasionally they would be curious about its sound, just as they'd be curious about lots of other sounds, wondering if it were cacophonous or sweet or insistent. During warm-ups before one road game, as a heavy-metal song blasted from the gymnasium speakers, Ronda Johnson made her jaunty, pigeon-toed way toward the scorer's table, a ball tucked under her right arm, and asked a hearing person who was grimacing from the noise, *"Does that hurt your ears?"*

"Yes. It's bad music, and it's loud."

"I thought so," she said, and then she pigeon-toed her way back. But mostly the world of sound is like somebody's wedding you pass by in your car: There's no reason to pay much attention because it has nothing to do with you.

Even in her third decade of coaching, Kitty still feels equal parts of excitement and trepidation in the early weeks of a season, at once enchanted by the possibilities and afraid of them, like an artist looking at a blank canvas. The uncertainty feels even greater this year because the expectations are so high. The previous spring, in the NCAA Tournament, the team had surprised everybody. Their tournament run was fun, but now the Bison's sneaking-up days are done. Teams that are ranked seventh in the nation may have a wealth of things going for them, but the element of surprise is not one of them. Indeed, in a span of six months, the Bison have gone from hunter to hunted, a team that opponents get fired up to play, knowing that a victory over Gallaudet would be a considerable achievement. Kitty isn't sure if her players are aware of how big a change this is going to be. She gets this vague sense of arrogance from the team, a feeling that the players think they've already accomplished something this season. She doesn't like it.

There are two promising freshman players: Natalie Ludwig, from Houston, Texas, and Cassey Ellis, from Boston, Massachusetts. But who ever really knows about how first-year players will work out? Courtney Westberg, a six-foot, one-inch transfer student from Anchorage, Alaska, is scheduled to arrive for the second semester, though here, too, Kitty maintains a half-wall of skepticism, not because Courtney didn't seem delightful (and tall) when Kitty met her the previous summer, but because things happen, kids change their minds.

Kitty will count on her when she sees her in practice uniform, stepping over the thick blue stripe that rims the Gallaudet court. There are other questions, too. Touria is ecstatic about finally being able to shed her clunky black knee brace, but now she is being asked to play point guard and direct the offense, a new and considerable responsibility. Will Ronda Johnson emerge as a steadily reliable force? Jenny Cooper has been diagnosed with mononucleosis and is not even enrolled in school for the first semester. Cooper is what Kitty likes to call "an igniter." She stokes the whole team's competitive fire, and everybody knows it. *"After I found out Jenny wasn't going to be able to play in the beginning, it made me concerned,"* Touria said. *"She means so much. Her style of play is an inspiration."* And for all their success the previous season, the Bison are a group that definitely needs inspiring sometimes, starting right at the top, with the resident All-American, Ronda Jo Miller.

There is not even a debate around Kendall Green that Ronda Jo is the greatest athlete, male or female, the school has ever had. In volleyball, she owns the NCAA record for kills and is the best player anyone can remember. She is a three-time All-American in basketball, and a three-time Capital Athletic Conference player of the year, the school's all-time leader in points, rebounds, and blocks. She was the second-leading scorer in the nation as a sophomore, with twenty-nine points per game, and was the No. 1 shotblocker with almost five per game. Routinely blanketed with double and triple coverage, Ronda Jo gets to the basket anyway, beating people with slicing spin moves and pull-up jumpers, and surprising them with her sinewy strength. Ronda Jo hates lifting weights but has lifted a ton of bales of hay. She is so smooth with the ball that she's forever pestering Kitty about playing point guard, eager for a temporary reprieve from the ball-and-chain congestion of the low post. Her combination of size and skill is being noticed more and more by scouts and executives in the Women's National Basketball Association; they are tracking Ronda Jo more closely than any player at the small-school, Division III level.

"She is a great athlete with tremendous versatility," said Renee Brown, the league's director of player personnel. "She can handle the ball as well as any player her size in the country."

From the time Ronda Jo showed up as a freshman, a spindly kid with arms and legs like linguine, she was the best player Kitty had. That was the coach's blessing, and her challenge. How do you motivate a student who is getting straight A's right from the beginning? What is she supposed to shoot for? How much incentive is there to get better? It's not as if Ronda Jo is lazy or apathetic. The best word for her, as far as Kitty is concerned, is *enigmatic*. Basketball is a sport that teems with so-called gym rats, players whose idea of a perfect July day is four ninety-degree hours with a ball and a rim. Ronda Jo's idea of a perfect July day is being on the hundred-acre family farm outside Little Falls, Minnesota, in the tiny hamlet of Flensburg (population 257 when Ronda Jo is home), riding one of her horses, Dusty Morning or Jasper, or walking the grain field across the dirt road from the house, or maybe even napping in a bed of straw with a few of her piglets. She is still good at naps. She can drift off anytime, anywhere. On nearly every bus trip, she falls asleep with her body folded like a V, legs propped up on the seat ahead of her. She can sleep at night immediately after slugging down a caffeine-intensive can of Mountain Dew. She's an inveterate nail-biter, but otherwise Ronda Jo just seems to glide on through life, with a pointy poker face and deeply set eyes, not letting much rile her, with an unstated mantra: *Everything in its time.* Ronda Jo likes volleyball in volleyball season, basketball in basketball season, and doesn't typically play either once the season is over. It is a reasonable attitude, maybe even a healthy one, but not necessarily the best way to reach your full potential. Kitty has always considered herself an able motivator. She has a gift for finding the right button to push to get a player to do more, but Ronda

Jo's buttons are harder to find than rush hour in Flensburg. Kitty has tried earnest sit-downs. She has tried booting her out of practice, yelling at her. She has tried the straight, spare power of logic *("How can you say you want to play in the pros, when you don't put in the work to get there?")*. Ronda Jo's response would never be defiant, but it wouldn't be compliant, either. Part of the problem is that she simply doesn't like practice much. She finds the repetition tedious, and though she would never say it, the tedium is compounded by the fact that there is nobody to push her seriously, in the way Jenny Cooper, for one, is constantly pushed *by* her.

Jenny and Ronda Jo came in together as freshmen. Jenny was a good player at the Indiana School for the Deaf, but she was thoroughly unprepared to go against someone as tall and quick and high-jumping as Ronda Jo. *"Every time I took a shot, she would smash it back into my face,"* Jenny said. *"I cried over it, it was so bad. I wanted to quit. I was such a baby."* With practice and doggedness, Jenny found ways to use her strength to move Ronda Jo around, to get her shot off. The competition made her a much better player. Ronda Jo has never had anyone who could do that for her. Games are her thing, forty-minute crucibles that peel off her layers of laid-backness and summon her spirit. Ronda Jo's style of play is intuitive, improvisational, grounded in a jazzy fluidity, an ability to spin and bend whatever way she needs to. Like an actress who needs the camera to be rolling to be at her best, Ronda Jo can never quite take the game seriously until she's in her No. 23 uniform in blue and gold and the clock is ticking. She occasionally drives her teammates crazy by not even coming out onto the floor until pretty close to game time. She prefers to spend her time in private, visualizing herself doing what she needs to do in the game. *"It really would make us nervous sometimes,"* Nanette said. *"We'd be warming up, wondering, 'Where's Ronda Jo? Is she okay?' And then she'd come out, looking totally calm, and play really well. I've known her a long time, and Ronda Jo is still always full of surprises."*

A team's best player is typically its emotional linchpin, its locker-room leader, a stature that flows directly from what she can do on the court. But that's not how it is with Ronda Jo and the Bison. She isn't much for making locker-room speeches or getting in the face of somebody who's goofing off. She shows little emotion, whether Gallaudet is up by twenty or down by thirty. She has no desire to lord her stardom over people. Before each game, after Kitty and longtime assistant Ben Baylor leave the room, the players form a circle and go around it, each player signing a thought or quote for the day:

"Let's play with heart today."

"Don't forget what this team did to us last year."

"The woman I'm guarding isn't going to score a single basket."

"Hustle."

Ronda Jo chimes in but never dominates. She is content to be just another Bison, an equal in every way, no matter how much Kitty sometimes wishes she were more like the player who inspired her jersey selection, Michael Jordan. It has always struck Kitty as ironic that the very qualities she finds maddening about Ronda Jo are the same qualities that make her admire her so much as a person: She is fair-minded, humble, content with what she has and who she is. When it comes down to it, Kitty would rather coach a player she enjoys being around than a gym rat she doesn't like. Still, there's a part of Kitty that feels she has failed Ronda Jo by not finding a way to get through to her. It's hard not to think about how much better she could've been. Coming out of high school at the Minnesota State Academy for the Deaf, Ronda Jo got a stack of recruiting letters from Division I and Division II schools, places that could offer a scholarship and a higher level of competition, but she doesn't even remember opening them. Ronda Jo only considered one school, the one campus in the world where her deafness would not isolate her.

"It was always going to be Gallaudet for me," Ronda Jo said.

With her country-girl roots, Ronda Jo was a mismatch for Washington, D.C., from the outset. She was terribly homesick her freshman year. She missed rubbing Dusty Morning's back and the Millers' snug white farmhouse. The homeless people and the congestion and the way the row houses were wedged together like Monopoly houses were all a jolt to her. Most of all, she couldn't fathom the D.C. pace, the palpable political hunger, the ambition that is as thick as the air in August. Every time she went off-campus, she would see people she didn't know, rushing for reasons she couldn't comprehend. For quite some time that first semester, Ronda Jo was sure she had made a big mistake. It was only when the familiar rhythms of volleyball and basketball seasons kicked in that she began to warm to Gallaudet.

For her parents, John and Dolly Miller, life in the big city was just as strange. Even after four years of visiting, they still look at the trip as a twenty-four-hour drive into the edge of the abyss. It is just *so* different. There are no people of color in Flensburg, and there is no feed store in the District of Columbia. There are so many locks and gates in northeast Washington. When the Millers went to Sweden for the Deaf Olympics in 1997 (Ronda Jo Miller was on the U.S. team that won the gold medal), they not only didn't lock their house, they left the keys in the car. On the corner of West Virginia Avenue and Florida Avenue, across the street from Gallaudet and a few steps from Ronda Jo's off-campus apartment, there is a dingy convenience store with a low-watt bulb and a crust of dirt on the bulletproof Plexiglas at the counter. John Miller, a six-foot, three-inch, three-hundred-pound farmer and shipping clerk, strong as he is wide, doesn't feel fear when he walks in the place so much as a detached amusement. He had a similar feeling when he visited a hole-in-the-wall barber shop one Saturday. It was on a desultory side street. There was a dog sleeping on the floor amid tufts of hair. The place had an aroma all its own, a weird, ripe combination of Alpo and hair tonic. John Miller has unruly hair that sticks up at an assortment of angles. It looked a little like an ear of corn when he got up from the chair, almost bare in some spots, with a patchwork of gray niblets on top. He paid the man his $8 and stepped over the dog on the way out and gave the barber the benefit of the doubt as he ran a meaty hand over his head. "I don't think he's had a customer with this kind of hair in a while," John Miller said.

It was against her father that Ronda Jo learned to play the game, on a hoop over the garage. The court was a quirky composite of grass and gravel, just across a dirt road from a cornfield, up the hill from the pen where Ronda Jo kept her horses. You never knew which way the ball would bounce, an unpredictability that was a pain at the time, but that made Ronda Jo's nimble hands and ballhandling skill what they are today. Ronda Jo would frequently play pickup games against her older brother, Robby, and her father, who laid his big body on people, more barroom bouncer than ballplayer. They'd play year-round, snow and subzero temperatures be damned. One time, Ronda Jo drove against her father and wound up getting bodied into a snowbank, gouging her elbows and shaking her up. "We didn't draw blood, but people did hit the ground," John Miller said. A mischievous smile conceals the method of his paternal madness; his desire was to toughen up his daughter and make her as independent as possible. Ronda Jo is the first deaf person on either side of the immediate Miller family. Like virtually all hearing parents, John and Dolly initially had no idea about how to raise a deaf child. The Millers didn't even know of the existence of the Minnesota State Academy for the Deaf until Ronda Jo's interpreter told them about it. John Miller just believed in his gut that it was important not to overprotect his daughter. If he was going to pass along anything, it would be a resilience that might help her find her way in a hearing world.

Ronda Jo was about ten months old when John and Dolly first suspected something was wrong with her hearing. A close friend of Dolly's, a woman who had a baby the same age, was looking after the girls one day and noticed that Ronda Jo did not seem to be responding to sound.

There was a loud noise on TV; the friend's daughter jumped when she heard it. Ronda Jo kept right on playing. The more the woman watched Ronda Jo, the more convinced she became that there was a problem.

"Dolly, I don't think Ronda Jo can hear right," the friend said.

"What do you mean?"

The friend explained. Dolly Miller's insides went cold and tight. It couldn't be, Dolly told herself. Ronda Jo always comes when she's called. How many times had she crawled across the room to her? How often had she smiled when Dolly had cooed her name? Dolly searched for proof that Ronda Jo could hear. Even when she took Ronda Jo to a hearing specialist, Dolly was armed with her arguments, explaining how responsive her daughter was. "She's coming to you because you are her mother, not because she heard you call her," the doctor said. Dolly finally decided to conduct her own test. After a bath and a diaper change, Dolly put her baby in the crib. She stayed in the room until Ronda Jo was asleep, a sentry in the dark. And then she walked to the edge of the crib and began to shout:

"Ronda! Ronda! Ronda Jo!" She kept saying it: "Ronda Jo! Wake up, Ronda Jo, wake up!" Dolly Miller stared at her sleeping baby, praying that she would start to cry, or at least stir. In the next room, Robby woke up and came in rubbing his eyes.

"Mommy, what are you doing?"

"I'm talking to Ronda Jo," Dolly said. She walked Robby back into his room. Dolly sat back down again next to her deaf daughter's crib, and she sobbed.

Dolly Miller is a self-reliant, self-contained woman, with ringlets of blonde hair and a strong preference for blue jeans. She's a fastidious keeper of her house, her garden, her daughter's bulging basketball scrapbooks, each page laminated and protected for posterity, the sort of woman who seems to be able to do anything. A few Christmases back, she made Ronda Jo a quilt out of all the T-shirts from all the teams she has ever played on. Dolly is not one to spill out her innermost feelings, a reserve her daughter has taken on, too. Ask Ronda Jo a direct question on the phone or by e-mail, and more often than not she'll give a truncated answer and say she'll tell you more when she sees you, but then never really does. Dolly gets that, too, but she's used to it, used to everything about Ronda Jo and her deafness. They talk on the TTY, sign at home. Even the family cocker spaniel, Bailey, knows some sign: If you hook your two index fingers together—the American Sign Language sign for friend—Bailey will raise a paw to shake hands. Dolly seems embarrassed now about the reaction she had the night she found out her daughter was deaf. It seems so overwrought.

John Miller is from a family of thirteen children, Dolly from a family of eight. Family gatherings aren't reunions so much as conventions. It was always Dolly's plan to have a lot of children of her own. She changed her mind after Ronda Jo was born and has just one boy and one girl. Dolly Miller is not a woman who indulges in much second-guessing, but her one regret is not having a bigger family.

"If I would change anything, I would've had more kids," she said. "And I wouldn't have cared if they were deaf. The deaf can do and be so much more than people think. When you see deaf people together, they are so close, and so friendly. They are not like the hearing. They can teach hearing people a lot. Having Ronda Jo for our daughter has been a joy and I wouldn't trade the experience for anything."

GAME

2

TIME

GALLAUDET UNIVERSITY IS separated from its northeast Washington neighborhood by a black iron fence, bordered on the east by West Virginia Avenue, on the west by Sixth Street, and on the south by Florida Avenue. Beyond the fence is a residential hodgepodge, a patchy mix of row houses and apartment buildings, with no discernible pattern except that a Baptist church never seems more than a block or two away. On one street, there are immaculately kept homes with burnished brass numbers and weedless flower beds. On the next, there are dangling gutters and porches sagging beneath the weight of decomposing sofa beds.

A few blocks away is the tawdry bustle of H Street, a commercial strip dotted with fast-food joints, liquor and clothing stores, and one of the world's most amiable panhandlers. He works the door by a Rite-Aid and wishes people a good day coming and going, whether they contribute or not. Murry's, a supermarket at the corner of Sixth and H, has a tiny, pitted parking lot and a sign that salutes itself for serving the neighborhood for decades, and another that implores its customers not to make off with the shopping carts.

The neighborhood has the feel of a place in flux, an undeclared battle-ground between the nurturing force of community and the angry encroachment of urban blight. The one constant is the striking lack of connection between the neighborhood and the mecca of Deaf culture that sits less than a half-mile away from H Street. You don't see signs in stores welcoming Gallaudet students or congratulating the latest graduates. The big corner sporting-goods store at Eighth and H has color-ful gear from the Washington Redskins and Washington Wizards in the window, but not a Gallaudet baseball cap or sweatshirt in sight. The students, for their part, go get their Big Macs and prescriptions and then make the short trip back to campus. It's not as if there's any sort of ill will, an uneasy alliance, between the school and its neighborhood. There is no alliance at all, as if residents and businesspeople still don't quite know what to make of people who communicate with their hands and eyes, nearly one hundred fifty years after they began coming to northeast Washington to study.

"I used to go by Gallaudet on the bus just about every day growing up," Ben Baylor said. "I couldn't tell you what the school was about, or what the students were like, or really much of anything. It was just a col-lege in the neighborhood that wasn't really part of the neighborhood."

Fitting into the hearing world has never been easy for the deaf. His-tory does not even record a deaf person by name until Quintus Pedius, son of an imperial Roman family, shortly before the birth of Christ. A painter, Quintus Pedius had no language or ability to speak, thus con-firming the prevailing wisdom that muteness was not a result of deaf-ness, but part of the same physiological impairment. Writing in *The History of Animals,* Aristotle said, "Those who are born deaf all become speechless; they have a voice, but are destitute of speech." Because the word *speechless* derived from the same root as *stupid,* Aristotle's meaning was widely mistranslated to be that deaf people are effectively idiots. Nor did the emergence of Christianity provide any respite. While the Old Testament of the Bible depicts the deaf as part of God's creation, the New Testament casts them as souls who have been overtaken by an evil spirit. Paul's letter to the Romans, chapter 10, verse 17, reads: "So then faith cometh by hearing, and hearing by the word of God." The upshot for literal Bible readers was that deaf people were incapable of salvation.

Centuries passed, and such ideas only seemed to get more entrenched. A commission installed by the French Academy of Sciences in 1749 said that the congenitally deaf could neither understand language nor "become capable of reasoning and acting like others." In his book, *Education of Deaf-Mutes* (1888), Thomas Arnold wrote of how the deaf were regarded as a disgrace even in their own families and "lived in deplorable isolation, looked upon as useless, a burden. . . . No other class suffered so much." Arnold's words were especially true of those who were born deaf, or who lost their hearing in the first few years of life. As David Wright, a deaf man and noted South African playwright, wrote in his compelling autobiography, *Deafness,* "Loss of hearing involves loss of the only means by which a child acquires language. The blind can at least hear, and so pick up speech and language like other children. But the deaf child, left to his own resources, must grow up not only unable to speak but denied even a concept of language, that indispensable instrument of thinking and reasoning. Not only is he unable to communicate with himself—he has no language with which to think about what he sees and experiences."

It was not until the sixteenth century that deaf people were considered capable of being educated. The breakthrough came in large measure from an Italian Renaissance thinker, Girolamo Cardano. Intrigued by a written account of a deaf Dutch pupil who had learned to read and write, and inspired to look further on behalf of his son, who was deaf in one ear, Cardano explored the notion that the deaf could compensate for their lack of hearing with their other senses, notably sight. He came to believe that thought and ideas could be conveyed without speech— and a Spanish missionary named Ponce de Leon proved him right. De Leon had befriended Gaspard Burgos, a deaf man who aspired to be a monk but was rejected because he was unable to make a spoken confession. He became Ponce de Leon's first pupil and apparently learned well. De Leon followed a method pioneered by Cardano, whose first step was to create a conceptual linguistic base by writing down words and then pointing to the objects that they signified until the association was created. De Leon had even more success with Franciso and Pedro de Velasco, two deaf brothers. Like nearly all of the early deaf students, the de Velascos were the offspring of an aristocratic family, being schooled for more than humanitarian reasons; throughout history, legal codes of most societies forbade deaf-mutes from owning property and entering into contracts. To ensure that wealth remained in the family, hearing forebears had keen fiscal motivation to educate their deaf scions. Through their study with de Leon, the de Velasco brothers were able to participate fully in Mass, learn Latin, and read prolifically.

Several hundred more years would pass before education of the deaf would expand beyond the gilded domain of royal families. Despite de Leon's remarkable results, the plight of the deaf remained something that few people even thought about. Still, there is no mistaking the magnitude of the change wrought by Ponce de Leon, and even more so, by Girolamo Cardano. It was he, after all, who had the intellectual courage to defy long-standing philosophical and medical conventions, who posited the heretical notion that maybe the deaf could be educated and that their lives need not be far different from those of people whose ears happen to work. Like a rock in still water, Girolamo

Cardano's boldness got things moving, and the ripples are still being felt today.

The bus is revving, the Bison are on board, and everybody agrees: This is really weird. It is sunny and almost seventy degrees in late November, and people are walking around Kendall Green in shorts, basking on benches. Even the grass smells sweet again. The players are scattered in the back of the white windowed bus, ready for the first games of the season, a tournament at Dickinson College in Carlisle, Pennsylvania. Except it doesn't feel like basketball season at all, which is maybe why Ronda Johnson forgets her Air Jordans back in her dorm room. Sitting in her seat, the first one on the right, Kitty rolls her eyes for exaggerated effect, and Ronda runs back to get them.

"Good way to start the season," Kitty said to assistant Hillel Goldberg, across the aisle. A shrieking police car races by on Florida Avenue, siren blaring, an arresting noise but only if you hear it. Ronda makes a breathless reappearance, sneakers in tow, and a few teammates raise their arms overhead, the sign-language equivalent of sarcastic applause. Ernie Young, in a blue-and-gold Gallaudet baseball cap, puts the bus in gear. It warms Kitty to see him, her favorite driver, a fiftyish man of deep faith and good humor, behind the wheel. Kitty still remembers the time Ernie bailed her out after she forgot the players' $15 per diem. The Bison love their junk food. The team stops at a 7–11 or similar store on just about every trip, disembarking en masse, fanning through the aisles, reboarding some ten minutes later with a high-cal, low-nutrient assortment of Slurpees, sodas, and chips. At one stop a few years ago, Kitty realized she didn't have the players' food money. Ernie pulled out his wallet and handed the coach $100.

The bus climbs through the hills of northern Maryland, into Pennsylvania, clouds thickening as they go. It has the feel of a pajama party on wheels. The team only makes a handful of overnight trips a season, not enough for them to cease being an adventure. Players stream on with their pillows and their blue-and-gold bags and revel in the time to nap or joke around. For three hours, the only sounds are periodic bursts of laughter and the steady drone of tires on pavement. From the back row, Nanette Virnig makes her way forward by walking on the inside edge of the seats, as if they were stilts. Touria Ouahid is sitting backward, watching Ronda Johnson holding court, as Ronda Jo stretches out, her feet sprawled across Touria's lap, bodies easily and unthinkingly overlapping, intermingling, as they habitually are, at practice, in the dorms, at lunchtime in the Ely Center. You can't stereotype the deaf any more than you can the hearing, but to Professor Donalda Ammons, it is inarguable that Deaf culture is a much touchier, feelier place than hearing culture.

"We're physical people who enjoy physical contact," Ammons said. *"If I'm in an airport and I see someone signing across the terminal, I'll practically trample people in my way to go over and greet that person. It's almost as if it's an extension of sign language, which is a physical, intimate language. Your hands are out there, your gestures are out there. It's all very open, very unguarded. I think that with the isolation so many deaf people have experienced over time, there is a tendency to embrace each other's presence, literally and figuratively. There is just a very strong need to be together and to feel camaraderie."*

The urge to reach out physically is mirrored by a desire to reach out socially. There are hundreds of deaf organizations in the United States, from local bowling clubs to vast advocacy groups, such as the National Association of the Deaf, the National Fraternal Society of the Deaf, and the USA Deaf Sports Federation. The first such group was The New England Gallaudet Association, formally launched in 1854. According to John Vickrey Van Cleve and Barry A. Crouch, authors of *A Place of Their Own: Creating the Deaf Community in America,* the rapid growth of deaf organizations was a natural result of the isolation Ammons spoke of. *"Hearing people have the opportunity to become friends with those they meet at the health club, in their neighborhood, with fellow PTA parents and so on,"* Stacy Nowak said. *"For deaf people those kinds of opportunities are not available—and deaf clubs were often the answer. We find kinship with other deaf people, and there's nothing better than a night with good friends, laughter and fun."*

Ernie drives through quiet streets with antique streetlamps and old stone houses, then turns onto a commercial strip on the outskirts of Carlisle and arrives at a Hampton Inn, a homogenous and well-kept place with a lobby thick with the smell of new carpet and potpourri. As the players trundle in, the first thing they see is a group of women in blue sweats. They are from Kean University in New Jersey, Gallaudet's opponent in tomorrow's season opener. The two teams immediately begin sizing each other up, like kids on the first day of school, except the focus isn't on clothes or hair styles, but on getting an on-the-spot read on who the *real* players are. Kean has three women who look to be six feet or better, which right away sets Kitty to worrying. She is an avowed pessimist. If a traffic light just ahead is green, she's pretty sure it'll go red on her. If her team gets off to a good start, she worries about whether it's going to peak too early. Now she's getting bad vibes about how the rebounding is going to go tomorrow night. "Man, they're big," Kitty said to Ben Baylor. Ben has a deep voice with a slight southern inflection. "I'm telling ya," he said. It is his stock statement of affirmation.

Kitty gets an extra copy of everybody's room key, the way she always does on the road, in case of fire or emergency or an unscheduled nap. Pounding on the door or calling on the phone are not options. Outside every Gallaudet dorm room there's a doorbell that isn't a bell at all, but a switch to flash the lights and get the occupant's attention. The hotel on campus has similar light flashers. This Hampton Inn doesn't, so extra keys are important. Kitty takes a fistful of them, and the team heads for the elevator as the Kean players, sprawled on sofas and chairs, watch the whole scene intently: the hands that are flying, the faces that are gesturing, a seemingly random tangle of signs and signals. A few Kean players avert their gaze, not wanting to get caught gawking. Others do gawk, their faces a study in bewilderment, as if they're wary of getting too close. The few Gallaudet players that notice are unfazed. They are used to it.

The only one signing now is Kitty. It's Saturday afternoon, November 20, a half hour before the season opener. She's in front of a green blackboard in a cinder-block locker room the size of a walk-in closet, preaching the three C's—concentration, confidence, and control—words she writes on the board before every game. The players are lined up on two benches in front of her, pregame jitters as thick as the walls. Nobody has it worse than freshman Cassey Ellis, who's about to play her first game for Gallaudet. *"I have butterflies, and they may turn into eagles by gametime,"* she said. The only African-American on the team, Cassey has a head of cornrowed hair, little brown stalks shooting up in varying directions. Her eyes are fixed on Kitty. You can tell it's game day, because Kitty is out of her Gallaudet warm-ups and in her coaching clothes, a neatly pressed pair of black slacks, button-down shirt, and print vest, the only concession to her occupation being the little orange basketballs dangling off her belt like ornaments.

Kitty goes over some last-minute reminders about helping out one another on defense, getting out in transition, playing high-speed Gallaudet basketball. "No silly fouls. You've got to play defense," Ben said, forming the sign for letter D with each hand. Kitty's signs get more emphatic, and her eyes are wide with energy. She scans the anxious bodies on the benches and says, *"The time is now. Let's go out and kick some butt,"* and in an instant the room is raucous, the Bison standing, whooping, clapping, hands together in a locker-room scrum.

The Bison make a short walk upstairs and run into the Dickinson gymnasium, a vast place that is one part field house, one part ski lodge, with a rubberized brown floor and a sloping, chalet-style roof. When the P.A. announcer begins the player introductions, Kitty motions the players to the bench and moves a few steps onto the court. One by one, the Bison are introduced:

"From Stockholm, Sweden, a five-foot, six-inch guard, No. 14, Touria Ouahid . . . From Deer River, Minnesota, a five-foot, eight-inch guard, No. 22, Ronda Johnson . . . From Mendota Heights, Minnesota, a five-foot, six-inch forward, No. 25, Nanette Virnig . . . From Boston, Massachusetts, a five-foot, six-inch forward, No. 33, Cassey Ellis . . . From Little Falls, Minnesota, a six-foot, two-inch center, No. 23, Ronda Jo Miller. . . . As each player is announced, Kitty points at her, signs the words being spoken, and motions to her to run on the court. She does this before every game, right after she meets at center court with the officials and captains of both teams, so she can interpret the instructions. Kitty reminds the officials that her team cannot hear, so if they play on after a whistle, it's not out of disrespect. She also asks the officials to be sure to point in one direction or the other when the ball goes out of bounds, instead of merely yelling, "Blue," or "Red," the way lots of officials do. Otherwise her players won't know whose ball it is. In the course of a game, officials often will talk to players, give them verbal warnings: "Watch the three seconds, 23 . . . Keep your elbows in, 14 . . . Next time you do that, 22, I'm giving you a technical. . . ." Kitty reminds them if they need to get a message through, they need to go through her. Most officials are accommodating about it. A few act annoyed. Kitty has radar for the latter type. She can tell by the roll of the eyeballs, the heaving sigh beneath the striped shirt.

"This guy's going to be trouble," she'll say to Ben.

"I'm telling ya," Ben will reply.

Kitty can live with a bad attitude, as long as the game is called fairly. Just about every Gallaudet player can cite an example when it wasn't. One Bison player recalls a high-school game when she actually saw a ref talking to the opposing coach and making fun of their sign language during a stoppage in play. Rival coaches have been overheard more than a few times yelling to their players during a huddle, "Are you going to lose to a bunch of deaf girls??!!" In a way, you can forgive a coach for saying something like that. Coaches are wired to win, to yank whatever motivational string they can think of, whether it's sociologically correct or not. But for a supposedly unbiased official to mock you, that's a much deeper cut.

The ball goes up, the season is on, and before forty seconds go by, the whistle blows. The official points at Ronda Jo. He calls a reach-in foul. Kitty pops up from the bench and mutters, "Oh, man." Ben is thinking, "Not this already." Foul trouble has been the one blot on Ronda Jo's career. In most games that have gone wrong, the reason has been Ronda Jo picking up early fouls. What makes it worse is that usually they are what coaches call cheap fouls—a reach-in, a swipe for the ball. Ronda Jo has astonishingly quick and nimble hands. It's a great gift for a basketball player, and she gets lots of steals. But she also gets lots of fouls because many officials automatically call a foul when a player reaches in, whether she makes a clean play or not.

It is not an auspicious start, and it gets worse. Ronda Jo scores inside on a feed from Ronda for the first basket of the year, and Ronda sinks a three-pointer from the left corner. Ronda Jo scores again on a well-placed bounce pass from Touria. But Kitty's observation about Kean's size turns out to be unhappily prophetic. The Kean frontline is getting all kinds of rebounds and second-chance baskets. The Gallaudet interior defense is atrocious. The Bison allow three layups off in-bounds plays and compound the trouble by missing a half-dozen layups of their own. The offense is rushed and disjointed, players circling like satellites with no destination. With Ronda Jo slow to get started, Touria and Ronda Johnson, the next offensive options, both play as if they're trying to do too much, forcing drives, taking imprudent shots. Cassey's nerves make her tentative, and Nanette is so upset at halftime that she barrels through the locker-room door and lets out a cry of disgust.

During intermission, Kitty addresses the defensive breakdowns and implores everyone to box out. She preaches poise and patience on offense, her tone analytical and reassuring. Down by seven, 43–36, Gallaudet rallies to take a 51–50 lead on a three-pointer and jump shot by Natalie Ludwig, but moments after Ronda Jo scores on a swooping drive, the whistle blows again. Ronda Jo is called for a push. It is her fourth foul. Almost seventeen minutes remain. Kitty stands up, her face clenched and annoyed. She has to sit Ronda Jo for a long stretch, and though the Bison stay close, Kean's inside dominance is too much. The final score is 89–79. In the locker room, the Bison slump on the two benches, faces flushed, bodies sagging. Kitty looks under rebounding on the box score and shakes her head when she sees that the margin for Kean was 63–32—the ugliest rebounding stats she has ever seen. Probably more than any other part of the game, rebounding is about energy and desire; the player who wants the ball the most usually gets it. To be outrebounded by almost a 2–1 margin is a joke. To Kitty and Ben, it's proof that the team wasn't ready to play. Natalie showed energy and poise off the bench in her first game. Ronda Jo, who finished with twenty-four points and fourteen rebounds despite the foul trouble, still never really dominated the way she can. Ben is more irritated than Kitty when she asks if he wants to say anything.

"Nobody cares about your No. 7 ranking, so you might as well forget about it. That's not going to win you any games. You have to play defense to

win games. You have to rebound to win games." Kitty can forgive first-game nervousness, even the tentativeness that can be wrought by high expectations. But what burns her is the lack of resolve she saw. The Bison, for prolonged periods, looked soft. The tournament hosts from Dickinson have a stack of pizzas delivered, and while her Bison dive in and watch the second game of the day between Dickinson and Allentown, Kitty is still bothered by her team's effort.

"I hate losing, but I especially hate it when we do it to ourselves," she said.

On the bus trip back to the hotel, Ernie stops at a convenience store. Kitty stands up by her seat and begins balling up tournament T-shirts she got from their hosts and tossing them one by one toward the back of the bus. The players surge forward like groupies, boxing each other out, jostling for optimum position.

"Where was that during the game?" Kitty said, her voice and signs emphatic. It's a joke with a moral. That night, the team gathers in a conference room and watches a videotape of the game. Ben, Gallaudet's director of technical services, a man with a magic touch around machines and wires, sets it up. The game looks worse the second time. Kean players get inside position with minimal resistance. The ball doesn't move. The Bison anxiety is typified on one fast break by Touria, who takes the ball to the basket but crashes the ball so hard against the board it doesn't even hit the rim. Kitty has a rolled-up box score in her hand and playfully whacks Touria with it. *"What was that?"* Kitty said. Touria begins to explain, then understands the fruitlessness of it and laughs.

The next day, waiting to board the bus for the consolation game, Ronda Jo is sitting in Stacy Nowak's lap. Nanette and Ronda are cavorting in the lobby arm in arm. "It's a Deaf culture thing," Kitty said, hoping the energy carries over into the game this time. In the pregame meeting, just beneath where she has written "The Time Is Now," Kitty draws two pictures: one of a basketball player falling down, the second of the player falling down and getting back up. Talking to the team, she makes her plea, efficiently and emphatically, every sign seeming to convey what it would take three spoken sentences to get across: *"We fell down yesterday. We did it to ourselves. Now we have a choice: Are we going to get back up, or are we going to stay down? Everything right now is up to you. You have to make the decision."*

Ronda Jo wins the opening tip, flicks the ball to Nanette, who hits Cassey Ellis for a layup. Three seconds into the game, the Bison have scored. Ronda follows with a jumper. Touria hits a drive and a three-point play. When Shanada Johnson sinks a pair of outside shots, the lead is up to twelve (28–16), and it's clear the Bison have made their decision. They are rebounding, running, playing energetic defense.

A few minutes into the second half, Ronda hits a three-pointer from the left wing, then converts a fast-break layup. Touria hits one, too, and makes a steal to find Natalie for one more score. The Bison are on a 15–0 tear, and in of those blissful zones athletes dream about. Everything feels free. The ball is zipping around. The passes are sure, the dribbles quick and purposeful. The Bison rarely think about being deaf when they are playing, especially at times like this. Without even the vaguest awareness of it, their other court senses become sharpened, fortified, like muscles gathering and strengthening around an injured body part. Ronda Jo doesn't need audible proof that someone is coming up to spring a double-team on her; she can feel the vibrations from the floor, see it somehow, her peripheral vision honed from years of heavy reliance on it. Nanette doesn't need to hear a voice to know a teammate is wide open, or that Ben is on her about giving up inside position under the boards; she can sense it. Ronda has never heard the clean snap of the net when her shot hits no iron. But she can see it, feel it in her follow-through, the snap jumping like a cricket into her extended right arm, a sweet bit of basketball biofeedback.

The Bison do not think about what they are missing, because it's impossible to miss what you have never had.

There are times, of course, when their inability to hear *does* work against them. Switching defensive assignments can get messed up because they can't simply shout them out—*"Twenty-one coming through," "I got her," "Pick left!"* No matter how frantically Kitty and Ben wave their arms and point to their watches, sometimes possessions and halves will end with time expired and a Gallaudet player, not having heard any warning, still bouncing the ball, unaware of the urgency. But such instances are more the exception than the rule. In the waning moments of the first half against Dickinson, Kitty gets Ronda Jo's attention with a waving arm, signs to her that fifteen seconds remain. Ronda Jo winds up going to the basket and getting to the free throw line.

One new Gallaudet fan, after watching her first game, said she expected to see striking evidence that she was watching a deaf basketball team. She discovered that, except for team huddles in sign language and Kitty's constantly moving hands, she saw no clues that the team in blue and gold was in any way different from its opponent. "I'd find myself yelling out things to them in the heat of a game, and then I'd catch myself and say, 'Why am I telling Ronda Johnson to look for the drive when she can't hear a word I'm saying?'"

The Bison beat Dickinson by forty-eight points. Touria crashes no more layups against the board, scores twenty-one points, and has seven assists. Ronda Jo has twenty-two points, eleven rebounds, seven blocks. Ronda, Nanette, Shanada, Stacy—everyone plays with much more commitment.

On the Sunday night bus ride back to Washington, the players vote to dine at Bonanza Steak House. A party of twenty fills up an empty dining room in a hurry. The players don't need Kitty to order because they each get a menu and point to show the waitress what they want. Ronda Johnson is making everybody laugh with her contorted faces and her ketchup consumption. Everywhere you look, hands are airborne and working and faces are animated, the high-energy language of triumph. Taking in the silent celebration is an elderly couple. They are still in their church clothes. They sit in their booth and bring their heads close together. "They must be deaf," the woman said to the man in a half-whisper. The Bison eat and pay, and Ernie drives through the darkness. Three hours later, he is turning inside the black gate, past the blue rectangular sign that says Gallaudet University at Florida Avenue and Eighth Street. Up the little hill, past the gatehouse, the bus rolls to a halt in front of the Field House and the statue of the Bison that is built of thousands of little strips of iron, oxidized to a reddish-brown. Across the street, outside the Ely Center, two students are locked in animated discourse, then sign good-bye to each other and hug. The players are happy to be home.

HOMECOMING
3

STACY NOWAK LOVES her car. It is a white Volkswagen convertible that she calls Gee, a nickname borrowed from her first license plate: 164-GGG. The summer before the season began, Stacy and Gee hit the road with a couple of friends, a trip that totaled six weeks, eighty-five hundred miles, twenty-one states, and four speeding tickets. Not encountering any state troopers who knew sign language, Stacy did not try to talk her way out of any of the tickets, not even the one in Nevada, where she was nailed for going four miles per hour over the speed limit. Stacy can lip-read well, but it's hard to do when a cop is standing at your window and you've never seen him speak before. So she went with pen and paper ("I'm deaf," she wrote for openers), paid for her excesses, and kept on rambling. Her last ticket was in Virginia, on a camping trip with Jenny Cooper and Ronda Johnson. It was a glorious summer day. Jenny was in the backseat, and three of them were signing songs, Gee a rolling symphony of moving hand and arms, Stacy never seeing the flashing lights in her mirror.

It took her three miles to pull over. *"He was so mad,"* Stacy said.

She apologized on paper for the chase. She knows she's got to be more careful about signing when she's driving. It's better that her hands be on the wheel.

When Stacy got back to Washington, D.C., she could feel the anticipation begin to build. She wheeled on to Florida Avenue and drove up to Eighth Street and turned into Gallaudet. As Gee ramped up the hill, she looked to the left and saw the spire of the Tower Clock, a Victorian flourish atop Chapel Hall, poking up into the Washington sky like an upturned ice-cream cone. She looked to the right and saw the row of doors in front of the Field House, the place where she has spent three years playing basketball and volleyball. Then Stacy did what she often does upon returning to campus after time away.

She started to cry.

Stacy attended the Model Secondary School for the Deaf, a high school that sits on a hill in the back of the Gallaudet campus. Her parents, Brent and Marcia Nowak, are both graduates of Gallaudet. Stacy has been around Kendall Green for years and still gets overcome when she comes back.

"The place just means so much to me. I think it will be like that with me forever. There's just so much history here. I know other schools have history, too, but it's not the same. Hearing people can go to lots of different colleges. If it weren't for Gallaudet, where would we go?" For a couple of years, Stacy worked as a Gallaudet tour guide, taking visitors and prospective students around campus, accompanied by an interpreter for the hearing parents. Stacy would like to be a writer or a journalist one day and own a bookstore. But for an undergraduate job, the tour-guide gig was about as good it gets, certainly a whole lot better than working the counter at the Abbey, the student-run pub in the Ely Center. She loved to surprise

people with historical nuggets, things she's known for years but would always try to relay with a hint of wonder on her full, freckled face: *"This original part of campus was designed by Fredric Law Olmsted, the landscape architect whose most famous work is Central Park in New York City. . . . The squareish brick building on the corner here is called Ole Jim, and it is just that: an old gym, dating to 1881. It is on the National Historic Register, and when it was built it was only the second gymnasium in the United States that had an indoor pool. . . . This is a statue of Edward Miner Gallaudet, the founder and first president of the school. The interesting thing about this statue is that this is where campus ended at the time, and yet you will notice that Gallaudet is facing backward, toward what was then open land. That's because Gallaudet was said to be looking into the future—into a time the school would grow and prosper."*

Stacy's favorite part of the tour, though, is in the front of campus, not even fifty yards inside the fence along Florida Avenue. Framed by trees and skinny houses is a bronze statue dating to 1887, weathered to a dark brownish-green. A work of Daniel Chester French, the leading sculptor of his day and creator of the Lincoln Memorial, the statue depicts Thomas Hopkins Gallaudet, the founder of deaf education in the United States, and a nine-year-old girl named Alice Cogswell, his first student. Gallaudet is seated on a bench, the child standing snugly against his left side, her head tilted back against his shoulder. The teacher's gaze is fixed on his pupil, his countenance kindly and encouraging. He is forming the sign for the letter A with his right hand, and she is doing likewise. Alice's face and body language suggest pride and gratitude, eagerness in a bashful sort of way, as she begins to spell her name. From this bronzed moment almost two centuries ago, the simple transference of a morsel of knowledge, a teacher teaching and a child learning, the lives of deaf children in the United States began to change.

On her tours, Stacy Nowak slows the pace when she arrives at the statue of Thomas Hopkins Gallaudet and Alice Cogswell. Then she looks right at them and signs, *"If not for them, we would not be here, Gallaudet would not exist, and I would not be giving this tour."*

Thomas Hopkins Gallaudet was born in Philadelphia in 1787, the year of the first Constitutional Convention. He graduated from Yale University, then completed seminary school at Andover. He became an evangelical Protestant minister. His mission was to spread the gospel of Jesus Christ. "No other object than the salvation of souls of the pupils can be named as of the highest moment," he once wrote. Then he met the girl next door.

Gallaudet was twenty-seven years old in 1814, living in Hartford, Connecticut. One day he noticed a child sitting off to the side while other neighborhood children were playing. Gallaudet learned that the child was the daughter of a physician named Mason Cogswell and that she was deaf. He approached her and showed her his hat, taking a stick and scrawling the letters H-A-T in the dirt. Gallaudet rubbed the letters out with his foot and wrote them again, this time pointing to the hat in Alice's hand. Alice nodded, and when he wrote H-A-T one more time, she pointed to the hat in Gallaudet's hands, and the preacher smiled. Next, Gallaudet scratched out A-L-I-C-E. She studied the dirt and then pointed to herself. When Dr. Cogswell came home, Alice eagerly showed him the first vocabulary words of her life. When she wrote A-L-I-C-E in the dirt, her father's eyes filled with tears.

Mason Cogswell had been seeking a way to provide for his daughter's education for some time. He was aware that several schools for the deaf had been established in Europe in the eighteenth century, but he was not thrilled about sending his daughter overseas. Sporadic attempts had been made to start a school in the States; none as yet had been established. Dr. Cogswell decided that the only sensible solution was to start one of his own. He floated the idea with an association of Connecticut clergymen and got an enthusiastic response. It was decided that the initial step would be to raise money and send someone to Europe to study the teaching methods there.

That someone was Thomas Hopkins Gallaudet.

Gallaudet was already informally teaching Alice, using a book by a Frenchman, Abbé Roch Ambroise Sicard, a disciple of a renowned French teacher of the deaf, Abbé Charles Michel de l'Epée, a man widely hailed for being among the first to recognize sign as the natural currency of deaf education.

Gallaudet's first stop was England, where he visited several schools run by Thomas Braidwood, who had drawn substantial notice for his success with the so-called oral method, educating deaf children by teaching them to lip-read and to speak. The Braidwoods, though, were a highly secretive bunch. They had plans to launch a school of their own in the States and weren't inclined to share anything. Gallaudet had a more agreeable experience upon meeting Abbé Sicard in London. A French cleric, Sicard presented a system of deaf education based on sign language and the manual alphabet. Underlying this method was the belief that sign language was the most efficient means of educating the deaf. Gallaudet was impressed by Sicard's presentation, particularly by the results the abbé achieved with Laurent Clerc, a deaf man and former pupil who had become a teacher himself. The abbé invited Gallaudet to return with him to Paris for further study. For three months, the preacher immersed himself in the silent system of communication. When it was time to return to Connecticut, Gallaudet convinced his new friend, Laurent Clerc, to join him, knowing that without someone with complete fluency in sign language, the school could not succeed. Clerc was reluctant to leave his family but felt great empathy for the deaf children of America, who, with neither a language nor an education, had to have the barest form of existence. Nobody needed to tell Laurent Clerc what that was like; until he was twelve years old, Clerc could not write and had no formal schooling or systematic means of communication. Most of his days were spent in his rural village, tending to cows, turkeys, and horses. Only when his uncle enrolled him in Abbé Sicard's school in Paris—*L'Institut National des Jeunes Sourds-Muets*—did Laurent Clerc gain access to a world of ideas and learning.

On August 22, 1816, after a fifty-two-day voyage, Gallaudet and Clerc arrived in Hartford. Later that day, Clerc met Alice. His impression was that she was an extremely bright child, but a girl who was "virtually without a language."

Laurent Clerc married a woman from New York, Eliza Crocker Boardman, one of the first pupils at the new school. They had six children. Clerc lived the rest of his life in the United States, devoting his life to the education of deaf American children.

Gallaudet and Clerc had much to do before opening their school. To raise money, they traveled throughout New England, making a compelling two-pronged presentation, Clerc impressing his audiences with his fluency in French, English, and Sign; Gallaudet, the trained preacher, supplying the rhetorical and spiritual flourishes. Gallaudet and Clerc raised $5,000, a sum matched by the Connecticut State Legislature, the first appropriation of public monies for a benevolent institution. The school was chartered as the "Connecticut Asylum for the Education and Instruction of Deaf and Dumb Persons," but it was later renamed the American School for the Deaf. It opened in 1817. The first of the seven students to enroll was Alice Cogswell.

Drawing students from a wide geographical area, the American School was a residential institution and quickly became a model for schools for the deaf around the country. By the 1850s, there were nineteen such institutions—and growing support for the idea of college for the deaf. Among those interested was Edward Miner Gallaudet, the youngest of eight children of Thomas Hopkins Gallaudet and Sophia Fowler, a young woman from Guilford, Connecticut, whom Thomas Hopkins taught at the American school and later married. The young Gallaudet, an unfulfilled banker at the time, received a letter from Amos Kendall, a wealthy man about Washington who made a fortune investing in the telegraph—an invention of his friend, Samuel F. B. Morse. Kendall had become the legal guardian for five deaf orphans and wanted to start a school for them. He got Congress to incorporate it as "The Columbia Institution for the Instruction of the Deaf and Dumb and Blind." He donated two acres of his northeast Washington estate and at the suggestion of Harvey Peet, the well-regarded head of the New York Institution for the Deaf and Dumb, contacted the twenty-year-old Gallaudet about becoming superintendent.

After receiving Kendall's letter on May 14, 1857, Gallaudet wrote back four days later, saying "enlightening the minds of Deaf-Mutes . . . occupies a warm place in my heart." Gallaudet met with Kendall in Washington and broached the idea of creating a college in addition to the residential school. Kendall liked the idea. Gallaudet came on board (his mother moved to Washington with him), commenced fund-raising, and, four years later, recommended to Congress that a college be established for deaf students.

In 1864, President Abraham Lincoln signed the legislation allowing the Columbia Institution to grant collegiate degrees. The collegiate division was called the National Deaf-Mute College—and the featured speaker at its opening was Laurent Clerc. Inside of two years, the school had twenty-five students from sixteen states. By 1893—the year in which the college was renamed for Thomas Hopkins Gallaudet—it had produced, by Edward Miner's reckoning, fifty-seven teachers, four ministers, a lawyer, and three educators who founded schools for deaf children in the west. John Carlin, an artist and longtime advocate for deaf education, hailed the establishment of the institution.

"The birth of this infant college will bring joy to the mute community," Carlin said.

Kitty has long viewed herself as more an educator than a coach, someone always looking for a teachable moment. From the outset of the 1999–2000 the season, the lesson she senses this team needs to learn is the importance of owning responsibility for its actions. She wants the players to be accountable, for themselves and one another. She wants them to be strong enough to stand up and say, "That was my mistake," and to expect their teammates to do the same. She wants them to be totally honest with one another, a quality that is the self-correcting sinew of almost every truly successful team: *"I think you dribble too much . . . You look like you're going through the motions . . . I've been open a few times and you haven't gotten the ball to me."* No coach wants gratuitous squabbling in her locker room, but honesty is a must.

Sometimes Kitty worries that the players are so close that they spare one another's feelings. The upper-class core of the team—Nanette, Ronda Jo, Ronda and Shanada, Stacy, Jenny, and Touria—are sisters in Phi Kappa Zeta sorority, the oldest deaf women's organization in the country. All but Ronda Jo (who has an apartment off-campus) live together on the sixth and seventh floors of Clerc Hall. *"We'll jump off a cliff for each other,"* Nanette said.

Kitty admires their closeness but doesn't want it getting in the way. As the Bison ready for their home opener, Kitty's aim isn't just to have a winning season. It's to underscore the importance of accepting responsibility. She doesn't have to wait long for the chance.

It's a sun-dappled Saturday, two days after Thanksgiving, a day of caressing warmth. Stacy, Touria, and Touria's boyfriend, Thomas Koch, spend part of it riding around in Gee, with the top down. As the temperature drops and dusk arrives, an orange half-moon hangs over the Field House. The Bison's annual Holiday Tournament is a couple of hours away. The other schools are State University of New York at Potsdam, Randolph Macon, and Capital University, the No. 2–ranked team in the country. Kitty calls Touria into her office.

"Did you do your extra shooting Friday?" Each player is required to take one hundred extra shots and one hundred extra free throws after every practice.

"No, I didn't. I'm sorry."

"Then you're not starting tonight." Touria is stunned and angry. Not starting the home opener? Because she didn't take all her shots? She doesn't think the punishment fits the crime, not remotely. Kitty sees the hurt on her face but is not buckling, no matter how much she feels inclined to. Touria has probably shown more courage and willpower than any player Kitty has ever coached. The way she fought back from her knee surgery was pure guts and diligence, grinding her way through the arduous process of rehabilitation. The way she held to her dream to play basketball and attend Gallaudet—despite fierce family pressure not to—is something Kitty respects immensely. "She's a very special person," Kitty said. Sometimes Kitty weakens when it's time to come down on Touria, but the coach knows she has to do this. She can't just talk about accountability and then not do anything about it.

For the first seventeen minutes of that night's game against Potsdam, Touria is parked on the bench. Natalie Ludwig gets the start. Touria resists the urge to pout or strike a pose of defiant disinterest. She roots hard for her teammates, and Kitty is silently appreciative of her maturity.

The Bison don't miss their point guard, and the main reason is her backcourt partner, Ronda Johnson. She makes steals, grabs rebounds, hits jumpers. She has four baskets in the opening minutes as the Bison surge to a ten-point advantage, and when she slashes through the lane for a layup late in the first half, Gallaudet has extended the score to 44–20. It is all going splendidly, until Ronda Jo gets clobbered on a drive to the basket, and there is no call.

Kitty springs out of her seat as if she'd been launched and signs, *"Is this referee a blind man or what?"* Paulina Wlostowski, keeping her stat charts on the bench, suppresses a giggle. Others on the bench and in the stands aren't so successful. If Kitty had voiced the words instead of signed them, she surely would've gotten a technical foul. Sometimes ASL comes in very handy for a coach, though Kitty knows she can't overdo it. King Jordan, one of the Bison's biggest fans, does not take kindly to the employment of sign language to gain any advantage, to willfully exclude the hearing from one's joke or aside. Kitty believes in proper sideline comportment. Sometimes her passions just get the better of her.

Kitty finally summons Touria late in the first half. She plays with aggressiveness bordering on frenzy, a kinetic force who seems here and there and everywhere.

"You sure made up for lost time," a friend said to her later. Touria twirls her short dark hair with two fingers, something she does scores of times during games and practices, a reflex as engrained as the deep breaths she takes before every free throw.

"I had a lot of energy to get out," she said, smiling. She has thought it all through and decided she's glad this happened. *"It shows everybody how serious Kitty is about holding people accountable. I think everyone on the team knows it now."*

Most of the second half is garbage time, the outcome decided, everybody loose and having fun. Center Amelia England, one of the last reserves off the bench, enjoys it as much as anybody, scoring as many baskets as she did the whole previous season. She racks up eight quick points and you can see her confidence grow with each success. Amelia keeps to herself in practices and games, but her positive body language is unmistakable. *"There's nothing like getting out there and playing."*

Touria winds up with fourteen points, six assists, and five steals. Ronda Jo grabs seventeen rebounds, and Nanette is quietly superb, with fourteen points and nine rebounds. But the night's unquestioned star is Ronda, who puts up eighteen points in the first half and has the crowd in a bleacher-stomping, arm-waving lather in the final seconds, when she sinks two free throws that get the Bison to one hundred points.

Game No. 1 in the Field House lives up to every bit of the season's advance billing. Well after the buzzer, fans are still marveling at the sequence midway through the first half, Ronda Jo going high to make a spectacular block, then saving the ball from going out of bounds and firing a strike of a baseball pass to Ronda, who finishes it off with a layup.

"That was one for the highlight film," Ben Baylor said. He told Ronda Jo the same thing. *"Ben is great. He's been such a big help to me,"* she said. She appreciates his consistency, his steady demeanor. All the Bison do.

Ben is as reliable as gravity. He has a wry sense of humor and a penchant for trash talk, a holdover from his days at Rutgers University in New Jersey, where he majored in computer science and played on the basketball team for two years. Ben works with the inside players mostly, and it's common at practice to see him playing one-on-one with Ronda Jo or Stacy Nowak or Cassey. Before he shoots a jumper, he loves to say, "Automatic," leaning slightly toward his tauntee for added emphasis. If he makes it—and he often does, because he can shoot—he'll come at them again. "I told you it was automatic," or "Why didn't you believe me?" The only thing better than burying a jumper over one of the women is blocking their shot. Ben hasn't gotten Ronda Jo's shot often in four years, but when he has, she hears all about it, in his slightly cumbersome but workable sign: *"Don't bring that garbage in here."* Or *"You're going to have to do better than that."* At six feet, two inches and about two hundred pounds, slightly thickened in the middle from his playing days but still a man with an athlete's moves,

Ben likes to lean on the bigger Bison in practice and does it with a purpose. He figures if they get used to pounding bodies with him, the average one-hundred-fifty-pound center is going to seem like a flyweight.

"He's made me a much better player," Ronda Jo said. *"He knows what to say and what to do to make me work harder on my moves. He'll tell me I'll never beat him, and even before games, tell me that such and such a player has whipped my butt and what was I going to do about it? I have to prove to him that I'm a better player than she is."*

Ben came to Gallaudet in the early eighties, after a short, unhappy stint in a computer job. He was in his field but out of sorts, discovering the depth of his distaste for desk work. He wanted to have a cubicle-free job, be able to ramble a bit. He saw an ad in the paper for equipment manager at Gallaudet. At the start, he did his uniform-cleaning and ball-inflating without knowing any sign language, or many students.

"When I first got here some deaf people were almost belligerent toward hearing people," Ben said. "It was almost like payback for what the hearing world did to them; a 'Now-that-you're-on-our-turf sort of thing.'" Ben had all kinds of things to learn, sign language being one of them. He had the hearing person's typically paternalistic attitude when he started assisting Kitty sixteen years ago. "Sometimes I'd catch myself feeling sorry for them. I'd think, 'Oh, I better take it easy on them, they can't hear.'" The players helped teach him sign and convinced him to lose the sympathy. With the zeal of the freshly converted, he gets as indignant as anyone on the team when the Bison encounter ignorance. He's not easily riled, but Ben got pretty hot last year when the Bison played another local school, and drubbed them, in the kind of game the Bison women like best: high-speed, in the open court, winning more with pulsing energy than half-court polish, the finely tuned execution of methodically plotted patterns. It's the style that made them one of the highest-scoring teams in the nation, averaging eighty-eight points a game in 1998–99.

During one break, Ben heard the opposing coach scream, "They can't even hear! How can you let a bunch of deaf kids do this to you?!!" Ben puts on his Walkman and listens to music, mostly jazz, on every trip, his eyes closed and his head back. The riffs from the game that night were as good as anything his CD player could serve up. It was a sweet, short ride home.

It can be an oddly unsettling experience for a visiting team to play in the Gallaudet Field House. Where else in America will you see fans not clapping, but throwing their arms overhead like a football referee after a field goal, with a flutter of their fingers? Where else do you hear no roars, but relentless stomping, the good vibrations carrying right down the pullout wooden grandstands to the floor? What other team gets on its hands and knees around the tip-off circle in the center of the gym, pounding the floor to a high-speed beat to get themselves fired up?

And how many times do you see someone like Linnae Gallano, alone on the floor moments before tip-off? A Gallaudet junior, Linnae is one of the regulars who signs "The Star Spangled Banner." She does it with feeling and flair, her hands and arms alternately moving swiftly and slowly, always surely, the spectacle packing the anthem with fresh power, no matter how many times one has heard it.

It's a surreal, silent world the hearing player finds herself in, devoid of all the cacophonous cues she's accustomed to on game day: no hip-hop or rock music blaring, no noise building, no overzealous P.A. person shrieking. The experience can make some visiting players go strangely flat, more observers than competitors.

"I've seen it happen plenty of times where a team comes in and because our team and our fans aren't making any noise, they kind of go quiet, too," Ben Baylor said. "It can be disorienting when you're not used to it."

Capital University, one of the elite Division III programs in the country, easily defeats Randolph Macon and moves into the championship game Sunday against the Bison. Capital has never played Gallaudet before and gets a thorough forewarning from coach Dixie Jeffers, who in her pregame talk with her players, tries to inoculate them against the flatness. She urges them not to underestimate Gallaudet, too, but sometimes kids just need to learn for themselves. As the national anthem begins, the Capital team is standing, the players' eyes fixed not on the flag, but on Linnae, as she unballs her fists, lifts them up, extends her fingers: the bombs bursting in air.

It is a game with the feeling of March about it, a sense of import not often found in November. Kitty doesn't want to play it up too much with her players, but she knows it's a significant test. She watches Capital run through warm-ups with a roster—twenty players—that looks more like a football team than a basketball team. Gallaudet suits up ten players. In Room 142, the Bison seem loose. Touria gives Shanada a noogie. Ronda and Nanette hold hands and skip down the corridor like schoolgirls, right into the classroom. Kneeling on the table with her chalk, Kitty writes "The Time Is Now," and her three C's (confidence, control, concentration), and some strategic specifics about defending against Capital's constant picking-and-rolling offense. The Bison are wearing their white home uniforms, with a V neck and blue and gold in a geometric weave along the sides. When the team huddles up and goes around the circle, Stacy lets out a whoop and says, *"No mercy!"* Kitty is already on her way to the gym in her black pantsuit, looking for her customized chair. It's the one she's sat in for years. It has a higher cross bar to rest her shoes on, a sort of booster seat for a grown-up. Her legs don't reach the bottom bar of a regular chair.

"Well, we've got all the ingredients. Now let's see if the cake rises or falls," Kitty said.

It is a game with the careening momentum of an amusement-park ride. Ronda scores the first eight points for Gallaudet, but Capital answers. The battle under the backboards is fierce, Ronda Jo and Kendra Meyer, Capital's own All-American, competing hard, taking turns getting the better of it. Ronda Jo hits a three-point play, scores off a rebound, and sinks a turnaround in the final minutes of the first half.

The Bison are up by twelve with seven minutes to go, but Capital, with all its depth, seems fresher and keeps closing in. Natalie hits a nerveless three-pointer from the corner. Ronda Jo muscles in a bank shot inside to make it 70–63 with under three minutes left. Capital keeps pushing, pressing, and gets within one. Every play, every possession, is huge now, tension building with each tick. Ronda has been driving all game, beating people with her crossover dribble, freezing defenders with fakes and stutter-steps. She's driving again, on the baseline, when she abruptly stops and pulls up. She fires up an eight-foot jumper. It's good. The crowd stomps the bleachers. The whole Field House feels as if it's quaking. The game moves into the final minute. The Bison play hard, swarming defense and move the ball well on offense. The Crusaders foul Touria, Ronda Jo, and Ronda, forcing them to make free throws under immense pressure. The three best Bison players take six pressurized shots. They make all six.

Gallaudet hangs on to win, 78–75. The crowd is berserk. The players are hugging and dancing on the court, Ronda Johnson, who finishes with twenty-seven points, in the middle of it. Alexander Long, *Buff and Blue* sports editor, signs from the scorer's table to a friend in the stands, *"That's one of the best games I've seen them play in a long time."*

Accepting hugs and kudos all around, Kitty walks out the gym door just as Touria walks in. They bump hard, Touria's water bottle soaking them both. They laugh and embrace, the benching all forgotten, and then Kitty corrals Ronda Johnson and rubs her blonde head and tells her how great she played. The Bison took twenty-one free throws in the game and made eighteen. They withstood a tremendous charge from one of the premier teams in the country. Victories always mean more when they come against great teams.

In the postgame award ceremonies, Ronda Jo is named the tournament's Most Valuable Player, but it is almost as if the choice were made out of habit more than empirical evidence. Ronda Jo was dynamic on both ends of the floor, but there's no way the Bison win this tournament without Ronda, who set a defiant, we're-not-backing-down tone against Capital from the start. Ronda is named to the all-tournament team and gets a big ovation when she's announced. She works hard at fighting her feelings of being underappreciated. She doesn't want to dampen a transcendent team moment with self-pity. She is happy for Ronda Jo, her longtime friend and teammate, all the way back to the Minnesota State Academy for the Deaf. Still, it's tough not to get recognized, even after the best game you've ever played. The team has an impromptu party with friends and fans in Room 142, cookies and brownies getting devoured, big moments in the game getting replayed. Ronda is by the window, talking with Shanada and Stacy, but she's not in high comedic gear. Something about her red-apple cheeks and pink skin hint at remoteness. Like a freshly spurned lover, she is going to need some time before plunging back into commitment.

Kitty makes a mental note to check back in with Ronda in a day or two, boost her up. She goes into the Phys Ed office and finishes her coaching day the way she does after every game, faxing the box score and a note back home to her parents, Paul and Peggy Baldridge, in Indianapolis. It's impossible not to think of her dad after a game like this, and impossible not to be sad, too.

Paul Baldridge suffered a stroke late in the summer, and it's been one thing after another since then. The motor function of his hands and arms, of his sign language, has been slow to return. His condition, and the strain it's putting on her mom, are worries that are with Kitty constantly. She's trying to get home once a month, but it's hard during the season. Basketball is one of the first bonds she ever had with her dad. Faxing the box score rekindles it a little. It feels good.

Just outside the office, the Field House lobby is still teeming with people, almost an hour after the game. It's a big, shell-shaped space, well-lit and welcoming, another Gallaudet place built for communing. A few hearing people are talking and signing, but mostly it is deaf people, their signs and gestures filling the lobby with motion and connection. Deaf people say that one of the hallmarks of their culture is the long good-bye, the reluctance to leave one another's company. It goes back to the isolation that Donalda Ammons talked about. Being together feels good and affirming. Good-byes can go on for hours, until someone flashes the lights repeatedly, incandescent shorthand for "It's time to go home." Nobody flashes the lights in the lobby after the Capital game, and the shell stays full for a long time.

COMEBACKS AND
CONSTERNATION

ASK ANY BISON, and she'll tell you: The best room in the house, almost any house, is the kitchen. It's the room where the lighting is the brightest and signing is the easiest, and lingering is a given. Shanada and Ronda Johnson grew up on a farm in Deer River, Minnesota, not far from Ball Club, Minnesota, a couple of hours from the Canadian border. Their parents, Ronald and Shirley, met at the Deaf Olympics. Shirley was a swimmer, and Ronald was a basketball player who was smitten the minute he spotted Shirley in her suit on the pool deck. The Johnsons have five children, four of them deaf. The only one who isn't deaf is the youngest of the five, Shawn, and everybody just assumed he couldn't hear either, until he was five years old and an interpreter in school saw him barking one day. Turns out he could hear and was imitating the sound he'd been hearing for years from the family dog.

"I was shocked when Shawn was hearing. Everybody was," Ronda said. *"Nobody ever thought there would be a hearing person in our family."*

In the Johnson home, as in many deaf households, the kitchen is more a social space than a cooking space. Shirley prepares a heaping mound of pasta and vegetables, and they gather round and eat and stay sometimes for two or three hours. It feels right. *"I've spent more time in the kitchen than all the other rooms of our house put together,"* Ronda said.

Whoever designed the gymnasium at Salisbury State University on Maryland's Eastern Shore was definitely not deaf. The lighting is dim. The floor is a rubber synthetic the color of mocha. The whole place is muted and monochrome. It wouldn't be a bad spot for a first date, but it's not so good for playing ball, and worse yet for signing.

It is the first of December, and the beach days of late November are done. The air is biting and blustery. Tonight the Bison begin the core of the season, their Capital Athletic Conference (CAC) schedule. As heartening as it was to knock off Capital and win the Gallaudet tournament, those games were just early-season appetizers. Now it's time for the main course. The players know it, but sometimes knowing isn't enough. Kitty wishes she could figure out why players show up flat sometimes—and why, when a couple of players are flat, it seems to spread through the team like poison ivy.

The Bison come off the two-hour bus ride in a deep fog. Ronda saunters onto the court in a hooded sweatshirt, wearing only the hood, the rest of it flapping behind her. She is eating a bag of Skittles and saying she doesn't feel loose. She lies on the floor, and Stacy and Nanette take turns sitting on her back, an impromptu spinal adjustment. Touria always likes to get on a Stairmaster to warm up her knee, but she can't find one. Ronda Jo seems typically aloof as she goes through pregame layups. Cassey Ellis is brushing her hands in an upward motion against her chest: "Fire up! Fire up!" She hollers, "C'mon!" for added emphasis.

Cassey has become the Bison's biggest spirit-booster. On the bench, Kitty doesn't like what she's picking up.

The first half is a study in carelessness, entropy in baggy shorts. There are turnovers, defensive lapses, and the dreaded foul trouble for Ronda Jo. When a Salisbury player slips inside Stacy for an offensive rebound and basket, Kitty said, *"I'm begging you to block out!"* Ronda is throwing risky passes, and Touria is having maybe the worst game of her career. She keeps losing her dribble under defensive pressure, keeps forcing passes that aren't there. She wears a white headband the width of a chopstick, and the head and headband are both hanging. Gallaudet is only down nine (41–32) at the half, and it's a miracle. The only one holding it together is Nanette, who hits an assortment of short jumpers in addition to her normal quota of hustle plays.

"I'm having a terrible day," Touria said, slumped on a halftime bench, hair matted in sweat. She rips off her headband. Her skin is flushed and her mind is running amok, replaying every single mistake, each one a fresh blow to her self-esteem. She's an All-Conference player, one of the top players Gallaudet has ever had, but she's never been much good at giving herself a break. Touria turns self-criticism into a full-body workout.

As they head out for the second half, Kitty says to Ben, "It sure would be nice if Ronda Jo got going." Ben nods. To Kitty, Ronda Jo has not seemed herself this year. Of course she's been the best player, but she's been lacking a certain spark through the early games. Wanting to check in with her, Kitty invited Ronda Jo up to the front seat on the bus ride over to Salisbury. Kitty asked her if the season's large expectations were weighing on her, or if her ankle injury from volleyball was bothering her.

Ronda Jo was as inscrutable as ever.

"I'm fine. I'm just getting into basketball shape. Things will be better in January."

The second half begins, and as if on cue, Ronda Jo seizes control of it. After Natalie drills in two quick baskets, Ronda Jo makes a steal and layup, hits a fallaway, hauls down an offensive rebound, and puts in a spinning reverse. She pumps in eleven straight points, and the Bison are suddenly within a point, 49–48. Touria hits a bank shot under pressure, Stacy puts in an offensive rebound, and when Ronda buries a double-pump hanger in the lane, Gallaudet has an 8–0 run and a lead it never relinquishes. Despite having two and three players hanging on her, Ronda Jo scores twenty-one points in the second half. For the game, she has twenty-five points and four blocks in only twenty-six minutes of time. She is the difference. Gallaudet wins, 85–78, to push its record to 4–1, but the headiness of a comeback triumph on the road is not universally shared.

Touria is miserable. She knows she panicked against Salisbury's press. Sometimes she actually ran away from the ball, even after Kitty pulled her out and said, *"Are you a good player?"* Touria nodded mechanically. *"Well, then start playing like it. Stop feeling sorry for yourself."*

Touria looks at a box score and crumples it up when she sees that she committed twelve turnovers. That should be four or five games' worth. She is sitting in the bleachers, showered and changed but not renewed. The way Touria's mind works, things are either very good or very bad. She is not someone who sees shades of gray. "Touria's the only person I know who thinks you have to break up with your boyfriend if you have a fight with him," a friend said. Just as quickly, they patch things up, and she shows a sweet picture of them arm in arm during spring break in Key West. Kitty and Ben go at Touria after the game, double-teaming her with humor.

"OK, you've had your one lousy game for the year. You're finished with it. You understand?" Ben said.

"Were you trying to set the NCAA turnover record? Was that your goal?" Kitty said. She rubs a hand back and forth over Touria's black hair. Touria has a full smile, the kind you can see from across a gym, against her toffee-colored complexion and small dark eyes. She wears her unhappiness just as openly. Her eyes get smaller and her mouth opens

slightly, enough to look aghast. Next to her on the bleachers, Ronda Jo has an ice pack on her ankle and Nanette has one on her knee.

"Maybe we need to get an ice pack for your head," Kitty tells her. Touria stays deep in replaying mode. *"I never got so panicky in my life. I don't know what was wrong. How can I play like that?"* The fast-food stop on the ride home is Burger King, done in retro, with vintage Coca-Cola signs and Elvis pictures, trying way too hard to impersonate an old diner. Kitty almost expects the guy handing out Whoppers to be dressed like James Dean. There's no feel-good nostalgia for Touria, in any case; she's from Sweden. She's farther from home than anyone on the team, in all kinds of ways.

It is after midnight in Clerc Hall, and Touria Ouahid, the resident adviser on duty, is alone in an office next to the front door, a schoolbook open behind a desk. She's fluent in five languages—Swedish, Swedish Sign, English, German, and American Sign—and is studying in English at the moment. She is wearing faded jeans and a gray pullover and sneakers, bearing the fitness of a varsity athlete even in a sedentary position. At twenty-three, Touria is in her fourth year at Gallaudet and her seventh year away from her home. She goes back when her schedule and finances allow, usually once or twice a year. She does not stay long. There are too many memories, even though part of her feels as if she should be used to it by now. During her visit the previous summer, Touria went out to eat in Stockholm with two of her brothers, both of whom are hearing. They talked and talked, doing minimal signing, and when Touria protested they said, "Wait a minute, we'll fill you in," but they never really did.

She felt left out and inconsequential.

It was an old feeling.

Touria is the fourth of ten children, one of four deaf girls born to hear-ing parents. It's hard enough for a child to get her needs met when she has nine siblings. It's harder yet when she is deaf and female, not a favorable combination in a traditional Muslim household. "You should be married. You are getting old," Touria's father says. "You shouldn't go to an American college. You will become like an American woman instead of a Muslim woman," her parents tell her. They disapprove of almost every choice she has made in her life, from her American boyfriend to her desire to go to college to her wardrobe. Touria doesn't pay any mind. She has not worn a veil since she was a little girl. She got to Gallaudet by telling them she only planned to stay one year.

She does what she has to do. She sticks by her choices.

The toughest part of being away is not seeing Jamila and Amina, her eight-year-old twin sisters. They are both deaf. Sometimes it really feels as if her heart is breaking, she misses the twins so much. Their pic-tures are on Touria's dresser, on the wall. In the wrong mood, just glancing at the pictures can bring on a bout of melancholy. Her parents know how to push that button. They have been telling her for years that she belongs at home, that she is the only one who can help Jamila and Amina find their way. It is a wrenching conflict for Touria. Her parents are right; she could do so much to nurture the girls if she were home. Her parents are wrong; there's so much more she wants to do and experience in her own life.

"I want to be a part of their lives. I want to be there for them and help them, but life has to go on," Touria said. *"I have to keep moving forward."* The twins aren't old enough to understand yet, but in time Touria will explain to them why she went away, and she's sure they will under-stand. Soon she will have her college degree. She thinks she'd like to work as a recruiter for Gallaudet, traveling around the country and the world, seeing new places and spreading the word of the university. Isn't it better to show, not tell, Jamila and Abina that they don't have to let

deafness stop them? Wouldn't it be great for them to experience Deaf culture for themselves, to be a part of a place like Gallaudet and get wrapped in an embrace of acceptance?

Like the overwhelming majority of deaf children in the world, Touria comes from a family with two hearing parents and a home life of enormous loneliness. Of almost forty-four thousand American deaf students surveyed by Gallaudet Research Institute in the 1999–2000 school year, 84 percent said that both their parents can hear—and 69 percent said that family members do not regularly sign. So in more than two-thirds of the cases, deaf students grow up cut off from full communication in their own families. As one Gallaudet student said, *"You never feel like you're totally included. You feel like you're always getting the Cliff Notes version of things."* Coming to a place like Gallaudet is a revelation for many students. But it also leaves some people struggling to come to terms with the split lives they lead: feeling terribly impaired in their own homes, and greatly empowered by the environment at school.

Touria's parents, Chaib and Fatima Ouahid, grew up in the remote village of Temsamane, in the Rif Mountains in northern Morocco. They moved to Sweden when Touria was a baby, in part because Chaib has a deaf brother and saw how abysmally he was treated in Morocco. Touria's brother, Abdallah, a medical school student, recalls a family trip back to Morocco when Touria was reading a novel and people believed she was simply doing it for show.

"They thought there was no way that a deaf person could be reading a book," Abdallah said. He is a narrow-shouldered young man, with dark eyes and a body like a blade of grass. When he was a kid, he was embarrassed to have a deaf sister, let alone four of them. He learned Swedish Sign language but did not like signing in public, the self-consciousness of youth wanting no part of something that would brand him as different. Separated by only a year, he and Touria have seen sibling rivalry and distance evolve into tenderness. Now Abdallah is embarrassed that he was embarrassed. When he made his first visit to Gallaudet, it didn't take long for him to see what Touria had been telling him for years: how alive and connected she felt there, and how happy she was not to have to make do with the linguistic table scraps she got at home.

"I understand now why this means so much to you," Abdallah told her. Abdallah's friends often used to express their condolences to him upon learning of Touria's deafness. Now he tells them, "Why are you so sorry? She has done more in her life than I have and she will do a lot more."

Touria learned her love of sports, especially basketball, from her sister Memount, who is also deaf and seven years her elder. Memount didn't teach Touria specific skills of the game. It was more the pure passion that Memount passed on, the joy of competing and sweating and learning to do things you couldn't do the day before. Memount stopped playing when she was about seventeen. She pleaded with Touria to do the same, hoping to spare her sister the abuse she got. Touria understood Memount was trying to protect her but would not listen.

"I can be a little bit stubborn," Touria said. It is the same way on the court. When she decides she is going to the basket, she pounds the ball into the hardwood and drops her shoulder. Her face draws tight and her eyes flash: *I'm coming at you, and you're not going to stop me.* Sometimes she drives too hard and puts up an off-balance shot. Most of the time she makes the basket or draws a foul.

Touria's father is a former railworker who retired twenty years ago with a disability that forced him to walk with a cane. To Chaib Ouahid, the notion of a young woman playing basketball, or any sport, was much worse than a frivolity. It was a disgrace to the family, an unspeakable affront to Allah, to their faith. Muslim girls were not supposed to run around in shorts. They certainly were not supposed to do it in front of boys and men. Hassiba Boulmerka, an Algerian who became the first African woman to win an Olympic gold medal, used to have to dodge tomatoes, rocks, and saliva on her training runs, so outraged were fundamentalist countrymen by her running around with bare legs. Chaib Ouahid could understand the depth of their feeling.

One of his long-standing regrets in life is that his children have grown up to be more Swedish than Moroccan. He believes if the family had stayed in Morocco, the children would've remained truer to Islam. They would not have been corrupted by the secular forces of the Western world, and his daughters never would've acquired this desire to play sports. Chaib Ouahid has built a big house in northern Morocco. His dream is that one day the whole family will return there to live.

Touria was eleven when she became interested in basketball. When her parents forbade her to play, she would make up stories about doing something else, then borrow shorts and T-shirts and sneakers from friends. The harder her parents disciplined her, the more she resisted. She ran away from home a couple of times. Her father became increasingly irate over his daughter's defiance. She was disrespecting him as a man, as a father. She was also disrespecting their religion, and so he felt he had no choice but to take matters into his own hands. Touria doesn't like to think about it, but the images do not go away. She can still see her father chasing her around the house. She can see herself finally letting him catch her, as much to get it over with as anything else. She can still feel the kicks and slaps and punches, all over her body. She doesn't hear him, but she is pretty sure he's screaming. For at least four years it went on. She tried to get him to stop, and so did her mother, Fatima. She is a kind woman in a quintessentially maternal way, someone who has stroked Touria's head and held her and been there in every way. Her mother tried to reason with her father but ultimately could not cross him.

Touria was good at hiding her bruises and welts. When the school authorities asked, she'd tell them, through an interpreter, that she had fallen or bumped into something. *"Oh, it's nothing,"* she'd say. One day the police showed up at the house and spoke to her father. The way it was explained to Touria, the authorities made it clear that if Touria ever showed up at school again with marks on her body, there would be serious consequences. She was never struck again. When Touria was sixteen, her parents saw her play for the first time. It was a national junior tournament in Sweden, against all hearing players. Touria scored thirty points and was named the most valuable player. She was so happy her parents were there. She thinks that even her father must've been a little bit proud that night.

Chaib Ouahid has had health problems the last few years. Touria sees him softening, becoming more accepting of things. They had the best conversation they've ever had when she was home last summer.

"When are you going to get married?" her father asked.

"You know me. I'm headstrong. I have to find a guy I really love." They talked a long time. Touria told her father that she knows how hard it must've been for him when she was growing up, how much it must've hurt him to have a daughter who was so determined to reject his beliefs. *"I understand that you probably felt that you did not have a choice,"* she said. *"I do understand that."* Her father looked old to her, vulnerable. She told him that she knew he did the best he could, and that she loved him. By the way her father looked back, his face sad and heavy, and by the way he kissed her, she knew that he loved her, too.

Kitty is looking out on the floor and not believing what she is seeing. The Bison are a team that loves the fast break. They rarely miss an opportunity to push the ball downcourt. But tonight they look as if they're stuck in porridge. It is early in the first half against conference-rival Mary Washington College, in Fredericksburg, Virginia, and the team is totally listless. Kitty had a bad feeling about this trip when Ernie pulled up to the

Field House in Gallaudet's old blue school bus, a rough-riding vehicle with seats as hard as park benches. "Oh man, not the prisoners' bus," Kitty said. "Ernie, you can't do better than that?" The regular bus was in use by another team. It happens once or twice a season. Kitty has never figured out what the team's record is in prisoner-bus games, but her gut says that it's not good, and fresh evidence is before her. Ronda Jo is in a daze, one hundred eighty degrees from where she left off against Salisbury State. Her moves are stiff, her inside game absent. It's almost as if her dark blue road uniform were being filled by an imposter. Executives from WNBA teams have already begun to call Kitty, asking her about Ronda Jo's game and planning when to scout her. It is a good thing nobody is scouting this game. Kitty calls time-outs. She brings in Natalie Ludwig and Shanada Johnson early to try to shake things up. *"You're playing with no emotion. Your body language says it. Your performance says it,"* Kitty said to Ronda Jo during a break. Ronda Jo hits the side of the backboard with a jump shot. Gallaudet is playing a 2–3 zone defense, which has two players aligned at the free throw line and three across the lane under the basket. Correctly played, the zone keeps the ball out of the middle and forces teams to shoot from outside. Mary Washington is shredding it, getting whatever shots it wants.

When the official blows a whistle on a questionable foul call against the Bison, Kitty pops up. "Got some home-cooking going tonight." She says it with her voice, not her hands. The whistle blows again. Kitty has earned her first technical foul of the season.

After playing from behind the entire game, the Bison finally begin to rally midway through the second half. Ronda Johnson sinks a fifteen-foot jumper. Touria converts two free throws and a drive. Getting the ball in the lane, Ronda Jo spins and scores. A fourteen-point lead gets sliced to two when Ronda Jo hits a hanging jumper. The Bison are coming hard now, swarming, committed, resurgent.

And then they fall apart in the final twenty-three seconds. They fail to get a shot off on a possession. They make a couple of ill-advised fouls. As Mary Washington comes down with the ball in the game's most critical possession, Kitty and Ben are standing up, waving their arms and stomping the floor, desperately making the sign for foul (a forward flicking motion with the hand against the ear), but nobody notices. The clock keeps ticking. When Touria *does* notice, she shoves a Mary Washington player and gets called for an intentional foul, meaning that Mary Washington gets to shoot two free throws *and* keep possession of the ball. The Bison lose, 70–66. It is an abominable loss, one that Kitty knows will be eyed deliciously by every team in the conference: If Gallaudet can lose to Mary Washington, not an especially strong team, everyone else will believe they can beat them, too. One game after Touria played *her* worst game, Ronda Jo does the same thing. Afterward, the team meets in a lounge adjacent to the gym, with ugly overstuffed furniture and a wall of vending machines on one end. Even players the size of Amelia and Stacy look like schoolkids as they sink into the gigantic cushions. Kitty tries to get a read on the team and figure out what will get through to them. She invites comments.

"Our minds weren't here tonight," Nanette said.

"We were tired. We've had a practice or game eight days in a row," Ronda Johnson said.

Ronda Jo waved her hand. *"We started the game at too slow a pace. We just weren't ready."* Kitty listens, and then it is her turn. She speaks with a calculated calmness. Words that sound as if they belong in a tirade are delivered evenly, with restraint.

"We got what we deserved tonight. They wanted to win this game much more than we did. We played like we were going at half-speed. We let them dictate the style of play, and the result was that we played at their tempo, not ours. We did this to ourselves."

The Bison stop at Arby's on the way back, and Kitty stands at the counter and orders for everybody. She has the appetite of a sparrow on her most ravenous days, and even less of one now. She has a few disinterested bites of a burger before getting back on the prisoners' bus.

She does not know what's going on with her team, but she doesn't like what she's seeing. It's not their record—they've won four of six games. It's the way they've looked getting there, the seeming disinterest at times. After twenty-five years of coaching, Kitty doesn't need anybody to explain the concept of the wandering attention span, or the gap between kids' words and kids' actions. But whatever happened to "The Time Is Now"? She writes the twelve letters on the board before every game. They're on the gray T-shirts the players wear during pregames— shirts that have become the Bison warm-up gear because none of them likes the school-issue ones. Have the words lost their meaning already, hollowed out by repetition? Whatever happened to the commitment to go farther than the 1998–99 team, to show every ignoramus who had ever belittled them how wrong they were?

The day before the Mary Washington game, Ronda Johnson had asked Kitty if she could skip practice. She was one of the finalists for the Miss Gallaudet pageant and needed some extra preparation time. "Now a beauty pageant is more important than practice," Kitty said. She told Ronda no. Nanette said that on the bus ride to Virginia, she sensed that people were thinking about everything *but* basketball. There was talk about a campus skating party later that night and some dismay over Kitty's rumored plan to ban jeans on road trips. Ronda Jo did a long interview about her experiences growing up deaf in a hearing family. Kitty figured that maybe that's why her head was in Minnesota instead of Virginia. The coach understands the media fascination about her team, but now she has a new rule: no more pregame interviews.

When Ernie stops the bus alongside campus to drop Ronda Jo off at her apartment, Kitty stands up and gives her All-American a hug, the coach's head barely making it to chest level.

"You better do some thinking this weekend. We need you."

Kitty believes Ronda Jo is trying to do too much, to surpass what she has already done. It's not easy to do when you are one of the top scorers, rebounders, and shotblockers in the nation. Ronda Jo grabs her No. 23 equipment bag and disembarks. Kitty watches her cross West Virginia Avenue, a ponytailed silhouette against the streetlight, looking tall in the blue parka she got for being a Kodak All-American. Without turning back, Ronda Jo slips into the lobby of her building, a red brick place with so many Gallaudet tenants that the landlord has painted the trim in blue and gold.

Two games remain before winter break, a swing into upstate New York. Ernie makes the right turn onto Florida Avenue. The transmission groans in downshift. Kitty's mind revs up, her thoughts hopscotching everywhere: *"Is this just going to be a quick stumble? Am I being unreasonable in what I'm expecting? Could it be that the grind of exams and papers has them feeling overwhelmed? What more can I do to help them understand that the time really is now?"*

Like a parent of a wayward child, Kitty's feeling equal parts of love and frustration for her charges, these ten Bison women. She goes home to light a candle, her wondering lasting far into the night.

Cassey Ellis didn't have one of her best games against Mary Washington, but after just a few months of coaching her, Kitty has come to regard her as an asset even when her shot isn't falling and rebounds are eluding her. If there was ever a woman with the ideal temperament to join an established team, it is Cassey. "She's just got one of those personalities you always want to be around," Kitty said. Cassey's not going to get too worried about being a newcomer, either. She's dreamed of coming to Gallaudet her whole life. Now that she's here, she's not going to let anything—not being the only African-American on the team, and not her history of heart trouble—get in her way.

"It feels so good to be back on a team," Cassey said.

At twenty-three, Cassey is no ordinary freshman. She is the second-oldest player on the team behind Touria. She graduated from her high school, The Learning Center in Framingham, Massachusetts, in 1996 but wasn't admitted to Gallaudet right away, needing to work on her English skills. That was a blow to her, but nothing like the word that came down from her doctors, who discovered that Cassey had a heart abnormality and made an initial prognosis that Cassey should not play basketball anymore.

Devastated, she went for another opinion and ultimately had a corrective procedure done. The second doctor said it would be fine to keep playing ball. Cassey had a much harder time convincing her mother, Sherry Ellis. Cassey stayed involved with The Learning Center as an assistant coach on a team that finished 26–1. She finally persuaded her mother to let her resume playing. She just has to promise to get on the TTY and let her know she's fine.

With her braids, black wire-rim glasses, and orange baseball cap, Cassey looks like a cross between a professor and a hip-hop diva. But there's really nothing split about her. Cassey has always been a joiner, someone active in groups, whether ones for children with divorced parents or Christian youth fellowship. Her natural gift for mediation is as much a trademark as her cornrows, helping her navigate through all kinds of potentially turbulent situations. *"If you put Cassey in a room with the Hatfields and McCoys, they'd come out being friends a half hour later,"* one Gallaudet friend said.

When Cassey was in junior high school, she felt estranged from her father, William Ellis. She wanted a closer relationship with him. She met with him and didn't sugarcoat anything. She told him she was hurt he wasn't more involved in her childhood after he and her mother divorced, and that she felt he was embarrassed to have a deaf daughter. But she also told him she loved him and needed him in her life. They've rebuilt their relationship, and it feels great.

When the Olympic Torch Relay came through Boston in 1996, Cassey was the one who carried it down Blue Hill Avenue. As she ran, all the people who were standing alongside her just started running with her. She has that impact on people, with a cheerfulness that seems to be as reflexive as brushing her teeth.

Her personal mantra is "Being negative is just not worth it. It's much better to be positive." Cassey learned plenty about that from Sherry, who once took in three foster children, in addition to the two daughters she was already raising. The kids belonged to a friend in the throes of drug addiction. Cassey couldn't believe how much love her mother gave them.

When tough times come and it's hard for even her to be positive, when she's struggling with English or feeling as if she's way behind the rest of the world, Cassey will sometimes ask her mother, "Why do things have to be so difficult for me all the time?" Sherry Ellis, a woman of deep faith, always knows exactly what to say: *"When you succeed, all the trouble you've gone through means that you're going to appreciate it that much more."*

The hardest time Cassey ever had was in junior high school. For two years, her funding for The Learning Center ran out and she was forced to transfer to a mainstream school.

"I didn't fit in anywhere," Cassey said. *"Not in school, or on the team. When the other players would go out to eat or be together, I'd be left out, and without being able to communicate, I always felt alone, no matter how hard I worked at it. Communication is the key to everything. Without that, how can you understand other people and make yourself understood?"*

Cassey grew up as the only deaf child in the Mount Olive Temple of Christ Church in the Roxbury section of Boston. The family lived in Brockton, Massachusetts, before that, a hardscrabble city famous for its two hometown boxing champions, Rocky Marciano and Marvelous Marvin Hagler. Even when she was surrounded by hearing people,

Cassey kept her sunny spirit. "She'd somehow turn the page and be okay with it," Sherry said. "She's always had this sparkle about her."

Sherry first had an inkling Cassey was deaf when she was about two. Cassey was staying with her in-laws during the day. When Sherry came to pick her up, she called out, "There's my little girl!" Cassey did not turn around. She did not respond at all until she saw Sherry. Sherry took her to a doctor.

"Cassey can't hear," she told him.

"OK, let's check her out. She's probably got some fluid in there."

"That's not what I mean. I mean that she can't hear at all. I mean that she's deaf." Sherry took Cassey to an audiologist. This was twenty years ago. Sherry remembers the equipment seeming very rudimentary, boxy and almost crude. But that didn't matter. Her daughter had a profound to severe hearing loss, and no amount of bells and whistles was going to change it. When the audiologist confirmed that Sherry was right, she and her husband were standing in a small, stark office. Cassey was playing in the next room. The walls felt as if they were closing in. Sherry remembers her world going soundless in that moment. The quiet was overpowering.

Cassey likes to do frequent gratitude checks, and her mother is always near the top of the list. She knows plenty of deaf people whose parents don't or won't deal with it. They refuse to learn sign language. They treat it as if it were an enormous burden. From the time she realized Cassey's deafness could not be reversed, Sherry Ellis's attitude was, "What can I do to help my little girl?" When the audiologist told her they could do tests to try to isolate a reason for Cassey's deafness, Sherry Ellis spared her the trouble. Her only concern was helping her daughter have as full and rich a life as possible. Sherry thinks she should've done a better job acquiring ASL, but her faith and devotion and belief that things would work out for the best have all been steadfast. It's almost as if Cassey and Sherry have a language all their own, without words or signs: They are in tune with each other. When Cassey calls home during the season, frustrated about not getting more playing time, her mother knows just how to get her centered again. *"Don't you worry, Cassey. Things will happen in time. Your time will come. Trust in the Lord."* When Cassey is concerned about her financial-aid situation, one conversation with Sherry makes her worries melt away. It all comes from Sherry's faith; it's an anchor. Once, when Cassey was five, the family was on a busy street in Brockton after a church service. Sherry's sister walked out to get into a car, and Cassey immediately ran after her, not seeing a speeding car bearing down on her. Sherry watched it all unfold but had time to do nothing. She saw her daughter and the car and as she heard the sick screech of tires was certain the unthinkable was happening. When Sherry opened her eyes, grief already spilling everywhere, Cassey was in her sister's arms, unharmed.

Sherry prayed and thanked the Lord. She did not know why He spared her child, any more than she knows why her child is deaf. But she trusted in His plan, and she felt incredibly blessed to have her two girls, and that has never changed.

THURSDAY
NIGHT BLIGHT

I'M REDECORATING," KITTY Baldridge said from behind her desk. She is surveying Room 102 in the Physical Education department, making her standard joke about her little office, a place that always looks as if a horde of barbarians has just stopped by. Her wooden desktop is buried beneath papers. A dozen coffee and travel mugs are scattered about, and a lineup of Post-its and phone messages are stuck by the computer screen and doorway, rectangular reminders of things to do, people to call. Stacks of basketball books bulge from the bookcase. A toy hoop is on the floor in the corner, surrounded by boxes, bags, and a carton of Gallaudet warm-ups. This is the detritus of her coaching life, and if it seems suffocating to others, it works just fine for Kitty. She's not afraid of being different. In the basement of her row house, she has a an entire bathroom done in the red and white of Indiana University, a porcelain Hoosier shrine. It features a bright red tub, and sink and toilet to match. "How could I resist?" she said.

Wedged between her office desk and the bookcase is an old wooden rocker. Whenever someone comes to visit, Kitty sweeps the debris off it and invites her guest to sit down, then takes a folding chair by the door for herself. That's how she is, generous without even thinking about it. When she knows a regular visitor is coming to a morning practice, she shows up with an extra cup of coffee and homemade bread.

"I figured you didn't have time for breakfast," she'll always say.

Before many road trips, the team orders submarine sandwiches from Litteri's, an Italian deli in a gritty warehouse strip adjacent to campus. It's a store known for fat sandwiches and skinny aisles, and an aroma thick with roasted peppers and fresh bread. Kitty makes sure all hungry parties get their faxed orders in. She is always including everybody, in everything. She's constantly having players over for dinner and conversation. If somebody can't make it home for a holiday, she's got a place reserved at Kitty's table. Kitty can be elusive at times, and not inclined to return calls or keep up with her mail, but when a player needs her, she's there. Two young hearing children—a seven-year-old girl and her five-year-old brother—adopted Gallaudet as their team while their father was working on a research project during the school year. The kids were learning about sign language in their school. Kitty invited them into the locker room for her pregame meeting, and the kids were awestruck, surrounded by the Bison and more signing than they'd ever seen. The players, following Kitty's lead, started including the kids in all kinds of ways, sending them e-mails, teaching them how to write "I love you" in sign shorthand (V,,/), giving them sweaty hugs after games.

Kitty is keenly sensitive to the stabbing pain of exclusion. She has spent most of her life around deaf schools and in most ways considers herself more deaf than hearing. ASL was her first language, English her second. On the top of her office door, K-I-T-T-Y is spelled out in the manual alphabet. The door tells a lot about the person inside; it is covered with sayings about the rights of women in general, and the rights of women to play sports in particular. To Kitty Baldridge, the passage in 1972 of Title IX, the law that mandates equal opportunity for men and women at institutions receiving federal funds, was more of a watershed moment than the moon landing that took place three years before. Kitty has the fine print of Title IX on a two-foot by three-foot poster in the center of her door, the blueprint for gender equity. She's so zealous in her support of women's athletics, she refuses to describe her defense as *man-to-man*. At Gallaudet, the term is *woman-to-woman,* as in, "We'll start in the two-three zone, but be ready to go woman-to-woman." After awhile, it sounds as natural as inbounds play or free throw or any other piece of basketball vocabulary.

As an undergraduate at Indiana University, Kitty competed in the last years before Title IX, memories that are as unpleasant as they are vivid. She was captain of the women's basketball team in her junior and senior years, an honor that entitled her to spend more money than everybody else. The team played the prevailing style at the time—six players per side, only two of whom (the so-called rovers) were free to run all over the court. It did not have varsity status and was entirely self-sufficient. This meant players paid for their own uniforms, arranged transportation to games, and took care of everything from gas and tolls to laundry expenses. When Kitty goes through old pictures and sees the team in its ragtag uniforms, it's as though she's looking at some gauzy black-and-white print from the nineteenth century. Could it really have just been three decades ago, at a major university?

"It's hard to believe we did that to ourselves—that we would placate society just so we could do something we wanted to do," Kitty said. "I think the sad thing in retrospect is that we didn't feel like we had any power to enact change. Nobody cared. Who was going to listen? Who wanted to bother with women's basketball?" And whoever thought that in the same lifetime she'd coach a team on equal footing with the men—a team that gets the same quality uniforms, the same buses, the same gym access? At Gallaudet the last few years, the women's team has been a much bigger draw than the men's team, sometimes attracting a thousand or more fans.

Kitty has been the head women's basketball coach at Gallaudet since she was twenty-nine. She started a women's team at the Indiana School for the Deaf after she graduated from IU and had it going strong until Gallaudet called in 1977. Then it seemed to be a momentous move, one she admits she wasn't quite prepared for. How many head college coaches get hired in their twenties? Now it seems as if it were all but predestined. Her parents, Paul and Peggy Baldridge, met at Gallaudet, Paul coming from Utah, Peggy right from D.C. Kitty is not just a coach's daughter; she's a Gallaudet Hall of Famer's daughter. Growing up, Kitty had no sense of being different from any other child until the family moved to Indianapolis when she was in grade school. It was her first experience living outside a residential school campus.

"To me, having deaf parents was normal. That was the first time I was around kids who didn't know what being deaf meant."

The only plausible career options Kitty felt that she had when she graduated were as a nurse or teacher. She couldn't see herself in one of those little white uniforms and matching hat. She *could* see herself as a teacher, and indeed, that is her principal job even now: professor of physical education. Coaching basketball is her $6,000-a-year side job, a part-time position consuming full-time hours.

Kitty grew up playing basketball with boys, because few girls played then. Peggy remembers Kitty organizing games when she was seven, shrewdly assessing players' talent level, selecting the best boys to be on her team. By then she was already a fixture around her father's varsity teams. He coached at deaf high schools in Arizona and Missouri, and Kitty, the second of the five Baldridge children, would do whatever he asked, one part mascot, one part gofer, even if she saw it differently: "I thought I was his assistant coach." Kitty would get towels and ride the bus and loved the bright lights and the smell of the gyms. The best part, though, was being part of a team, sharing the inside jokes and the signs on the bus rides, and the sense of common mission and of being together.

She still loves the feel of a team. Even after a loss like the one at Mary Washington, it felt good to be on the bus, in the right-hand front seat, with Ben Baylor and Hillel Goldberg across the aisle, and her players scattered in the back, the Bison of Gallaudet, in *it* together. Gallaudet's record the two seasons before Ronda Jo arrived in 1996 was 3–22 and 6–24, and Kitty felt that way then, too. Winning percentage may be society's benchmark for success; as long as there are coaches, they will probably spout aphorisms about winning being everything. But Kitty's own yardstick is much more finely calibrated. She measures success on an individual basis, by how hard a player tries, how far she has come, how much she has gotten out of her ability. The ultimate battle is not played on the external scoreboard, but on an unseen one, between a player and her own desire, a player and her frustration tolerance, a player and her capacity to not give into fatigue, self-criticism, and all the other demons that sabotage the pursuit of excellence. It's the same for a team. Some of Kitty's most rewarding years were when victories were not much more common than a lunar eclipse. One of her favorite coaching moments came in one of those seasons, inside the gymnasium of Mary Baldwin College, in Staunton, Virginia. Kitty had eight players on the roster. Because of injuries and academic conflicts, only five could show up one night, two starters and three subs. Gallaudet was up by twelve at the half, but the inevitable weariness set in and Mary Washington rallied. Still, the Bison kept fighting and took the game into overtime. Fifteen seconds into the extra session, a Bison player fouled out. They were down to four. Then another player fouled out, and they were down to three. Woman-to-woman defense was no longer an option, since there were five of them and three Bison. Kitty called for a 2–1 zone defense and a spread-out offense. Gallaudet hung in. A couple of players hit huge baskets in the waning moments. They played defense like madwomen. They won the game.

"We were totally focused on what we needed to do, and the other team was worrying about how they absolutely could not lose to a team with three players," Kitty said. You never know when kids are going to stun you with their composure and resilience and leap to a place they've never gotten close to. When it happens and all the hours and drills and caring have taken root and yield this kind of return, there is no better feeling. None.

"It's why you coach," Kitty said.

It's the Monday after the Mary Washington game, and Kitty's having a hard time letting go of her disappointment. Even after having a weekend to decompress, she still finds the spotty effort almost unforgivable. Usually losses don't linger so long; she's able to tie them up and be done with them, like a garbage pickup left at the curb. Kitty's not sure why it's different this time. It probably goes back to her expectations, and maybe to Indianapolis, too. Here is her dad, at seventy-nine, waging a daily fight to reclaim his body from the stroke, while her Bison, with youth and health and a precious opportunity before them, are half mailing it in. No matter what year they are in school, players sometimes act as if they think their college careers will go on forever. "Of course I know what's happening with my father has nothing to do with the team, but it's hard for me not to think about it," Kitty said.

The Bison have a full week of practice before going on a two-game weekend swing to upstate New York, the final games before Christmas break. Kitty has a lot she wants to get done. She wants to work on defense, and attitude. The practices are hard and long. For years Kitty has had a running contest with the team, having them line up single file at the free throw line and shoot for dinner at her house. If every player makes her free throw, Kitty cooks. It has never happened, and Kitty loves teasing them about it. She's not into contests right now. Her arms are crossed in unamused detachment. Right after stretching, the Bison do suicides—wind sprints up and down the court. They will be put through more later. In between, Kitty steps forward, waves her hand to get their attention, and calls for more conditioning and drills, and then half-court sets to go over offense and defense. The Bison's preference is always to scrimmage fullcourt, to simulate games and play without interruption. Half-court situations, full of stops and corrections ("No, you have to set the pick higher so Ronda Jo has room to come around it") and endless repetition, is more boring to them than C-SPAN. Kitty knows it, but to her, running fullcourt is a reward, a carrot she dangles in exchange for hard work. Before she lets them do what they want, they have to do what she wants—pay attention to detail, play smart, box out and move their feet on defense. They have to avoid silly fouls and move the ball and make good choices, not hoisting up a shot after five seconds.

It is one of the grimmer practices of the season. The Bison do not appreciate it. Nanette, for one, thinks Kitty has changed from past years, is more unrelentingly serious. Nanette doesn't get why Kitty's still so upset over the Mary Washington game. Sure they were pretty poor, but it's not like it's a trend. They're still 4–2 for the season. They've beaten the No. 2 team in the country. And besides, the Bison have always been a slow-starting team, because of the late arrivals from volleyball. "I think after we beat Capital some of us were hoping that our effort would be acknowledged more and we might even get a day off," Nanette said. "But it was right back to work. We still love Kitty as a person, don't get me wrong. Things just seem a little different sometimes."

A short time before Wednesday's practice, Kitty develops a sharp pain in her stomach. She consults with Ben about practice and heads home. When the players show up and ask where Kitty is, Ben runs a semiclenched hand over his midsection. He intends to say that Kitty has a stomachache, but the way he signs it, the meaning is more that Kitty is disgusted. Ben is not the most fluent ASLer on campus. A slight change in gesture or its placement can alter the meaning of a sign. It is an innocent mistake, but the wrecking ball has already hit the building. To the players, the upshot is unmistakable: Kitty is so fed up that she can't even stomach being at practice with us! She's bailing out! She's turning on us!

Almost to a player, the Bison are indignant that Kitty isn't there. She's been cranky all week, and now this. Anger and defiance build as the practice goes on. Ronda Johnson is probably the most upset and has no trouble getting company from her sister Shanada and Stacy Nowak, both of whom are not thrilled with their lack of playing time, anyway. Nanette is miffed, too. Ronda Jo feels kind of betrayed. Touria isn't sure what to think, but seeing that all her sorority sisters on the team were pretty worked up, well, she gets tugged along, as well. Natalie Ludwig and Cassey Ellis can't believe what's happening. Natalie, a transfer from Pratt Community College in Kansas, endured all kinds of upheaval the year before, her coach getting fired by the administration, and she's thinking, *"Oh no. What is it with me and coaches?"* Amelia England, never the most vocal of team members, takes in everything warily.

It's a hard time of year. Everybody feels stretched thin, end-of-the-semester pressures fraying nerves, clouding judgment. With beleaguered spirits and spinning heads, a bunch of players talk that night on the sixth floor of Clerc Hall, the floor where Touria is the R.A. and where her responsibilities include making over a bulletin board on topics ranging from exam preparation to cold prevention. Chinese food and pizza delivery people make their regular trips. Students queue up to use the TTY in the dorm lobby. The players share their feelings and hurts, and somehow the idea comes up that if Kitty really is so disgusted, maybe she shouldn't come back to coach the team right away. So what if she's coached the team since 1978 and coached the team to its best season ever and had them two games from the Final Four last year!

The next day, the players ask Kitty to meet with them at four o'clock, the time practice is supposed to start. The meeting is held in the Hall of Fame Room in the corner of the Field House. It is Thursday, December 9. Kitty has no idea what to expect.

It's hard to say how these things unfold, except to say that the impetuosity of youth and the sting of rejection are a combustible combination. The players begin and go around the room, and there is anger and accusations and tears and yelling. Kitty is way beyond disbelief. She explains that she was not disgusted the day before; she was sick. But it's gone way beyond a malformed sign now, to a deeper wound. Nanette tells Kitty she thinks she has been too hard on them and has taken some of the fun out of basketball. Several others say that practices are tedious because the drills never change and that the offense is too predictable. Ronda says that she feels shackled, Kitty having stripped her game of flashiness, the between-the-leg dribbles and bowlegged jukes and no-look passes—things Ronda considers not just stylish but effective, and Kitty sees as needless showboating. They've been having this debate for three years, but now it has become a basketball line in the sand.

"You don't let me play my game," Ronda said.

"That's B.S.," Kitty shot back. *"Your game is much better without all that stuff."* Ronda Jo, offended by the rebuke of her teammate, stands up and is ready to walk out. Stacy calms her down. And so it goes. Kitty knows better than to try to rebut point after point. After ninety minutes she opens the heavy wooden door and comes out into the lobby. Ben and Hillel Goldberg are waiting for her. She looks as if she has gone fifteen rounds with Mike Tyson in his prime. Except that most boxers see the punches coming.

These are her kids, young women she'd do anything for, even when she is ticked off at them. This is Gallaudet, the only college she has ever coached at, and the only one she wants to coach at.

"They want me to resign," Kitty said to her assistants. A small bear of a man, Hillel has eyebrows as thick as a hedge. The hedge furrows as Kitty goes on: *"They said they don't want to play for me anymore."* Kitty's voice is thin, her eyes glassy. She looks small and frail in her warm-ups with Kitty stitched over the heart. Ben glances around the lobby, so often a happy gathering place after games.

"Anybody got a gun?" he said.

The players continue to meet for another half hour. The gripes keep flying like shrapnel. Touria is upset that Kitty had gotten on her about missing practice for an R.A.-related commitment. Ronda brings up the Miss Gallaudet pageant, and how summarily Kitty shot that down. Nanette feels as though Kitty has been beating them up for the Mary Washington game for days. As worked up as everyone is, it has more the feel of vengefulness—you hurt me, so I'm going to hurt you—than a full-blown mutiny. The players finally emerge, rigid and stone-faced. Nanette and Ronda Jo, the captains, ask to speak to Kitty in her office. They close the door. Their faces are taut and pale. There are no jokes about clutter. Nanette is wearing a yellow slicker and faded jeans with a big rip in the right knee. She tells Kitty the team has decided the best thing to do is table the subject and go ahead and make the trip to upstate New York. Kitty is businesslike but unmoved. She grabs a stack of itinerary sheets for the trip, with information about departure time, hotels, practice and game schedules. She hands one to each player, saying nothing. It is almost 7:30 by the time Kitty walks out in the cold and damp night and gets in her Subaru station wagon. The itinerary says the bus will leave at two o'clock the following afternoon. The destination for the rest of the season is much less certain.

The laboratory of their years of coaching at Gallaudet has taught Kitty and Ben that what they say to the players may not be as important as how they say it. When it's time to come down on them, they need to do it in moderation. The players inside the uniforms change; the sensitivity is pretty much a constant. Screaming and demeaning may work fine for such top women's coaches as Pat Summitt of the University of Tennessee and Geno Auriemma of the University of Connecticut, but it won't work in large doses on Kendall Green.

"We've learned that if you really rip our players, it'll backfire because they will turn on you," Ben said. "Hearing teams that I've been on and been around, coaches can scream and yell and say all kinds of stuff, and teams usually respond. These girls, I'm telling you, it just doesn't work that way. They'll go into a shell or take it personally, like you really don't like them when all you want is for them to improve. That's just not what you do."

Maybe that's what's going on here. Maybe the sting of the perceived rejection from Kitty is so sharp that somehow the players, emboldened by their numbers, feel compelled to lash back.

Ben isn't sure why the players react differently from other teams he's been with. Are the players more sensitive to rejection and disapproval because they have experienced great amounts of both in their lives? Kitty and Ben don't give it much thought. It is what it is. It gets into the issue of the psychology of deafness, which, depending on one's viewpoint, is either a useful way of assessing the deaf experience or an odious stereotype that effectively takes the full range of a human being and filters everything about her through a single disability. For those with the latter belief, the notion that deaf people tend to be affectionate or egocentric or naïve is as misguided as talking about the psychology of blackness or Jewishness. On the other hand, aren't all of us whittled from the wood of our experiences? Aren't those experiences shaped by the world we move in? More than twenty-five years ago, scholar and author McCay Vernon wrote: ". . . The environment is a major factor in the psychological development of all of us. When environment is systematically altered in a significantly consistent way for any given group of people, these individuals will tend to be different in some shared ways from those whose environments has not been altered in this systematic manner."

The question is not whether deaf people exhibit a particular trait because they are deaf. It is whether the experiential differences in their lives that have flowed from their inability to hear have shaped them in some way. Ben Baylor has no doubt that the Gallaudet women he has coached are easily bruised by what they perceive to be harsh criticism, anger, or disappointment. Look at the early-season game when a loyal Gallaudet fan stepped out of the gym in the final minutes while the Bison were blowing a big lead. Several players noticed the fan's departure, and right away thought the worst.

"We thought you were fed up and had given up on us," Touria Ouahid told him. During her unusually pointed remarks at halftime of the Mary Washington game, Kitty told the players she hoped they weren't thinking about the skating party that night. More than a few players thought it was a cheap shot.

Kitty's mind is reeling. Her hurt is deep. There will be time for analysis later. It seems as if six months have passed since the Bison played. Kitty just wants to get to the next game already. Nanette and Ronda Jo and the players are thinking the same thing. It's about the only consensus in sight at the Gallaudet Field House.

ROAD 6 WORRIERS

A THOUSAND MILES is a long time to think. Kitty and Ben need it, and so do the players and managers and even scorekeepers, like Ronnie Zuchegno, a stocky, short-necked young man with an amiable manner and the thick forearms of a former baseball player. Ronnie Z., as everyone calls him, represents the seventh generation of deafness in his family. His name sign is simply the finger spelling for his initials, RZ, traced in the air. Everybody in Deaf culture has a name sign, a visual way to identify themselves. Kitty's name sign is the letter K held against one's mouth, and then tugged away to the side, as if one were pulling the whiskers of a cat. Touria loves zippers: zippered sweatshirts, zippered jackets, zippered warm-ups; her name sign is made by simulating the motion of zippering. Ronda Johnson's name sign is her initials, RJ. Natalie Ludwig's is the letter N (thumb tucked beneath the index and middle finger), running wavily through the hair, in deference to her long, coarse blonde locks; and Ronda Jo's is an upside down R, tapped on the heart.

The Bison are en route to New York State, riding a chartered coach with cushiony paisley seats, a toilet in the back, and a VCR up front, right behind the driver. It's a couple of weeks before Christmas. Darkness seems to come right after lunch. The ground is as hard as stone, and the trees are barren, branches sticklike against the sky. Stacy is wearing a Santa Claus cap. Ronda is wearing a green Halloween mask. Somehow they don't look like revolutionaries anymore.

It's a nine-hour trip to Rochester, the first stop for the weekend. The Bison luck out because Interstate 81, running up the gut of Pennsylvania into New York, is free of ice and snow, not a common occurrence this time of year. The VCR is playing *Full Metal Jacket,* with subtitles, the volume cranked up loud. Four rows from the front, Touria's eyes are set on the TV, the light flickering across her face. She has a navy-blue zippered sweatshirt on. On the screen, a profanity-spewing sergeant is physically and verbally abusing a recruit. She has always hated violent movies. She had no idea what this movie was going to be like. Twenty minutes into the film, tears are rolling down Touria's cheeks. A few more minutes pass, and finally she has seen enough. She sweeps her cheeks dry with a finger and moves to the back. She doesn't say a word.

The bus rolls on, into New York State, and passes a sign welcoming them to Chemung County, and someone jokes, "Is this *the* Chemung County?" At a rest stop the Bison get off the bus, few of them bothering to put on their topcoats. Kitty looks out the window to see most of her team in the parking lot, T-shirts and shirtsleeves against twenty-degree air, turning the asphalt into the set of a kung-fu movie, letting fly with leg kicks and hand chops and shouts, deaf martial artists on the loose. She admires their resilience on a certain level. She wishes *she* could bounce back so fast. At the close of maybe the hardest week of her entire coaching career, Kitty's feeling as light as a manhole cover. She's thinking about what she will say to the team before they head to the game against Roberts Wesleyan, and about how great it would be to win.

Forty-eight hours have passed since The Incident, as Kitty has come to call it. She is sitting on a lumpy bed in Room 260 of a well-worn Holiday Inn, hard by Interstate 390, across from the Rochester Airport. It is not a property Holiday Inn will likely feature in an advertising campaign, with its worn walls and circa 1960 furniture and cars on the highway for background music. Kitty has assembled the players in her room. She begins going for closure by closing the drapes. She turns off the lights and puts two candles, one red and one white, on a table in front of her. She is still plenty angry about what happened, that the players would have the audacity—The Audacity!—to ask her to quit a job she's had since before they were born. It ticks her off that they would lay the blame elsewhere—on the boring practices and the supposedly stale system, and in the case of Ronda, Kitty's refusal to let her shimmy and shake to her heart's content. Kitty and Ben are in complete accord: Maybe the most disappointing thing of all is that nobody was willing to stand up and say, "You know what? We're not playing well, and that's our own fault. It's not the coach or the plays or that Ben doesn't know how to sign bellyache. It's us."

The more she thinks about it, the more convinced Kitty is that the entire confrontation was engineered by a couple of players who aren't off to a good start and managed to whip their sorority sisters into a frenzy. Next thing you know, you've got The Coup on Kendall Green. Kitty wonders if The Incident ever would've happened if the team's missing sorority sister, Jenny Cooper, had been around. Kitty could easily picture Jenny standing up in the Hall of Fame room and shouting everyone down with the moral weight of her passion, a quality that has been the team's spiritual mortar for four years: *"Just suck it up and play."*

Still, Kitty recognizes that she's the adult here. She doesn't want to mirror the behavior of the players and simply cast blame. She *has* been pushing harder, and she *has* been less patient. Her thoughts often drift to her father's bedside in Indianapolis. Who knows how much that's taking out of her? Maybe she should just listen to Nanette, who isn't just a cocaptain but a lovely, loyal young woman. And Nanette thinks she has changed.

With the drapes tight across the window, Room 260 barely has enough light for the players to see Kitty signing. They are gathered around her in a loose circle, in sweats and jeans and fleece, apprehension across their faces. Kitty begins.

"Red is the color of love and passion, and that's what this red candle signifies. It is a symbol of my love and passion for you all as people and players, and also for the game. The white candle signifies purity and honesty. I'm guilty of doing something I've always told you not to do, and that is taking things personally. When I get on you about a sloppy pass or a forced shot, I say it's not about you as a person, it's about the game. I get upset if you take it personally, but that's what I've done this year. I've let myself be hurt by the up-and-down play and some of the attitudes I've seen, and because of that, my own flame of passion and love have been burning more dimly. The best way to get the flame back burning brightly is by being honest and owning it, and igniting the flame of purity and honesty. Sometimes families go through this, and sometimes teams do, too. To get the flame and the fire back, you can't have walls up, you can't have barriers. You have to be together. And that's the only way this season is going to be what we want it to be: if we all have our candles burning together. If we do that, we'll be fine."

Kitty scans the faces before her. Her eyes are moist. She takes out a book of matches and lights the red candle and then the white candle and brings them next to each other, and the flames flicker in ten Bison faces. Kitty asks them to come in closer, and she puts her arms out, around Cassey and Natalie and then they all share a big circular hug. When they are done, Kitty pulls out a small treasure chest. Inside is a timepiece.

"Time is precious," she said. "The time is now. This is the only time we have." Beyond the drapes, cars whiz by on I-390. The Bison board the bus and ride to the game. In a locker room of stark white cinder blocks, Kitty flicks off the lights to reveal her two red and white candles. "See the light and feel the fire," the coach said.

"*Miss ... Miss ... Miss ...*" Touria Ouahid is at the side of the free throw line, doing some silent trash talking to a player from Roberts Wesleyan. It is late in the first half, three hours after the candlelit air-clearing in the Holiday Inn. Touria is running a cupped hand in front of her face, then snap-closing it, as if she were trying to catch a fly, the ASL sign for miss, as in miss this free throw. She knows the shooter doesn't get the import of her gesture, but that's okay.

"*Maybe it will help anyway,*" Touria said with a conspiratorial smile. And it does. The player misses.

Touria does not miss when she has her own chance at the free throw line. That's nothing new; she's one of the best foul shooters on the team. She's also the most consistent in sticking to her routine: a few bounces, a deep bend of the knee, a caress of the ball in her hands, a deep breath, and the shot. She makes four in a row near the end of the first half, then gets an outlet pass from Ronda Jo Miller and scores on the fast break, as fearless as ever as she pushes the dribble toward the basket. King Jordan, Gallaudet's president, knows it is probably a presidential faux pas to have a favorite player, but he can't help himself. From his seat behind the Gallaudet bench, Jordan knows he may not see another Bison player as athletic and dominating as Ronda Jo. He admires Nanette's selflessness and is invariably entertained by the inventiveness of Ronda Johnson, cherub-faced queen of the unpredictable. But he has always been most taken by Touria, because of the way she puts it all out there. You see in the set of her jaw, the eagerness to take on her defender, the baring of her teeth when she's fighting through a thicket of arms and legs in the lane.

The Bison go up by ten points (47–37) with sixteen minutes to play. Kitty is thinking: *Why does there always have to be so much time left when your team is on a roll? Why does the time tick off twice as fast when you're behind?* Her pessimism is blowing strong, a sure signal that this is no ordinary December game. This is one Kitty wants badly. She's been at the head of the bench long enough to know that candles and clocks are fine, but there's no healing agent like winning. You just have to have faith that it will happen.

Kitty's faith has been tested already in the first seven games. Now it is being tested again. Roberts Wesleyan starts connecting from outside. The Gallaudet lead is trimmed to six, then to three, and then it is tied. The Bison begin to get tight, and loose with the ball. Ronda Jo throws one away. Ronda double dribbles. Touria fires a fastball to Shanada Johnson, too high, too hard. Too bad. With each turnover, self-doubt and discouragement get more and more palpable. Natalie Ludwig drills a three-pointer from the left wing, but the Bison look tentative. They're always at their best when they are playing freely, totally unself-conscious, in a good way. Nobody's trying too hard. Nobody is worried. They're just clicking.

Now they are clacking. They're firing up shots too quickly, not keeping track of a forward named Krista Damann, who is killing them from outside. She hits a string of three-pointers, and the game remains tied with under three minutes to go. Damann hits two free throws to give Roberts a 71–69 lead. Ronda Jo hits a jumper from the baseline to tie it. And then Damann comes down, sets up on the left wing, and drills one last three-pointer. Roberts scores the last eight points. The Bison do not score again. They walk off the far end of the court, into the locker room. A few lockers get slammed, and the sound collides with the cement wall, a cold, hard crash. It is another game they could've won, should've won. Kitty looks drained and small. Ronda Johnson has her chin cupped on her knees, her face red and her body slumped. Shanada looks pale and vacant, upset that she got into the game for only four minutes. The Bison didn't play badly; they just didn't close it out.

The charter bus rolls up next to the gym and gets on the New York State Thruway and heads west. There isn't much talking, even though the lights are on. Natalie, the most serious student on the team, is not doing schoolwork for once. She is staring out the window. She's watching frozen farms rush by, decorated with festive dots of Christmas lights, reds and greens and blues and yellows. She wonders who lives there, and if they are happy.

One of the perks that comes with the longest road trip of the season is the chance to tour the National Technical Institute for the Deaf, or N.T.I.D. The unofficial guide is Amelia, who used to attend N.T.I.D. before transferring to Gallaudet. The school is on the campus of the Rochester Institute of Technology and has provided vocational training for the deaf for decades, sharing both a rivalry and a kinship with Gallaudet. Each spring the students from both schools throw a big weekend gala, alternating between Washington and Rochester. There are parties, meetings, concerts, and maybe an ASL-based theatrical production or poetry reading. It's more than the prototypical collegiate beer blast, though liquor is rarely in short supply. It's a chance for the students to feel connected to one another, to find another safe harbor in the choppy waters of the hearing world. Whenever the Bison's travels take them near a school for the deaf, it inevitably stirs a similar reaction.

Deaf schools have a unique place in Deaf culture. It has been that way for most of the last two centuries, since Thomas Hopkins Gallaudet and Laurent Clerc opened the American Asylum in Hartford in 1817. Many other schools for the deaf followed, an ad hoc reform movement that did not merely provide the deaf with their first formal places of learning, but an incubator for an entire culture. Learning and literacy were paramount, certainly, but because the schools brought deaf people together, en masse, for the first time, they also spawned a way of life—customs and mores, jokes and games, traditions and attitudes, all communicated in their native language of sign. The culture became so rooted that it even survived a ninety-year assault from proponents of oralism, people who believed that the focus of deaf education should be to teach students to speak and lip-read. Oralists did their best to dismantle the sign-based school system founded by Clerc and Gallaudet, going so far as to forbid students from signing and to discourage activities of Deaf culture. The signing and the culture didn't die. They just went underground, in the dorms—the locus of deaf students' lives.

Residential schools continue to occupy a central place in Deaf culture, but the current educational climate has not been hospitable to them. In 1975, Congress passed Public Law 94–142, the Education for All Handicapped Children Act, the upshot of which was that mainstream public schooling should be available to all children whenever possible, and that children deserved to be educated in the "least restrictive environment." The law, in essence, was the offspring of *Brown v. Board of Education,* trumpeting the idea of open access and reaffirming that separate never means equal. It was well-meaning and has served millions of disabled children effectively. Just not deaf children.

Nobody stopped to think that for a deaf child, the so-called least restrictive environment—public schooling and mainstream classes—may in fact be the *most* restrictive environment. How is it least restrictive if a child is shunted off to the corner of a classroom with her interpreter? How is it least restrictive if the class is conducted in a language that she struggles with on a daily basis? What is the gain for a deaf child to be taken away from her peers and removed from an educational setting that is both positive and empowering?

According to a study by the Gallaudet Research Institute, the year before the law was passed, 55 percent of deaf students surveyed were educated in residential and day schools for the deaf—and 10 percent were in a mainstream classroom. By 2000, 29 percent were in schools for the deaf and 45 percent were in a mainstream setting. Declining enrollment has forced some residential schools to close, but the schools remain as entrenched as ever in the souls of so many who go there.

Ronda Jo's whole life changed when she found out about Minnesota State Academy for the Deaf (MSAD). She left her mainstream school in sixth grade. It was such a relief not to feel weird or impaired any more. *"It was the best thing that ever happened to me,"* she said.

From kindergarten through twelfth grade, Nanette Virnig was in MSAD for all but one course—freshman reading in ninth grade. Her parents mainstreamed her at that point, believing that being surrounded by hearing readers would help elevate Nanette's reading. She felt dumb and hopelessly different from everyone else. She was the deaf kid everyone whispered about and made fun of. She couldn't get back to MSAD soon enough: *"Everyone there is deaf and we communicate twenty-four hours. Dorm life was the best. Sharing everything together made for a great social life. Why would you go to a place where there are barriers to learning everywhere you look?"*

Amelia doesn't get much playing time, and often when that's the case, it's hard for a player to feel a part of the team. Maybe that's why she savors her time as N.T.I.D. tour guide, pointing out the dorms and student center and gymnasium, touting a great submarine sandwich place that they all go to for lunch.

This is Amelia's second year on the basketball team. In the fall, she is a goalie on the Gallaudet women's soccer team. The team isn't very good, but the fun part is that she stays busy with all the shots on goal. She is six feet tall with the sweet, fair-skinned face of an English schoolgirl, and wisps of light brown hair that don't want to stay off her forehead. She has a big-framed body that she feels much better about now that she's taken fifty pounds off it over the last couple of years. Last year, she could not even finish suicide sprints in practice. Now she does, even when it's not easy. In the first week of the season, she sprinted to the final baseline and kept going, right out the back door of the gym. She threw up.

Foot speed is not Amelia's strength, but she has hands like clamps, strong and sure. The first time she started a game in goal for the soccer team, she made forty saves. Gallaudet lost 10–0, but Amelia was proud of how she overcame a wicked bout of nerves and didn't get discouraged in the face of the onslaught. Her brother—he's also deaf—would've been proud. He's the one who taught her how to catch by throwing balls and toys and assorted other objects to her when they were kids. Amelia is surprised she wound up liking goalie, because usually she doesn't want to be noticed. That's not easy to do when you are a broad-shouldered, seventy-two-inch-tall woman, but Amelia learned how, not by slouching so much as slip-sliding, honing the art of getting in and out of places unnoticed.

Amelia is mostly from Asheboro, North Carolina. The family moved around quite a bit when she and her two brothers were young, but wherever they lived, home was a minefield. There was lots of anger, and fights. Amelia's parents are both deaf and planned to stop having children after having the two boys. Then came Amelia. *"I thought all the troubles were my fault. I thought I should be able to do something to make things better."*

Her mother graduated from the North Carolina School for the Deaf. Her father dropped out in ninth grade. Amelia calls them "old-fashioned deaf people," because they didn't believe that they could really do anything with their lives. She liked to teach her parents new words and signs she learned in school. She felt as though she had to look out for them. Who else was going to?

Her parents divorced when Amelia was seven, and the sadness and guilt just kept flooding into her. In the fifth grade at the North Carolina School for the Deaf, she spent more time in suspension than she did in class. She got in a lot of fights. One time she got caught stealing some money from a teacher's pocketbook. She knew she was in for it this time. The principal already hated her. Now what would happen? The principal was a stern, stout little woman, and she summoned Amelia to her oppressive little office.

"One more problem from you, young lady, and you will be asked to leave this school. Do I make myself clear?"

Amelia's mother decided the family needed a fresh start, so they moved to La Grange, Georgia, where her mother got a job in the post office. Amelia was dropped into a sixth-grade mainstream class, with no interpreter, no signing teachers, no means to communicate at all.

Though she has a small degree of hearing, she was completely lost. She'd never been in a hearing class before. Overwhelmed and left out, she acted out more than ever.

"What I did was basically join a gang. They didn't call it that, but that's what it was, a bunch of low-class kids, freaks, misfits who everybody else looked down on. We did a lot of bad things. Shoplifted, got in fights, walked around with a bad attitude." Amelia went along with all of it, the price of admission to belong somewhere. About the only time she felt comfortable and happy was when she was with her cat Whitey. He's deaf. That's one of the reasons she got him. Whitey is sixteen and now has two black kittens to keep him company in Amelia's off-campus apartment. The kittens can hear, but they know that Amelia can't. When they're hungry or want attention, they don't meow. They knead their claws into her hair.

After the two worst years of Amelia's life, the family moved back to North Carolina. Amelia enrolled at North Carolina Central School for the Deaf. She was relieved to be out of LaGrange, but things got steadily worse. She still felt as though she didn't fit in, even though she was surrounded by deaf people again. She was still acting out, quick to turn belligerent. One day she stopped a classmate in the corridor.

"I'm deaf like you. Why aren't you nice to me?"

"I don't care whether you are deaf or not," the girl replied. *"You're not acting like a nice person."*

Amelia felt as if life kept dropping boulders on her. How was she supposed to get out from under them all? What was the point of trying? One day when her parents were out, she went in their bedroom. Next to the bed was a two-drawer nightstand. She opened up the top drawer and pulled out her stepfather's handgun. She had played with a BB gun before but never had held a real one. It felt cold and hard. She turned away from the bed and put the gun in her mouth. Her finger was on the trigger. She was sure she was going to pull it, until she saw her parents driving up to the house. She pulled the gun from her mouth. She put it back in the drawer.

Amelia's self-critical voice says that she didn't have the courage to do it. A gentler voice allows that the trigger was too final a solution, no solution at all. After she met Glenda Small and found the Lord, Amelia came to understand that what really stopped her that day was the love of God.

Glenda Small is a teacher at Central, a person who goes about her work with profound kindness and compassion. She was one of the first people who ever really made Amelia feel special. Amelia has always found reading a struggle. She has dyslexia, and she gets headaches from reading. Glenda let her learn at her own pace, in the glow of encouragement. If Amelia only felt comfortable reading comic books, that was fine. Outside the class Glenda looked after Amelia, too. She brought her home with her and they started to read a picture-book Bible together. A devout Christian, Glenda had a grace and contentment that Amelia could tell came from someplace deep. Soon the words of the Scriptures felt as though they were flowing right into Amelia's soul. It's hard to describe, but she just started to feel like she was one of God's children, and that she mattered.

"I felt the peace of the Lord come over me," Amelia said. "And from then on, my life changed."

Amelia's second year at Central, eighth grade, could not have been more different from her first. She did much better in school. She made friends. The old stout principal from her grade school was now principal of her high school. Amelia was sure what the principal was thinking when she saw her: "Oh no, not this kid again." After a few weeks of ninth grade, the principal called her in.

"What's happened to you?"

"What do you mean?"

"I haven't seen you in here. You seem to be a very different girl."

"I am different. I am completely different." Amelia told the principal about Glenda Small and how she wanted to do good things now, not bad things.

The principal smiled and said, *"That's great. I want to see you succeed. I want to help you. And I am so happy to have you in the school."*

Everything in Amelia's life changed. She went out for sports and emerged as a star player. She was elected student council president. She attended youth-leadership conferences, happily surrounded by the same kinds of kids she used to mock, and hate. She graduated as salutatorian from the North Carolina School for the Deaf. She was proud of herself, and so grateful for Glenda Small and the grace of God for saving her.

Amelia probably has more residual hearing than any player on the team. She can hear the rumble of the engine on the bus, and some blaring noises. She has worn hearing aids most of her life, and they work for her, turning up the volume of everyday life, allowing her to take in sounds—the chirping of birds, the cackle of laughter—that she wouldn't hear without them. Some people who wear hearing aids at Gallaudet say they are treated as pariahs, but Amelia hasn't had that problem. It all depends on your own attitude. If someone wears hearing aids and doesn't sign and acts like she wants to be a hearing person, then she's going to have trouble. But if she calls herself deaf and signs and embraces Deaf culture, then using a hearing aid is no more an issue than your hair color.

Natalie Ludwig, who has a profound hearing loss, wears hearing aids much of the time, too. They don't do much to help her understand speaking voices, but she can hear loud noises and knocks and sometimes ringing phones a little, and she likes having that alert. It has nothing to do with wanting to be hearing, or to be able to avoid signing. She just likes being able to make out a few sounds. It's a very individual decision, and one that is often determined by the nature of one's hearing impairment. Some people can only hear static, and a hearing aid does nothing but make the static louder. Ronda Jo used to wear them, and they would help her hear sound, but she found it more unsettling than anything else.

"I couldn't identify what the sound was—it was just sound—so what good was that? It didn't help me at all."

No Bison has less use for hearing aids than Nanette. She was forced to wear them as a youngster at the Minnesota State Academy for the Deaf. She brought one home one night, took it off at bedtime, but forgot to turn it off. It hummed and hummed until one of her Boston terriers, annoyed by the sound, traced its source and chewed on it until it was silent. *"I don't think they believed me in school, but that's really what happened,"* Nanette said. *"The dog ate my hearing aid."* Nanette hasn't worn one since, and never will again.

"I am in a quiet world. That's where I live. That's what I like. The world of noise is for hearing people."

It's a clear, cold morning in Amherst, New York, a suburb of Buffalo. The Bison check out of their roadside motel, not too broken up about saying good-bye to the green shag rugs and the knotty pine furniture. They head to Daemen College for a Sunday afternoon game. On the locker-room blackboard, Kitty draws a picture of a maze. Beneath it she has written, "AMAZE." The red and white candles are lighted and sitting on a stool.

Kitty points to the maze and tells the Bison, *"We keep running into the same hedge. Instead of turning around and finding another way, we just keep butting into it. We need to find a new way. We can get amazing results if we look at what we've been doing, and find a new direction."* The players nod and seem to like the analogy. They can see how hard Kitty is working. Kitty, Ben, and Hillel depart, and the players huddle up, around the candles.

"No more letdowns," Nanette said.

"Let's play hard and smart," Touria said.

"This is our last game in this semester," Cassey said. *"Let's make it a good one."* They put their hands in and shout "Whoooo!" and run out into the gym. More than a hundred fans from nearby deaf schools have come out to cheer the Bison on.

The Bison start impressively. Nanette takes a feed from Touria and puts in a short jumper. Touria sinks two straight spinning drives and Ronda Jo hits a leaning one-hander under pressure. The Bison go up by a dozen, and then, just as quickly, they hit the hedge again. They start with the turnovers and rushed shots and go six minutes without scoring a point, before Shanada Johnson hits a pretty, scooping drive. Down by one at the half, the players look rattled by their sloppiness, their faces fretful. The second half is a debacle. Ronda Jo's shot is off, and she lets out a scream of anguish after one open jumper misses badly. Nanette is wide open underneath and is waving her hand on one possession, but Stacy doesn't see her and winds up losing the ball. The defense is weak, half-hearted, devoid of commitment. One of the refs seems to have a big edge on, right from the start. He tells Kitty at the pregame meeting that if his players don't hand him the ball right away after a whistle, they'll get a technical. During the game, he keeps talking to the Gallaudet players, as if they could hear him. The guy has a thick neck and a mustache that looks like a piece of electrician's tape. The Bison are sick of him by the end, but not as sick as they are of themselves. The fans are waving their arms and stomping the bleachers, but it doesn't help anyone take better care of the ball.

The Bison have the body language of defeat. Except for Nanette and Cassey, who are poised and productive, nobody plays up to their ability. Gallaudet is outscored by more than thirty points in the second half and gets walloped. The locker room feels like a tomb, heavy and vaulted. Kitty asks if anyone has anything to say.

"*Merry Christmas and Happy New Year,*" Cassey said. Everyone laughed, a wonderful and instantaneous load-lightener. It was the highlight of the weekend.

The Bison's record is 4–4. As the charter makes the long return trip home, nobody is thinking about national rankings or Final Fours. They are thinking about how they might salvage their season.

It is Christmas break. The Bison scatter around the country. Touria, her boyfriend Thomas, and other friends head for the Florida Keys. Ronda Jo, Nanette, and Ronda head for their homes in Minnesota. Bound for Indianapolis, coach of a .500 team, Kitty is more convinced than ever that everybody, maybe herself included, is trying too hard to make good things happen. Everybody sees the team struggling and they want to fix it and pretty soon they're all trying to do things they can't do, forcing things. It's no way to play or coach. Pretty soon your head starts spinning. You're thinking instead of just playing. Look at Ronda Johnson. She was brilliant in the finest game of the season, against Capital, and has mostly looked lost ever since. Her instincts and judgments seem askew. Kitty knows that behind Ronda's jokes and hijinks, there is a young woman who loves the game passionately and wants desperately to prove herself. The team needs her to be the player she can be. It needs everyone to be more consistent. In the final days before the year 2000, Kitty isn't worrying about anything so global and apocalyptic as Y2K or impending technological meltdowns. Her wish list is much more basic. She just really, really wants to have her team back.

SIGNS OF
AWAKENING

NOTHING IS BETTER than Christmas on the farm. This year more than most, the timing is a blessing. The team needs to gets away, and Ronda Jo needs to be home, feeling the crunch of the snow underfoot and seeing the benign beauty of the landscape, blanketed in white. In Washington, Ronda Jo rarely wears anything heavier than her All-American parka in the winter, though it's little more than a windbreaker. How can you take the D.C. winter seriously after growing up in central Minnesota?

Sometimes the sameness of small-town life feels confining, but not now. The moment the pavement ends and the old country cemetery comes up on the right, Ronda Jo starts to savor the familiarity. She can't wait to rub the strong chestnut backs of her horses. Just walking through the door of the old white farmhouse gives her a rush of comfort. It's always tidy, unchanged. The wooden cupboard Ronda Jo built in shop class in high school is still in the corner of the living room. There's the lacquered wall of Ronda Jo's trophies and plaques and clippings. Upstairs in her bedroom, the pile of sneakers is the same as ever, a hi-top tangle at the foot of her closet.

Ronda Jo figured she'd take time off at home and rest her ankle, but sometimes a player just has to play. She goes to the YMCA in nearby Little Falls one day with her father. They play one-on-one for awhile—a major mismatch—and then John Miller spots three guys across the way and asks if they want to play two-on-two, with Ronda Jo as the fourth. They say sure. Two of the guys are pretty good players and they stay together, and put Ronda Jo with the guy who isn't so good. They play for an hour. Ronda Jo is in one of those places where everything feels right. She feels strong and quick and confident. She hits jumpers and fallaways, spins around them for layups. She drives and blocks a few shots, and a couple of times she fakes them out so badly, they fall down. She wishes Renee Brown or one of those WNBA general managers who are always calling and asking for tapes could see her now, not because the caliber of competition is the best, but because she's doing everything. Ronda Jo and her teammate win every game. When it is time to go, they all shake hands, and the two opponents watch Ronda Jo gather her stuff and slip on her sweats. John Miller hears one guy say, "She's good."

Two days into the year 2000, Jenny Cooper walks onto the Field House floor for the first time since last season, with her familiar sturdy swagger and her new chipped tooth. She broke it on a glass door, which she was pressing her face against at the same time that someone was opening it. It hurt, but that's okay. She has other teeth.

Campus is deserted. The Bison, the men's basketball team, and a few other assorted students are around, but the other students are not due back for a couple of weeks. Kendall Green has the surreal feel of a movie set; all the buildings and hangouts are in place, but nobody is in them.

The sight of Jenny in her blue/gray reversible practice uniform is the best thing to happen in weeks. Her mono is gone, and her infectious energy is back. The Bison can use her fire. They can use her rebounding. They definitely can use her goofy sense of humor, a leavening agent that any team can benefit from. Jenny is a ferocious worker on the floor, effort she puts forth with no demands attached. She doesn't have to get a certain number of shots. She doesn't have to score points. Her reward is wearing the Gallaudet uniform, muscling around the basket for loose balls and garbage points, and stirring everyone up as she goes, with her bushy ponytail and mischievous brown eyes. Her teammates still crack up about the time Jenny hauled down a rebound away from a player she'd been jousting with all game, and in a momentary bit of excess, drove her shoulder into the player, knocking her down and getting whistled for an intentional foul. The play was more overzealous than dirty, not that you could convince the opponent of that.

Later Jenny explained herself.

"You know, I talked to my shoulder before that happened, and I said, 'Shoulder, don't do it. Don't do it.' But then my shoulder did it, anyway. It just wouldn't listen. So what are you going to do?" Jenny is a force that draws people in, without trying. A big part of it is her comfort with herself, her gift for not taking herself too seriously. In her suite on the seventh floor of Clerc, she gets up in midconversation, grabs a magazine, heads for the bathroom, saying, *"When a woman's got to go, a woman's got to go."* At five feet, nine inches, she moves with a rugged easiness. She is quick to own her behavior if she messes something up, if a pass skids off her fingers or she forgets to switch on defense. When a fan says he's going to nickname her "Hatchet" after a series of games in which she's in foul trouble, Jenny laughs out loud.

Deafness goes back three generations in Jenny's family. Her parents both attended Gallaudet, and both played basketball. The idea of being immersed in a deaf world was why she came to the school. Still, she's not afraid to be in the minority. Almost all the other Bison say that when it comes time to have children, they want theirs to be deaf. Jenny's older brother, Marvin, who is six foot, six inches and was a standout basketball player for the Indiana School for the Deaf (the same school Jenny attended), has a hearing wife and a new baby girl, Holland. From the time the baby came home, Marvin would clap his hands over the crib, and if Holland didn't respond, he'd say, "All right!" Jenny understands where her brother is coming from; she knows he and her teammates are afraid that if the children can hear that, they will want to go off on their own and not be a part of Deaf culture. Jenny doesn't buy it. When she saw that baby Holland could hear and was responding to Marvin's noises, she thought that was great.

"To me it doesn't matter if children are deaf or they're hearing," Jenny said. "Either way they will have opportunities, and it will be fine. Either way, they will learn Sign and they will move easily between the two worlds. Love is a powerful force, and that transcends all."

It is a unique package Jenny possesses, with her zest for body-banging in the lane and her affability the rest of the time. She is studying elementary education and thinks she'd like to teach first grade, and she already knows how she can connect with her pupils: animals. Kids love them. Jenny loves them, all kinds, and reptiles, too. When she was three years old, she saw a snake get run over and tried desperately to reattach the flattened pieces. If she came upon an injured bird or a half-dead bug, she would do the same thing. She is sure she would have become a veterinarian if she were a hearing person. It's the only reason she ever feels a longing to hear. She's not someone who imposes limits on herself, but she doesn't think being a vet would work. "I am a deaf person, from a deaf family, from a deaf world. Being out in the middle *of nowhere in the hearing world, I just think it would be hard."* She doesn't agonize over it and doesn't wish she were someone else. Deafness to Jenny is like an old sofa. It's totally comfortable, and she knows all the best spots: *"If I were a hearing person, maybe I would have more opportunity and could do more things. But maybe I would be a nobody, just another person who blends in with the crowd. As a deaf person, I feel like I have an identity. I have a place. I don't think that's so easy to get when you are a hearing person."*

Jenny had mono for five months, and it was the worst. She recuperated at home in Indiana, agonizing about the volleyball and basketball games going on without her. She had recurring dreams about basketball and got a slew of e-mails from her teammates, especially Nanette and Ronda. That made her miss Kendall Green even more.

She was diagnosed in the late spring of 1999, when she was working three jobs and getting up at dawn to train for volleyball. She started feeling worn down. She went to the university health center, and nothing turned up. Her temperature went up to 103 one day. *"I could barely move. I just felt worse and worse."* She went to a hospital in Maryland, and they told her what she had. She was crushed. She was about to enter her senior year, her final go-round as a Gallaudet athlete. Jenny's not the sort of person who needs to see Kitty writing "The Time Is Now." She knows it and lives it. *"You have to enjoy every moment. This is a once in a lifetime experience. In the scope of your whole life, this is one dot, the chance to play on teams at Gallaudet. You have to give it everything because it will be gone before you know it."*

A fresh dusting of snow is coating Kendall Green, and the dome of Capitol Hill is shimmering in the clear light of morning. It is a pristine Saturday, the government is closed, the roads are unclogged, and the white frosting and deep quiet give Thomas Gallaudet's campus more the feel of northeast Vermont than northeast Washington.

To Kitty, to everybody, the New Year feels like a fresh start. First Kitty gets Cooper, her resident igniter, back. And then, finally, she gets Courtney Westberg, the long-awaited transfer student from Western Oregon, a Division II school in Monmouth, Oregon. Courtney is the best kind of Christmas present for a basketball coach: She is tall (six feet, one inch), she is skilled, and she is only a sophomore. She just has to get used to having fellow deaf people around her; in one of her first practices, she uses her voice to get her teammates' attention, a hold-over from years of playing on hearing teams. Then it hits her: *"They can't hear me, so why am I standing here yelling?"*

The Bison practice twice a day for their first game of 2000, against Wheaton College. Before a morning session, Kitty gets a call from Linda Hargrove, new coach of the Portland Fire of the WNBA. She has some questions about Ronda Jo and asks for a couple of game tapes. Kitty relays the news to Ronda Jo, who's standing in her doorway, in front of the Title IX poster.

"Maybe we should send her the Mary Washington game," Ronda Jo said. Kitty looks up at Ronda Jo's blue-gray eyes. Four years together has not made it any less of a comical sight, the five-foot-tall coach alongside her six-foot, two-inch center. Kitty laughs and gives Ronda Jo a push.

"Yeah, that will really make them want to draft you."

Kitty asks Ben to film ten minutes of a four-on-four scrimmage. That's all the Bison there are, because Shanada Johnson has quit the team. She expected to have a bigger role. She tells Kitty she doesn't have any hard feelings; she just hasn't been having that much fun, so why continue? Amelia England is also missing. She e-mailed Kitty and told her she has a terrible bout of flu and is still in North Carolina.

Done filming, Ben wheels a TV and VCR onto the floor, and the Bison watch themselves. "Maybe if they see it they'll start to believe what we're saying," Kitty said to Ben. Some good plays are interspersed with rebounding breakdowns and lazy passes. When she sees a half-hearted entry pass she throws to Ronda Jo, Ronda, sitting on the floor, said, *"Wow, I can't believe I threw that pass."* Ronda seems in good spirits, even with Shanada's departure. In a way, she feels relieved. It was hard to see Shanada not enjoying herself.

Before the game, Wheaton coach Cheryl Aaron reminds her players that Gallaudet was among the top-scoring teams in the nation the previous year. "They are going to come at you hard, so you have to be ready," the coach said.

Gallaudet starts in vintage, high-speed form, getting baskets in transition and racing to a 22–8 lead. They are rolling, and then, suddenly, they are not rolling. A couple of forced passes and a rash of turnovers create a scoring drought, and at the other end, Wheaton has started to penetrate the Gallaudet zone with disturbing ease. The mysterious inconsistency has surfaced yet again. Jenny Cooper scores the last five points in the half for the Bison, but the game has tightened up and Jenny, dragging a leg muscle she'd strained in practice, can't understand why. She gets up before her teammates during halftime and pleads with them: *"We need to play with heart. We can't go through the motions and win. Please, please don't take this for granted."* She looks around the room and is about to say something else and then she stops and starts to cry, her chest heaving, her mouth gasping for air. Kitty puts an arm around her and kisses her on the head. Later, Jenny tells Kitty, *"I feel so limited by my leg. I'm trying to do so much, and I can't, and they're all healthy and they're doing nothing."* Jenny feels even worse afterward, the Bison losing a ten-point lead in the final five minutes and dropping their fourth straight game.

In Room 142, Kitty's patience and gentleness have been exhausted. Her signs are strong and abrupt. *"They outworked us and outhustled us in the end, and I'll tell you why: because we played the way we practice. I am the coach of this team. You are the players. If you don't want to practice hard and listen to the coach and turn this season around, you will be asked to leave.*

"I am not afraid of any opponent," Kitty said. *"But I am scared to death of you."*

The more Kitty sees of Courtney, the more she likes her. She has good agility for her size, and a soft touch. In time, she should become a dangerous threat in the low post. The problem is her confidence. She arrives at Gallaudet with almost none, the fallout from an unhappy year and a half at Western Oregon. She won a scholarship to Western and was excited at first. But once the season started, she felt like a spare part and had chronic communication problems with her teammates. Courtney was supposed to get a regular interpreter, but it turned out that she had a rotating group, all of them students who were still learning. Half of them didn't know anything about basketball. When someone doesn't know an outlet pass from an offensive rebound, how is she going to interpret for a basketball player? Courtney longed to be a part of the team's jokes and triumphs but always felt as if she were stuck on the other side of an invisible partition. The low point came during a practice when the interpreter didn't show. Courtney tried to read lips and use gestures to communicate, which was more than anyone else was doing. It was almost as if her teammates were freezing her out. Courtney has a long neck and creamy skin. She could feel herself turning red. The point guard called out a play. Having gotten no signal about what they were running, Courtney set up in the wrong place. It happened two more times. The coach got so mad, he had everyone run suicides. A bunch of the players glared at her. Courtney went out that night with her boyfriend. He's deaf, and he understood how angry she felt. She was quiet the whole night, fogged in by a bank of hurt, the only breaks coming when her mind went back to the previous summer and her time at Gallaudet. Courtney had been on Kendall Green for the tryouts Kitty was running for the U.S. Deaf National Team. She met Ronda Jo and Ronda and Natalie and a number of other Bison players. Every place she looked, she saw people using ASL. Kitty wished Courtney well at Western Oregon but told her that if she ever changed her mind, she would love to have her on the Gallaudet team.

Courtney had changed her mind.

And was she ever ready.

Courtney comes from Anchorage, Alaska, and has never been a part of Deaf culture until now. She'd always played on hearing teams and been surrounded by hearing people, in her family, her neighborhood, everywhere. She went to Robert Service High School, the largest in Alaska, the only deaf person in a student body of four thousand. She has a perky grace and good sense of humor and she made friends, communicating with a rudimentary sort of sign language, but she'd sometimes get out of class and see the swarm of kids and the bustle in the hall and feel envious of how effortlessly they blended with one another. In four years of playing ball, she was never invited over to a teammate's home. Nobody came over to her house, either.

"They wanted me to teach them dirty words in sign language. They thought that was hilarious. But that was about it. I said to them at one point, 'Here I am, the deaf girl, all alone. You want me to play or you want me to quit?'" They said they wanted her to play, but the answer felt hollow, scripted. It wasn't as bad as the first team she was on. Courtney was ten, playing in a local youth league. Nobody passed her the ball. She dreaded going to games. *"I'd bawl my eyes out and tell my parents I didn't want to play, but my father wouldn't let me quit."* After five games, he relented.

Courtney is a young woman of deep faith. The wooden cross over her bed is her most prized possession. She knows the Lord will not give her anything that she can't handle, that He has a plan for her.

The first day she put down her bags in Room 309 in Peet Hall, her dorm room at Gallaudet, she felt as though she belonged. Her parents, Wayne and Dottie Westberg, accompanied her on the trip and stayed at the Kellogg Conference Center, Gallaudet's on-campus hotel. It was a strange experience for the Westbergs, being among the hearing few. Dottie is good at signing, but she felt like a beginner when she was at Gallaudet. Wayne carried an ASL instructional book with him all over campus. He's heard about fathers who have nothing to do with their deaf children and thinks it's deplorable. Courtney was glad her parents were there.

She was also glad that *they* were the ones who didn't fit in for once. *"I didn't want them to be uncomfortable, but it gave them an idea how it has always been for me,"* Courtney said. Her dad, a ruddy-faced man with white hair brushed up like a fence, cried when he hugged her good-bye.

Courtney learned the game from her father, a former player and coach and onetime owner of a minor-league basketball team. She liked going to University of Alaska-Anchorage games with him, at least until she got older and began getting embarrassed when he'd pull out his little magnetic board and diagram plays. She'd give him the "Oh, Dad" look, and he'd put it away.

Being the only deaf person in a home with two hearing parents and two older hearing brothers wasn't easy. Dinners were the hardest. *"We'd say grace and bless the food and then the conversation would take off like a train leaving the station, and I would be left at the platform."* Dottie would remind brothers Wade and Kris to include Courtney, but it was the same as it was for Touria at her home. Courtney loved her family but couldn't wait to be excused.

Maybe even more than Ronda Jo, Courtney is a country girl, a woman who much prefers wilderness and mountains to museums and monuments. She skis a lot, and though a few coaches along the way have tried to discourage her (it's not the most knee-friendly activity), it's still one of her greatest passions, along with Peanut M & M's and chicken fajitas. She started skiing at age three.

"She had absolutely no fear," Dottie said. "She would ski down that hill just as fast as her brothers and her father."

Dottie Westberg has a voice of velvet, a kind maternal face and coiffed hair, a Betty Crocker advertisement come to life. Her emotions are so present that she can cry almost on demand, out of sadness or happiness. Dottie figures it's because she has known so much of both. She lives with the joy of her three children, and the pain of her six miscarriages. She almost lost Courtney, too, to a rare blood disorder when she was an infant. Praying for the grace and strength to deal with it, she would rock Courtney in her arms and sing, "Turn Your Eyes Upon Jesus." Courtney's eyes would widen, and Dottie would keep singing. The disorder—supposedly a fatal condition—began to respond to treatment. When Courtney lost her hearing due to complications from whooping-cough serum, Dottie found the grace she had prayed for.

"What was Courtney's deafness, after the possibility of her dying? It was nothing. I did not know it then, but it was such a blessing, because she has taught us a whole new way of life."

Two years ago, Courtney and Dottie talked in depth about her deafness for the first time. They sat on Courtney's bed in a third-story alcove of their home, in front of the two big windows, the pink-orange Alaskan sunset filling the room. Dottie told her about how she sang to her and what her voice sounded like, and how sad Dottie felt when she took Courtney to a parade one afternoon and knew Courtney could not hear it. Then Dottie's mother reminded her: "She's not missing anything, because she never had it. The band doesn't mean anything to her. She sees things you'll never see and I'll never see. She'll look at the marchers' precision, their legs going up and down. She just has a different experience of it, that's all." They talked for two hours. Tears flowed, but they were good tears. They finished with a hug, not an ordinary one, but something much stronger.

In her first game for Gallaudet, Courtney doesn't score and acts as if she doesn't even want to touch the ball. Kitty knows it'll take time and encourages her to take her shot. Kitty keeps nuturing her and Courtney keeps drinking it up, eager for her basketball to catch up to the rest of her life at Gallaudet.

"I feel like I've been let out of prison," Courtney said. *"I love that I'm in an ASL world."*

Courtney grew up communicating in Signed English, a language in which signs are employed with English grammar and word order. It is in the same family tree as ASL, but on a very distant branch, considered by many confirmed ASL users to be a diluted, even bastardized, form of ASL. Courtney started learning ASL in seventh grade but didn't fully appreciate it until she was seventeen, at a tryout in Iowa for the Deaf National Team. Most of the players were signing in ASL. Courtney loved watching them, finding it a much richer way of communicating. It was the first language she'd ever used that she felt could convey all her feelings.

To the uninitiated, ASL might seem to be nothing more than an amalgam of hand signals and gestures, the mysterious means by which most deaf people communicate. To those who use it, it is a way of life, a linguistic choice that speaks loudly about one's attitude toward not being able to hear. When someone says, "I speak Italian," it is a statement of fact. When Ronda Jo Miller says, *"I am an ASLer,"* it is a declaration of cultural independence. She is proud of who she is, and the culture she is part of.

If Deaf culture is a wheel, Nanette Virnig says, then ASL is its hub: *"It is much easier to express our opinions and emotions by signing in ASL as opposed to English. Hearing people may have a hard time understanding that, but Signed English is a longer, slower method and it doesn't let us express ourselves the same way. ASL is a beautiful language, too, the way we sign with our hands."*

The power of ASL stems partly from its remarkable economy; it's possible to put a paragraph worth of words in a few gestures and movements. "ASL takes full advantage of its spatial dimension and can pack a whole lot of information into a few signs," said Robert E. Johnson, a professor in Gallaudet's Department of ASL, Linguistics and Interpretation. "It's a marvelous language that way." As an example, take the sentence, "The car went by me on a windy mountain road." Those ten words of English can be conveyed in an instant by using the sign for car, showing it going through S-turns and moving it away from the body.

Much as English words are constructed of vowels, consonants, and syllables, signs are constructed of such components as hand shape, hand location around the body, and the direction and nature of their movement. The sign for vacation, for instance, involves taking both hands, open and fingers extended (as if you were holding up five fingers), and bringing them in toward each armpit, touching it with the thumb. Take the identical hand shape, and put it to your temples, thumbs first, and it's the sign for deer.

For all of ASL's intricacies and efficiency, though, the greater power of the language derives from its origin. It is homemade, baked in the hearth of Deaf culture. Once exposed to it, the Bison and many others find it impossible ever to be satisfied by store-bought again.

American Sign Language has its roots in the French sign language that Laurent Clerc learned from Abbé Sicard in Paris and exported to the United States when he came back to Connecticut with Thomas

Hopkins Gallaudet in the early nineteenth century. Like any other organic entity, Clerc's language changed as it took root in new soil, incorporating new signs, losing others, evolving to suit the needs of the nascent school and its pupils. The pupils themselves brought their own language to the mix, having an established, if uncodified, system of signs. "Some of us have learned and still learn signs from uneducated pupils, instead of learning them from well-instructed and experienced teachers," Clerc said in 1852. Still, the foundation of ASL remains undeniably French, and to this day, ASL bears a striking resemblance to its Gallic ancestor.

It is one of hundreds of sign languages in use around the world.

"More than a few times I've heard people comment, 'It's stupid to have all those sign languages. There should be just one universal sign language,'" said Robert Williams, professor of psychology at Gallaudet. "When I hear that, I say, 'OK, fine. We'll do that just as soon as we all *speak* one universal language.'"

As a network of residential schools began to form in the United States, it proved to be an ideal breeding ground for the language. The schools had a built-in community of users with a great incentive to learn it, and the day-to-day immersion so critical to learning a new language. Few pupils resisted, and why would they? They were learning their own language.

To stand back and watch a conversation in ASL is almost like having a window into the conversants' souls. It fills space not just with movements and gestures, but with feeling, with a sense of full presence, the speakers' eyes unfailingly locked in on each other. It is visible and visceral, its energy and beauty seeming to flow right from the speaker's soul. One of the rudest things one can do in Deaf culture is to walk in front of someone as she is signing. It is tantamount to cutting someone off from the world. Sign language seeks to avoid exclusion, not foment it. Or as J. Schuyler Long, a teacher at the Iowa School for the Deaf, wrote nearly a century ago:

Sign Language is, in the hands of its masters, a most beautiful and expressive language, for which, in their intercourse with each other and as a means of easily and quickly reaching the minds of the deaf, neither nature nor art has given them a satisfactory substitute.

It is impossible for those who do not understand it to comprehend its possibilities with the deaf, its powerful influence on the moral and social happiness of those deprived of hearing, and its wonderful power of carrying thought to intellects which would otherwise be in perpetual darkness. Nor can they appreciate the hold it has upon the deaf. So long as there are two deaf people upon the face of the earth and they get together, so long will signs be in use.

Every person's signing style is different, just as everyone's voice is different. The way someone signs often says a great deal about who she is and where she's from. The most fluent and facile ASLers, like Ronda Johnson, are invariably those who have been deaf since birth and who most often come from families with a long history of deafness. Courtney, by contrast, is a comparative novice. Her signing style is unbridled and zealous, her movements loud and sweeping.

There are geographical variations in ASL as well. Many deaf people say that they can recognize someone from New York City with no problem. In the east, the sign for the verb "to walk" is to hold two hands flat, palms down, in front of one's body, moving them slightly as if they were feet. In California, the movement is the same, but the hands are configured in the "OK" shape, index finger and thumb touching, the other three fingers extended. Across the country, there are about twenty different signs for birthday and some thirty signs for the color gray.

The finer shades of ASL are going to take time to master, Courtney knows. She wants to learn it all as fast as she can. Her long body is folded into a chair at a small square table in the Bison Eatery. Students are eating pizza and tortilla wraps and macaroni and cheese. Courtney's lunch will have to wait; it's hard to eat and sign at the same time. For the first time in her life, she doesn't feel in need of fixing. She is thrilled to be learning a language that lets all her emotions come forth.

"I never felt this way before in my whole life," she said.

As it comes up on its third century, ASL may be in more robust health than ever. While the media exposure gained during the Deaf President Now uprising in 1988 did much to circulate ASL to a wider population, its greatest gain has come from linguistic scholars, most notably former Gallaudet professor Dr. William Stokoe, whose studies determined ASL to be a complex, distinctive, and fully formed human language, as legitimate as any of the spoken variety. ASL has its own syntax and grammar and idioms, quite distinct from English. It has a vastly smaller vocabulary than the estimated three hundred twenty thousand words English encompasses, but it doesn't need as many words because of the amount of information that can be provided through motion and placement. It is a language able to communicate ideas, emotions, and even abstractions, Stokoe found, and soon others were picking up on his findings. In the same year as Deaf President Now, the Parliament of the European Community recognized the indigenous signed languages of its twelve member countries. In many states and in a growing number of U.S. colleges and universities, ASL is accepted as a way to fulfill a foreign language requirement. The image makeover has been striking and swift: In the span of just a couple of decades, ASL has gone from being dismissed by many as little more than homemade pantomime to being hailed as a fully developed, self-contained human language. A few deaf educators have recently come out in favor of Signed English instead of ASL, arguing that the use of ASL has impeded the English proficiency of deaf students and kept them from achieving their full potential. The most ardent members of Deaf culture are unmoved. They believe more than ever that deaf people need to use their natural language, that ASL alone can provide a deaf student with the sound linguistic base necessary for a good education.

The soaring credibility of ASL has been a source of comfort and even vindication to a great many people in Deaf culture. It has been a much less pleasing development to oralists, who believe that the mission of deaf education should be to cultivate the ability to speak, no matter how laborious the process might be (and even the most fervent oralist will not deny that the process is laborious). Nanette is just one of the Bison who had a disagreeable experience with speech. *"My parents had me go to speech therapy for two or three years and it was terrible,"* she said. *"The teacher would make me use my voice and tell me that I have a wonderful voice. That was B.S.! All speech teachers always say to deaf children they have a wonderful voice so they feel proud and good, but it's usually very ugly."* To Nanette, the experience was a waste of time that could've been much more profitably spent learning about geometry or the Roman Empire.

Sign versus speech? Oral versus manual? The debate has raged for centuries, in the Old World and the New, carried out more in diatribe than dialogue. In *Dancing Without Music,* Beryl Lieff Benderly likens it to a holy war, and it is a most apt analogy for an issue that is broached on both sides by religious fervor. Supporters of sign and speech agree on only one thing: that they have the best interests of people who are deaf in mind. To achieve that end, one group turns left, the other right, and two hundred years later, they are no closer to finding a patch in the middle to meet on.

To oralists, sign language is anathema. It is self-limiting, inherently isolating, a guaranteed way to cut a deaf person off from the great majority of the people on earth—socially, culturally, and vocationally. Why restrict yourself in this way? Why stamp yourself as different and consign yourself to a separate world? As one oral proponent said, "Sure, it is easier to learn sign language than speech, and certainly it is more convenient and efficient. But where exactly does that convenience take you, beyond the dinner dance at the local deaf social club?" Oralists believe deaf people need to communicate the way the rest of the world does: through speech. You must force yourself into the mainstream, by learning to lip-read and articulate.

To signing advocates, oralism is heresy. It is a method that is founded on illusion. Said Nanette, *What's the point in pretending to be hearing? Why deny the fact that you're deaf?* She thinks that oralists are chasing a life that will lead to frustration and humiliation, to being little more than a mumbling facsimile of a hearing person. Where's the wisdom of devoting endless hours engaged in the numbing repetition of speech lessons? Lip-reading is a famously hit-or-miss proposition, as the old joke about three elderly deaf men aboard a train portrays. When the train pulls into a station, the first man looks at the platform and says, "Ah, Weston."

"Wednesday?" the second man says. "I thought it was Thursday."

"Thursday?" says the third. "I am, too. Let's go have a drink."

Sign supporters believe oralists are living a lie. They believe oralists are obsessed with the one thing they cannot do—hear. *"We, on the other hand, accept our deafness,"* Nanette said. *"We love the culture it has brought us into. We know what we have and who we are, and we are content with both."*

Perhaps no oral advocate in history was more zealous than Alexander Graham Bell. While not busy with his inventions, Bell turned his genius against the sign-based residential school system that was the center of deaf education in the nineteenth century. By almost every account, these schools had done an exemplary job of educating deaf children. But Bell was unyielding in his conviction that sign language had to be driven from the schools, and by the time he was done, he had very nearly fulfilled his mission.

Bell came by his interest in deaf education honestly. His father and grandfather was well-known teachers of speech and elocution, and both his mother and wife were deaf. In the 1860s, a loosely knit group of oralists were beginning to assail the methods of the residential schools. They believed the oral approach was the way of the future, based principally on the success of oral schools in Germany. Bell, who emigrated from England to Canada in 1870 and came to the United States a year later, thought so, too. Teaching deaf pupils in Boston with a system pioneered by his father called Visible Speech, he became convinced that the use of sign language isolated the deaf and fostered a separate culture that was not in their best interest. Many hearing parents of deaf children, eager for their kids to be as "normal" as possible, were quick to support him, as were hearing teachers and some politicians. Nor was Bell hurt by his timing; he was advancing his theory in an era when the Industrial Revolution was spawning rampant faith in progress, and a Victorian parochialism was tugging people to conform to strict societal standards.

More and more, Bell and others persuaded people that sign language was archaic. Before long, these stirrings forged into a global movement that held that the goal of deaf education should be to teach pupils to speak.

Even Edward Miner Gallaudet, president of the new college for the deaf that would be named for his father, saw some value in learning speech, though not anywhere near to the extent that he was ready to abandon ASL-based education. Gallaudet toured more than a dozen European countries, visited schools both oral and manual, and came home as certain as ever that nothing was better than sign language to help students learn to think, acquire knowledge, and express themselves. Gallaudet was a rare centrist in the debate, but his voice of reason was increasingly being drowned out by Bell and his band of oral crusaders. Bell lobbied loudly for the outright ban of signing and the closing of the residential schools, and just as loudly against deaf intermarriage, believing that such unions would produce more deaf children and deepen the family attachment to sign language. An 1889 study by Edward Allen Fay, a professor of foreign languages at Gallaudet, proved Bell wrong, showing that while roughly 10 percent of marriages involving a deaf partner yield deaf children (a proportion considerably higher than the corresponding figures for marriages of two hearing people), there was no greater probability of having deaf off-spring if both parents were deaf. Even more illuminating in Fay's work was his finding that the rate of divorce and separation of mixed couples was three times that of marriages that included two deaf people. Fay traced the difference "to the strong mutual fellowship growing out of their similar condition, the ease and freedom with which they communicate with each other and the identity of their social relations and sympathies outside of the domestic circle." As Van Cleve and Crouch write in *A Place of Their Own*, ". . . Fay discovered what deaf Americans had come to know for themselves—that they were happiest among each other."

Still, Bell was unbowed. In Europe, the oral movement was gaining even more momentum. It all culminated in 1880 in Italy, at the world-wide Congress of Educators of the Deaf in Milan. The convention was attended by 164 people, 163 of whom were hearing. The tone of the meeting was set by the leader and organizer of the conference, Italy's Abbé Guilio Tarra, who thundered in his opening remarks, "Evviva la parola" (Long live speech!). The lone deaf delegate was James Denison, principal of the Kendall School in Washington, D.C., then and now on the campus of Gallaudet. Denison was joined in the five-person U.S. delegation by Edward Miner Gallaudet and his older brother, Thomas, a reverend who worked with the deaf in New York City. There's no record that anyone found it curious that an international conference about educating the deaf should include a total of one deaf person. At the close of the conference, a motion was passed overwhelmingly. It read:

The Convention, considering the incontestable superiority of speech over signs, (1) for restoring deaf-mutes to social life, and (2) for giving them greater facility of language, declares that the method of articulation should have the preference over that of signs in the instruction and education of the deaf and dumb.

Moreover, the conference's position was that the use of sign language should be forbidden in schools, lest students cheat and go back to their most comfortable form of communication.

The final vote was 158–6. All five Americans voted against it, but they were holding teacups against a waterfall. One European country after another adopted speech as its official method of educating the deaf. Even France, the nation where Abbé Charles Michel de L'Epée pioneered deaf education and sign language, went oral. The United States, with its sign-based residential schools, was slower to convert, but here, too, the oral onslaught was unstoppable. In 1882, according to the historian Van Cleve, 7.5 percent of the nation's estimated seven thousand pupils in U.S. schools for the deaf were taught orally. By the turn of the century, that number was close to 50 percent. By the end of World War I, 80 percent of deaf pupils were learning their lessons orally. The stunning reversal didn't just ransack an educational way of life; it stripped students of a powerful group of role models—the deaf educators who were teaching them. In the middle of the nineteenth century, half of the teachers of the deaf were deaf themselves. About a hundred years later, the percentage had shrunk to a little over ten.

Still, sign language did not go away, and neither did its advocates. One of the main thrusts of the switch to the oral method was that learning speech would help a deaf person rejoin mainstream society. Robert P. McGregor, founder of the sign-based Cincinnati Day School and the first president of the National Association for the Deaf, said this notion was a bad joke. He said he'd never witnessed a single example of a deaf person being "restored to society." Rather than readying the deaf for the hearing world, McGregor believed oralism left the deaf in a pathetic, linguistic no-man's-land: "With imperfect speech, they cannot mingle freely with the hearing, and knowing no signs they are equally at sea in a social gathering of the deaf."

After absorbing nearly eighty years of body blows, the manual method began to make a comeback in the 1960s. Parents and deaf educators increasingly started to question the value of the oral method, doubts that became an epidemic after the release in 1965 of the Babbidge Report on deaf education. Commissioned by the U.S. Department of Health, Education and Welfare, the report presented a scathing critique of oralism and the educational mess it had wrought. Other studies in the United States and Great Britain revealed that the average deaf high-school graduate was reading at approximately the fourth-grade level. There was no international conference held to trumpet it, but visual communication was unmistakably back in favor. In his account of deafness, *Seeing Voices,* Oliver Sacks maintains that the oral revolution did not just fall short of its goals; it was an abject failure: "Deaf students of the 1850s who had been to the Hartford Asylum, or other such schools, were highly literate and educated—fully the equal of hearing counterparts. Today the reverse is true. Oralism and the suppression of Sign have resulted in a dramatic deterioration in the educational achievement of deaf children and in the literacy of the deaf generally."

There are an estimated 1 million deaf children in the United States, and only one in ten of them is born into a family with deaf parents. Nanette Virnig is one of the 10 percent and has always been grateful for that. She never felt like a stranger in her own household. It always saddens her to think about her deaf friend from a hearing family in Minnesota. *"She's twenty-two years old and they won't let her do anything. They call her dumb to her face. They wouldn't let her come to Gallaudet. She basically has no life."*

For Nanette, there was never any doubt that her first language was going to be ASL. She doesn't know where she would be if she didn't have it. Deaf history is strewn with examples of children born to hearing parents who, whether out of confusion or heartsickness or misinformation, not only don't help their deaf child learn sign language, they don't help her learn any language at all early in her life. Such a child grows deprived of a way to fulfill the most basic human urges: to connect, to find her place, to understand the world around her.

The Virnigs read and write English, of course, but the pulse of the home is ASL. Nanette had the usual collection of first words—Mommy and Daddy, cup and cookie—the only difference being that to her they were signs, not sounds. Hearing children learn by listening; connecting sounds to people, places, and things; and repeating the experiences over and over. Deaf children learn by watching; connecting signs to people, places, and things; and repeating the experiences over and over. From Nanette's first days, Tom and Carole Virnig gave her a way to make sense of her world. They gave her ASL.

"If you cannot hear, the likelihood of developing your full intellectual potential is very small unless you have full access to a visual language," said Lynne Erting, a deaf-education researcher at Gallaudet.

"You have to have one language before you can learn another," Nanette said. "If you don't, it's like building a house without a foundation. It's just going to fall."

Once she has her elementary education degree and gets in a classroom, Nanette's students will learn about her passion for ASL, and her faith in them. One thing that has always incensed Nanette about deaf education is that too many schools don't aim high and don't push children. To her, it is the soft bigotry of low expectation. She sees it at residential schools and mainstream schools alike, administrators spoonfeeding students or barely feeding them at all. It is the most vile form of paternalism. It makes her crazy that people in the education business would do that to a child.

Natalie Ludwig had the almost identical experience. "I never had good English because teachers did not really teach us to get to a higher level,"

Natalie said. *"Deaf people have eyes. They should be able to read and do well in English, but I blame the teachers who didn't think we could."* Kids usually perform to the level that is expected, so the results become a self-fulfilling prophecy.

Nanette doesn't have an easy time reading her English textbooks. Her mind wanders, and the comprehension often seems to come at glacial pace. She stays with it. She's proud of the 3.6 GPA she had in the fall term. *"One of the reasons I want to become a teacher is to encourage kids to push themselves to find out how much they can do,"* Nanette said. *"Enough with pitying them and sending them a message that they can't do this and can't do that."* In Ms. Virnig's class, the bar is going to get raised. There will be lots of complaints and lots of misses, as there always are when standards are jacked up. She doesn't worry about that. She thinks about how cool it will be to see the end result, when all these deaf children are soaring over the bar.

The Gallaudet bus is motoring through southern Pennsylvania, but Kitty's thoughts are on Indiana. This has happened often during the season, but never more powerfully than now. Paul Baldridge has just had another setback. He and Peggy went out for breakfast on New Year's Day, and he slipped and fell and broke his hip. He's already had surgery. The break seems to have been clean, but Kitty wonders how much more he can withstand. Paul had been back walking before the fall, and now this. She thinks back to the start of this ordeal, August 23, when he had the stroke. Kitty got to the hospital as fast as she could. Her father told her he thought he was going to die because she was there, as if the presence of his old assistant coach meant it was time for the head coach to go.

Kitty set him straight.

Paul Baldridge stabilized and was moved to a rehab facility, but Kitty's worries have never stopped. When the phone rings, she braces herself, her insides freezing up, her voice getting clipped and wary. He's lucid but still has trouble with his signing. His recovery has been slow, triumph measured in maddeningly minute quantities, people fussing over his being able to hold a spoon or eat Jell-O or sign, "Good morning." It hurts Kitty to be powerless to help him. It hurts to see Peggy feeling overwhelmed and then guilty for having the over- whelmed feelings. Before the season started, Kitty thought of taking a leave of absence, turning the team over to Ben Baylor and going home. Her parents talked her out of it. They said she needed to be in Wash- ington. Kitty is not someone who glides through such decisions. Deeply loyal, she is a person who needs to know she's doing the right thing more than she needs to eat. Her mind became an endless, tor- turous loop, playing and replaying her options: go or stay? Ultimately she decided to stay. Her parents were right. There was only so much she could do for her father, anyway. She needed to live her life, honor the commitment she and her players made the previous spring in the soul- searching postscript of defeat against Salem State in the NCAA tourna- ment. They had all vowed then to do all they could to do even better next year and not let any mental noise about not being able to beat a hearing team deter them.

Maybe all this thinking about her dad is why Kitty turns the first week of 2000 into Bison Father Week. It's an undeclared policy, but John Miller and Wayne Westberg are both in town with their wives, both at practice, and Kitty recruits them for a fullcourt scrimmage at the end of a practice. They clamber out of the grandstands, gray-haired and thick in the middle, and take positions underneath the basket on a zone defense, part of an all-male team that is going against the starting five. Cutting, faking, driving to the basket, Ronda Jo and Courtney make their fathers look as mobile as lampposts. When Ronda Jo gets the ball on the right blocks, John Miller goes to lean on her with his three hundred pounds, just the way he always did at home. She slips by him, ducks under, and scores. She turns and gives him a teasing look after the ball slips through.

The clouds are thickening as Ernie steers the bus off an exit marked Harrisburg and pulls into a Days Inn, host hotel for the Elizabethtown College Tournament that has brought the Bison here. There is a sign out front that says, "Welcome Gallaudet University," and there are blue and yellow streamers hanging outside their block of rooms. The players are pointing at the decorations, touched by the welcome. The Bison check in, and Kitty gets her extra set of keys and sees another sign welcoming the team. "Isn't this nice?" Kitty says. She thanks the manager. She is glad she is with her players.

"Do you like losing? Do you have pride? Do you care?" The rhetorical questions come from Nanette, minutes before Gallaudet is to take on Delaware Valley College in the Elizabethtown College gymnasium. The Bison seem more ready to play than they have been in a long time.

"Be aggressive," Natalie Ludwig said in the pregame circle.

"Don't wish. Don't think. Do it now," Jenny Cooper said.

Delaware Valley is a strong, physical team. Their frontcourt players battle hard underneath, and the Bison battle just as hard. Ronda is hitting her jump shot early and doing a splendid job of moving the ball around. Touria makes a double-pump layup between two defenders as the Bison go up by seven, 39–32, at the half. What Kitty likes most is the judgment. The Bison are running, but doing it judiciously, showing good patience when there's not an opening. The only exception is when Courtney fires a pull-up jumper on the fast break with nobody underneath to rebound.

Kitty waves her hand to get Courtney's attention and puts her palms down to settle her. *"Don't rush,"* Kitty said. *"Wait for your shot."* Courtney nods and runs back on defense.

Midway through the second half, the Bison begin to take over. Playing some of her most effective minutes of the season, Stacy powers in two offensive rebounds. Ronda Jo is getting roughed up inside, and Kitty can see it's getting to her.

"Keep cool," Kitty said. *"The best revenge is to smile and keep playing your game."* Ronda Jo agrees, her ponytail bobbing, and then goes on a tear, connecting on a turnaround, a fallaway, a spinning drive, slicing up the defense from all angles. Ronda Jo is crushing them, and as the Bison pull away to an easy victory, one of her foes has had enough and lets fly with a forearm shove. Ronda Jo gives a shove back and then the whistle blows, and the official ejects both players from the game. Ronda Jo departs with thirty-one points and four blocks, but she may have just really hurt her team. The officials huddle afterward to determine whether Ronda Jo should be suspended for the championship game the following day against Elizabethtown. Kitty makes her case to the tournament director—that Ronda Jo was acting purely in self-defense.

"Even when things go right this year something goes wrong," Kitty thinks.

Ronda Jo is spared, and she puts on one of the greatest shows of her career against a deep and highly skilled Elizabethtown team in the championship game. Despite some shaky interior defense, the Bison stay close for most of the game before fading at the end. Ronda Jo winds up with thirty-six points and fourteen rebounds and has the fans applauding her even when the game is out of reach. After the buzzer sounds and the teams shake hands, a father and his thirteen-year-old deaf daughter approach Kitty and introduce themselves. He asks if his daughter can meet Ronda Jo. Minutes after a disappointing defeat, Kitty graciously brings the girl over to Ronda Jo, who asks her about where she goes to school and how much she likes basketball. They chat for a few minutes. The girl says she wants to come to the Gallaudet basketball camp.

"That would be great. I'll see you there because I'm a counselor," Ronda Jo said.

Before she can get to the locker room, there is someone else waiting for her. He's a tall man in his forties, with dark hair and a handsome chiseled face. He looks like an athlete, Ronda Jo thinks. Turns out he is the father of one of the Elizabethtown players. He extends his hand and says through a Gallaudet interpreter, "I just wanted to tell you what a wonderful player you are and what a pleasure it is to watch you." When he talks about her footwork and her ballhandling, she gets the sense that he really knows about the game. The man never mentions her deafness. Ronda Jo likes that most of all.

John and Dolly Miller, who made the trip to Pennsylvania, say good-bye to their daughter before their drive back to Minnesota. As much as she prizes her independence, Ronda Jo admits that she loves it when her parents are at her games. After scoring sixty-seven points in two games in Elizabethtown, she jokes, *"Maybe I should give them some money and see if they'll stay a little longer."*

The trip back to D.C. is quick and uneventful. Ernie stops the bus outside Ronda Jo's apartment, for her usual dropoff. As Ronda Jo drifts off that night, she feels much better about the season. The Bison only split in Pennsylvania, but they were more intense, more committed. All year the Bison have clung to an implicit faith that things would get straightened out. They have their best chance to justify that faith coming up in three days, against their biggest conference rival, St. Mary's

College. St. Mary's is undefeated, ranked among the top ten teams in the country. The last time the teams met, the Bison knocked St. Mary's off on its home court in the first round of the 1999 NCAA Tournament, one of the sweetest triumphs the Bison have ever had. After they danced and cut down the net, team stat man Ronnie Z. and a few associates smuggled a blue-and-white folding chair with St. Mary's written on it back into the bus. They wrapped it up and presented it to Kitty at their year-end party.

The teams have not met since. St. Mary's coach, Shann Hart, is undoubtedly going to have her players primed for payback. A victory over such a high-flying team could change the tenor of the whole Bison season. The last practice before the game is one of the best of the year, players fully attentive, movements crisp, execution spirited. When Kitty waves her hand, players stop and listen quickly. When she puts them through ballhandling and defensive drills, they do so uncomplainingly. The Bison look like a team with direction and passion. The sloppy practices have carried over into games. As she closes her office door the night before the most important test of the season, Kitty can only hope that this one will carry over, too.

OVERTIME, OVERJOYED

IN THE WEEKS leading up to the season, and oftentimes during it, Ronda Johnson would arise at six A.M. in her dorm room on the sixth floor of Clerc Hall. She'd climb out of bed, slip out the door, and run a route she's taken a thousand times in her three years at Gallaudet: down the ramp, by the circle in front of Benson Hall, past Hotchkiss Field, where the football team plays and the track team runs, to the fitness center in the basement of the Field House. Amid the mats and mirrors and vague smell of sweat, she would pump iron, working on her arms and pushing herself. Often she would be joined by Stacy Nowak and Nanette Virnig. She loved the company, finding strength in numbers, so it wasn't strictly a session between herself and her willpower. She'd gut out one more rep, one more set. Ronda would tell herself, "I'm making a deposit now so I can draw on it later, when I've still got legs and my opponent doesn't." Ronda started the year twenty pounds lighter than she did the year before. She might've been leaner still were it not for the postworkout breakfasts Stacy would make: a bagel topped with eggs, cheese, and green peppers.

"I feel so much better," Ronda said. She is quicker. She is stronger. She's hoping it'll pay off at the end of the season.

For some Bison, basketball is a seasonal pursuit, giving way to other diversions, depending on the time of year. Not for Ronda. Beneath the jokes is a woman who lives for basketball. Her attention outside the court flits around a lot. She has not much appetite for studying and wishes that English were not so difficult. So many rules, so many tenses. So little sense. And writing is the worst of all. She keeps waiting for it to become easier for her, but it hasn't happened yet. She knows she probably spent too much time with her ASL at home, and not enough with her second language. Ronda is self-conscious about her struggles with English. She'd much rather be busy, and her favorite way to be busy is by playing basketball.

It is, after all, just the way her father planned it.

Ronald Johnson has a slim, sinewy body; a square chin; and the handshake of a man who has spent years working the earth. He may be the only man in America with this three-pronged job description: farmer/herbalist/basketball coach. He and his wife, Shirley, have five kids, which Ronald always says is half the number he wanted to have.

"I really hoped to have enough to make two full teams," Ronald said. The Johnson kids' names all begin with either Ro or Sh (Robin, Shanada, Ronda, Shawn, Rochella), and they all learned to play basketball on the Nerf set in the living room. The location was no accident. Ronald wanted it right in the middle of everything. When the weather allowed, they'd go outside to a regulation court. Ronald made up drills for Ronda and the others, putting her in a small circle with a ball to dribble, and two defenders who would try to take it away. Like Ronda Jo, who learned her touch on the wayward bounces of a dirt driveway, Ronda

acquired her ballhandling skill early. It's wired into her, like riding a bike. Her father made sure. He makes a fist with his right hand then rubs his knuckles back and forth along his extended left index finger. It is the sign for practice.

"You have to practice, practice, practice," he said, voicing the word for added emphasis.

When the four deaf Johnson children enrolled at the Minnesota State Academy for the Deaf in Faribault, Minnesota, the Johnsons kept the farm but got another place near the school. Ron coached Ronda and Shanada on the MSAD girls team (he coached Ronda Jo and Nanette, too). With the keys to the gym, the coach had ample opportunity to preach his basketball gospel, which stressed dogged defense and a creative, free-flowing offense, encouraging players to treat the court like their own personal canvas—and express themselves. Ronald Johnson has always believed that if a coach tries to script every pass, shot, and dribble, he'll wind up with a bunch of automatons with no feel for the game. *"He'd never use a book of plays, or pull out a Concepts of Basketball book,"* Ronda said. *"He knows that books don't know us, or our styles and skills. He would make plays that worked for us, that fit us all. He's one of one of the greatest coaches I ever had."*

Ronald Johnson is a not a man bound by convention, or pragmatism. Not on the court, or in the car. The Johnson family has not had good luck in the state of Iowa. Their teams always seem to lose to Iowa teams. Rochella, the youngest of the five children, ripped up her knee in a volleyball tournament in Iowa. The one time their Volkswagen bus broke down on vacation, loaded up with gear and kids, it broke down in Iowa. Ronald Johnson has actually taken two-hour detours to avoid hitting a corner of Iowa. He believes in trusting one's instincts, in all matters.

Aside from basketball, Ronald Johnson's favorite subject may be Green Life, his homemade health concoction. It is a powdery mix of alfalfa, oats, barley, garlic, and other stuff, all grown pesticide-free on the Johnson farm. It supplies energy, fortifies the body, cleans the system out. Ronda gives an exasperated eyeball roll every time her father launches into the benefits of Green Life, especially the cleaning-out part. Ronald Johnson smiles and sets his chin and goes right on. To him, the stuff is a nutritional godsend. He is convinced that Green Life is why all the children were so healthy growing up.

Ronda didn't just appreciate the freedom her father gave her as a coach; she appreciated his faith. As much as she likes Kitty as a person, Ronda often feels constrained by her on the court. Every time she does her jump-stop maneuver—in which she drives, stops, and eludes a defender with a flashy hop and step move—Kitty gets upset. She thinks it's a show-off play, not good basketball. Ronda thinks Kitty might as well send her out there with ankle weights, she feels so limited sometimes. The stylistic gulf between coach and player sometimes seems to be widening by the week.

In all kinds of ways, the season is not going the way Ronda wanted it to. She hasn't really felt in a rhythm all year. She had the phenomenal game against Capital and has been up and down since then. And that's just the start of it. Ronda feels that she and Nanette have drifted apart. They're still roommates, and still have a deep bond going back to their days at MSAD, but it doesn't feel the same. Ronda feels hurt and abandoned because Nanette is spending most of her time off-campus at Ronda Jo's place. During Christmas break, the players each got meal money. Ronda Jo and Nanette pooled theirs and made dinner and hung out together every night. A part of Ronda wants to admonish herself: "Don't be such a baby." Another part feels jilted, dumped. It doesn't feel good.

The other thing bothering her is her caretaking. Ronda felt it was her job to make Shanada happy, before her sister decided to quit. Now she feels it's her job to help out Stacy, who think she's underused and is frustrated about it. Ronda tries to avoid carrying other people's burdens but sometimes can't help herself. She is happiest when she can make everything nice, for everybody. When she was a kid at MSAD, her team made a trip to a hearing school one day. The hearing kids started throwing snowballs at the bus and mocking their sign language. Ronda was furious and made it her responsibility to minister to the feelings of everyone who was hurt by it. She is not so good at ministering to herself. When she was ten years old, she tried out for a boys' team that played for the Worldwide Church of God. She was totally excited about playing and eagerly used her voice to tell the coach her name. He couldn't understand her. She tried again. He still didn't get it. Then the coach stepped back and looked at her and starting laughing at the sound of her voice, laughing right in her face. Ronda wanted to crawl under the floorboards. She made the team and became a starter, but the wound did not heal. It was too deep, too raw. It galled her that it happened, galled her even more that it happened on a Christian team. She never had any interest in being a hearing person before. She had even less interest now.

"I lost a lot of respect for hearing people after that," Ronda said. *"I just had a real hard time dealing with what he did."*

She did not use her voice again for six years. She made a sound in class one day to get her favorite teacher's attention, and the stunned teacher said, *"Ronda, was that you?"*

Ronda told the teacher how embarrassed she was about her voice. *"I'm glad you used it,"* the teacher said. *"It's a lovely voice."* Ronda didn't believe her.

Ronda is proud and protective of Deaf culture and those who inhabit it. Except for the church team and a few summers with a hearing AAU team, she has spent her entire life around people who are deaf. If she has children, she wants them to be deaf, because she's sure there would be deeper connection with them that way. The feeling of connection is one of her favorite parts of Deaf culture: the piles of pasta and leisurely dinners at the kitchen table, the vacations in the VW bus—two parents, five kids, and jars of Green Life crammed in together. It's not the same in the hearing world. Ronda is pretty sure of that. She sees it with Shawn, her hearing brother. He often seems to be running off somewhere or cutting out of the kitchen to go watch TV or listen to music. Without the distraction or enticement of sound, Ronda and the people in her world savor their time together and rarely are in a hurry to leave. *"You don't feel like you're missing out on anything when you're together,"* Ronda said.

Students have come back to campus, and the Ely Center and the dorms are returning to life. An icy wind cuts through Kendall Green but doesn't feel quite so harsh with dorm windows aglow again and the odd comfort of a semester's routine beckoning. As the Bison prepare for the big game against St. Mary's, one student who still has yet to resurface is Amelia. She has sent Kitty a few more e-mails, and it remains unclear when she's going to make it back to school.

Almost every basketball team has an archrival, the school it would rather face than any other. For the Bison, that opponent is St. Mary's College, a small non-sectarian school in southern Maryland, about two hours outside of Washington, D.C. St. Mary's is usually at or near the top of the Capital Athletic Conference. It also has an attitude. Or at least the Bison think it has an attitude.

"When we beat them, it always feels especially good," Stacy Nowak said.

Most of Gallaudet's opponents are long past the time when their fans or players would openly taunt the Bison about their deafness. St. Mary's is one of the holdouts. Something always seems to happen, and this year's visit to the Field House is no different. When the team barrels out of

Room 142 and comes onto the floor, Stacy lets out one of her war whoops. An instant later, at the other end of the court, a St. Mary's player mimics the sound. Someone on St. Mary's sets up a boom box, which they always bring with them to Gallaudet because they know there's no pregame music there. It's okay to put on music; plenty of teams do it. But this music is profane and misogynistic, a rageful rapper spewing four-letter venom. Wes Frahm, Gallaudet's sports information director, approaches the St. Mary's bench and asks them to please change the music.

"Nobody here can hear it, so why should they be offended?" a team member said.

St. Mary's is led by Felicia Harris, a star guard who is one of the quickest and most dangerous players in the league. The Bison have a habit that drives Kitty crazy—playing to the level of the competition. Against St. Mary's, that should be a good thing.

The Bison come out playing hard, but running haywire, like a circuit with too much voltage. They're throwing the ball away, playing too fast. Still, Kitty and Ben love the way they are competing and urge them just to throttle it back a little. It takes Kitty repeated waves of the hand before she gets Ronda's attention. Ronda's off to a great start; Kitty just wants her to relax. *"Don't push it if it's not there,"* Kitty said gently. Eight minutes into the game, Ronda Jo snares a rebound, dribbles out herself, and leads the break, delivering a bounce pass to Touria for a layup. A clever scooping shot in the lane earns Touria another bucket and a three-point play. She doesn't realize the whistle has blown and a foul has been called until she sees the St. Mary's players have stopped playing and are looking to the official. It's a reliable indicator that there's a stoppage—and what the Bison players almost always go by—but it's not foolproof. Some years ago, the Gallaudet men were playing against a hearing team that faked a stoppage in play, relaxing their bodies. When the Bison men did likewise, the opponents threw the ball downcourt for an easy layup. The official saw what happened and assessed the hearing team with a technical.

The Bison women are fluid and energized now. Ronda Jo hits four straight baskets, knifing layups and tough turnarounds. Gallaudet is within two at halftime.

As the second half begins, the Bison are getting some solid minutes from Stacy, who is starting in place of the injured Jenny Cooper. Courtney contributes under both baskets, and Nanette plays with her usual energy, getting rebounds and making assists. But as the teams battle and the end nears, it is Ronda who begins to take the leading role. She hits three-pointers. She knocks down big free throws, pressing the ball against her forehead before shooting each one, a basketball telepathy session from fifteen feet out. With the score tied at 74, Ronda Jo gets the ball on the baseline in the final moments, and the entire bench and the crowd is standing, poised to celebrate a buzzer-beater. Her shot looks good but rolls off the iron.

In the huddle before overtime, Kitty tells the team, *"Play loose. Have fun. This is our game to win if we play good defense and play our game."*

One minute into the period, Ronda launches a three-pointer from the left corner. It swishes through the net, and the Field House crowd erupts. She follows with two more free throws, and Ronda Jo hits two of her own. Felicia Harris sinks a three-pointer for the last of her thirty-one points to get St. Mary's within one (81–80), but Ronda has three more successful telepathy sessions from the free throw line, and as the clock ticks down, the Bison begin reveling in their achievement: an 84–80 victory over no-longer-undefeated St. Mary's.

Ronda finishes with twenty-seven, to go with Ronda Jo's twenty-four points and twenty rebounds. Touria also scores twenty. It adds up to Gallaudet's most important victory of the season. After they make their way down the corridor and turn into Room 142, Nanette grabs a piece of chalk and writes in huge letters, "WE'RE BACK!" on the board. She fires the chalk into the floor and it smashes into bits, and everyone goes crazy.

"It's nice to see the real Gallaudet team," Ben said.

"It was a beautiful game," Kitty said. She points to the heart she had drawn on the blackboard before the game. *"You played with heart. That was the difference."* She feels the lightness in the room and loves it. She looks into her players' faces and said, *"Remember how this feels."*

In the Field House lobby, the lingering goes on even longer than usual, a humming human tapestry of hugs and laughs. A few hearing parents and fans are talking. Everyone else is doing their exulting in ASL, hands dancing, arms waving, faces contorting. The victory is an elixir. For Ronda Jo, the day began with word from the Charlotte Sting, one of the WNBA teams that had been scouting her, that they would probably not be drafting her. Ronda Jo is not going to let it spoil the day's ending.

"I don't take it as a failure," she said. *"I have a goal to play in the WNBA, and I have to understand that it might take some time."*

The next day, the Bison are still floating. When they beat their opponents in a practice drill, Touria and Ronda fall to the floor in the form of letter "L," Touria playing the vertical part, Ronda the horizontal, full-bodied shorthand for "Loser." During a break, Jenny, Cassey Ellis, and Ronda array themselves on the sideline, bouncing up and down in dead-on imitation of perky cheerleaders, doing silly leg kicks and clapping demure little cheerleader claps. After making two free throws in an empty gym, Ronda turns to the rolled-up bleachers and does a shoulder shimmy and holds up her hands, acknowledging the cheers of a nonexistent crowd. She is the last one left at practice. She showers and changes and comes back upstairs, zipping up her blue Gallaudet windbreaker and walking out of the Field House. She turns right and retraces the route she's made all those mornings, when she'd put in the work in hopes of getting a payoff just like this.

Amelia is back in town, but she's not back among the Bison. She has decided to quit the team. She was sick over the break and felt weak and had neither the strength nor the desire to practice twice a day and dive back into basketball. It would've been different if she'd been playing, but when a player has been on the bench for two years, the sitting can get old. It wasn't worth the time commitment. What Amelia loves most about being the soccer goalie is the nonstop action, the way the team depends on her. In basketball, she doesn't have that. Kitty kind of figured something was up when Amelia still hadn't shown up ten days into the New Year, but she is still surprised. "You think you know what kids are thinking, and sometimes you find out that you have no idea what's going on with them," Kitty said. She reminds herself to check in with some of the kids who don't stop by her office as often as the veterans. Natalie, for one, is someone whom Kitty has a difficult time reading. She's quiet and stays to herself. And the truth is she hasn't felt all that connected to the team of late, either.

Three months into the season, Natalie still feels like a newcomer at times. Now that she's hurt, the feeling is even more pronounced. The injury came late in the final of the Elizabethtown tournament. Natalie made a turnover and was upset with herself and ran back hard on defense, tried to make an aggressive strip of the ball, and wound up rolling over on her ankle. She collapsed in an instant, writhing in her dark blue No. 12 uniform as the crowd fell hushed. As she was helped off the court, tears rolled down her face. Stacy came over to her at the end of the bench. Another freshman, Cathy Stutzman, whose own season was interrupted by health problems, gave her a hug. A trainer from Elizabethtown, with the help of an interpreter, explained to Natalie that she needed to ice it and elevate it on the ride home. Natalie brushed back a few hairs that had escaped her thick blonde ponytail. A cross-country runner in the fall, she has the taut physique of someone who can run all afternoon and not get tired. She is the fittest player on the team. Fitting in hasn't been as easy.

"I sort of feel like they don't have confidence in me as a player," Natalie said. "I know I can show these girls that I can do better." Natalie thinks part of the distance stems from her linguistic status. She grew up in a hearing family and had extensive oral training as a child. She does not have the ASL fluency that most players on the team have. From the start of the season, Natalie knew she was just going to have to prove herself.

There was nothing new about that.

Natalie's parents, Steve and Karen Ludwig, weren't thrilled at first about her coming to Gallaudet. They didn't want her to be so far from their suburban Houston home and weren't sure if it was the best idea educationally, either. But Natalie was ready to be in a place where the other students would not look at her as if she had a big D stamped on her forehead. She has been in mainstream schools her entire life, from kindergarten through twelfth grade. She spent her freshman year at Pratt Community College in Kansas, another mainstream place. She starred on the court and in the classroom. She was featured in a huge profile in the local paper. She was miserable anyway. She was the only deaf student. Just about every conversation had to be through an interpreter. She was so tired of being different.

"I knew from the first day at Gallaudet that I wouldn't be 'that deaf girl' anymore," Natalie said. *"I don't have to have people help me. My parents came up with me and for the first time I didn't need them to help me with registering for classes, getting a room and taking care of all the details. I really liked the feeling of independence."*

For most of her twenty years, Natalie has felt that people have looked at her as if she were brain-damaged, just because she can't hear and doesn't have normal speech. Others act surprised that she's able to play sports, as if the constitution of her inner ear has anything to do with her legs or her outside shot. She thinks even her parents sell her short sometimes. Natalie is the oldest, and when she was born with a profound hearing loss, her parents had nothing to draw on. Her mother uses Signed English and her father and younger sister know some homemade sign, but they don't use it that much. When she was younger, Natalie often felt that her parents were dumbing down to her, pointing to things, using simple words and short sentences. It was probably more their limitations with sign language than a reflection on her intelligence, but it still made her angry. She'd walk away sometimes saying, "Do even my parents believe that I can't think?"

Natalie is strong-minded and serious, her dimpled smile and golden locks a cutesy cover for a sturdy competitor's will. Steve Ludwig played big-time college football, part of a national championship team at the University of Oklahoma. Like her dad, when Natalie gets after something, she goes at it hard. Her academic career is a self-generated backlash, a statement against all those who have doubted her: *So you think I can't do anything and that I'm not smart? Just watch.*

A chemical engineering major, Natalie is partial to science and math. The most reliable event on every Bison bus trip is seeing her engrossed in a textbook, studying vectors and inorganic compounds. Her grade-point average her first term on Kendall Green was just under 3.8. When someone congratulates her on her grades, she says she probably should've done better. She keeps the pressure on herself, ever vigilant about slacking off, not wanting to jeopardize her summer internship at Duke University, where she will be taking Biomedical Engineering and Ethics. *"It's so easy to socialize and communicate here, I have to make sure I watch out for that."*

Beyond graduation, Natalie isn't sure what she wants to do, other than break ground. Maybe invent something, or discover a cure for a disease, do something to show once and for all what deaf people can do. Her greatest aspiration, though, is to be an astronaut. She loves technology and loves teamwork, the feeling of accomplishment that you get when people are working well together toward the same end. *"I would find that very challenging, because I know that it is highly competitive. I just know that I want to do something different from others."*

• • •

A recent study of e-mail patterns by an Internet consulting firm revealed that Gallaudet is one of the top three universities in the country in the amount of electronic correspondence generated. Natalie is holding up her share. She loves the speed and the ease of it, its ability to bypass the human ear. She does e-mail interviews, has e-mail chats with friends, and has regular on-line correspondence with her parents. It levels the communication playing field between them, and because they are more in touch, it has helped smooth over some of the swells of her adolescent years. E-mail is de rigueur on just about every college campus these days, but it's hard to imagine a place where it is more central to daily life than at Gallaudet.

"It has made a huge difference in the way I live," Natalie said. *"I never had such an effortless way to communicate with people."*

Other technological breakthroughs have had a significant impact on the lives of people who are deaf, too, in ways big and small. There are vibrating alarm clocks, with a device to slip beneath the mattress that literally shakes someone out of her slumber. Every room in the campus hotel is equipped not only with a TTY, but with a flashing light attached, illuminating when a call comes in. There are now relay operators who are a phone call away, intermediaries who can facilitate a conversation between a TTY-less hearing person and a deaf person, translating the deaf person's written TTY messages into spoken words, and the hearing person's spoken words into written TTY form. In the last few years, pagers have become as indispensable at Gallaudet as e-mail, allowing the deaf to have access to communication as never before. They are deaf people's equivalent of cell phones, without the annoying rings. Most people set their pagers to vibrate. *"I never go anywhere without my pager,"* Amelia said. *"It's something I can't do without."*

But perhaps the most far-reaching change has come with the advent of closed captioning in the 1980s, providing the deaf with instant, firsthand access to television. One can argue whether this is a good thing, but for those who have never been able to get any information or entertainment from their TVs, having words trailing along the bottom of the screen was a full-scale, small-print revelation.

Dr. Robert Williams has been a Gallaudet professor for twenty-five years. "I remember vividly when Ronald Reagan was shot in 1981, and all the televisions on campus were tuned in to the breaking news. Invariably there would be knots of students around each one, with some hearing person standing next to it interpreting what was being said and what was going on. Eventually the hearing person would have to leave and the deaf people would have to run and find another hearing person to interpret. Cut to the *Challenger* disaster, five years later, after live closed captioning was introduced. All of a sudden you saw deaf people sitting in front of the TV getting the knowledge of what was going on firsthand like everyone else. I find that my students come to Gallaudet with more knowledge about everything than they used to, and I attribute it in large measure to closed captioning."

Not all advances on the technology front are seen so benignly. Nearly two decades ago, modern medicine brought the cochlear implant, a surgical procedure in which an implanted device can provide a degree of sound sensation by sending electrical stimulation to the auditory nerve. Cochlear implants consist of a small microphone and transmitter, a speech processor that converts sounds into signals; and the implanted receiver, which is installed behind the ear and sends the signals it receives from the speech processor into the cochlea (a snail-shaped part of the inner ear) via electrodes. The electrodes stimulate the auditory nerve, producing a neurochemical exchange that the brain recognizes as sound. Profound hearing loss, in most cases, can be traced to damage to the infinitesimal hair cells in the cochlea, a malfunction that impedes the movement that transmits the neurochemical discharge to the auditory nerve. Stripped to their essence, cochlear implants attempt to circumvent the problem through artificial stimulation. Unlike hearing aids, which are strictly amplification devices, implants are proactive, engineering sensation where there was none before.

Research work on cochlear implant technology goes back almost a half century but has made significant strides in the last twenty years. An estimated forty thousand people around the world have opted to undergo the surgery, with wildly variable results. The procedure, most experts agree, works best with children who have experienced hearing and speech before going deaf (so-called post-lingually deaf children); and with adults who have lost their hearing later in life. Because such people have familiarity with sound, the adaptation to the technology is often facilitated. In nearly every case, though, the procedure requires intensive rehabilitation and training to get full benefit from the device. One must in effect program the brain to make sense of the signals it is suddenly receiving.

The explosion in cochlear implant surgeries has brought with it a deeply charged controversy. The debate is about choice and is at its most feverish on the subject of deaf babies and toddlers, whose parents, whether deaf or hearing, are asked not to make merely an in-the-moment medical decision, but a choice with lifelong repercussions, one that may well determine whether the child will embrace—and be embraced by—Deaf culture or will rather try to function as a quasi-hearing person on the periphery of the world of sound.

Advocates of cochlear implants view the technology as the engine of progress at work, bringing sound to those who did not have it previously. They are certain that implants will only get better and that ultimately the technology will bring down all sorts of barriers for deaf people. Opponents, though, see it as the latest instance of hearing people doing everything they can to make deaf people more like them, as a way to fix them. The most zealous opponents view implantation as a nefarious technological charade, a frontal attack on Deaf culture under the guise of making people hearing, when all they really are is a little bit less deaf. Others see it as tantamount to baby-stealing, as hearing (usually) parents rip their deaf child away from Deaf culture, implant them, and often imperil the child's acquisition of ASL, since the postimplant program entails spending hours each day getting accustomed to spoken language.

"It's one thing if a child is ten or twelve years old and wants to try it," Ronda Jo said. *"It's another when parents make the decision for a baby, and then ruin the child's chance to learn ASL and get a good, solid first language."*

Rory Osbrink, a graduate student at Gallaudet, received a cochlear implant at age four. He stopped using it at seventeen, feeling frustrated by spending half of his life in speech therapy and becoming increasingly troubled by a lack of identity. The more time he spent around other deaf people, the more disillusioned he became with the device attached to his body and his elaborate efforts to become less deaf. "I felt like I was a duck living in a world of chickens," he said at a panel discussion on cochlear implants at Gallaudet in February of 1999.

Harlan Lane is an author, professor of linguistics and the psychology of language at Northeastern University, and a longtime champion of Deaf culture. "Every responsible advocate for cochlear implants agrees that a child with implants is still deaf," Lane has said. "The message that parents ought to get is your child is deaf and nothing can fix that. You should have sign language and deaf role models, and you can embrace Deaf culture. Most parents want a quick fix. They want technology to fix it."

A great many people have had cochlear implants and are happy they did, just as a legion of parents have had the procedure done on their toddlers and are happy *they* did. Slowly, grudgingly, there is a greater acceptance of cochlear implants in the deaf community these days. There is a growing sense of inevitability about the technology, much as there was with the hearing aid several generations before. In the Laurent Clerc Center for Deaf Education at Gallaudet, there are programs to help families understand their options and offer support should they opt for implantation.

Still, for the staunchest supporters of Deaf culture—a group that includes the entire women's basketball team—cochlear implants continue to be seen as an invasive technology. Students who have the telltale mark of implantations—a C-shaped scar behind their ear—are frequently, if clandestinely, derided as "hearies" around Kendall Green.

"When my parents brought it up to me when I was twelve, I gave my mother a really ugly attitude: No! No! No!," Natalie said. *"I did not give myself a minute to think about it. I didn't want to wear that thing on my body, and I did not know how much risk it would be. I wear a hearing aid, and it helps me hear a little sound and I think that's helpful sometimes, even though I can't understand speech or a lot of other things. There was no reason to get a cochlear implant."*

Said Touria, *"If a child is born deaf, maybe the child was meant to be deaf."* Touria has friends who have had implants and have stopped using them, finding them more trouble than they are worth. She has no interest in having a cochlear implant and says she never will. She wonders whether decades from now studies will show that people who have a cochlear implant are actually worse off than those without, because they don't really fit into either the hearing or the deaf world.

Touria feels that throughout history, deaf people have been sustained by a cocoon of kinship. Anything that threatens that bond—by diminishing their numbers, or suggesting that their current lives are flawed—is nothing short of a scourge.

"Where does your self-identification come from? Where do you fit in?" Touria asked. *"The best thing you can do is know who you are and love who you are. You may not be able to hear, but that's not everything. There is more to life than hearing."*

CLEANING UP
THE SPILL

WHEN THE BUSINESS of his office isn't dispatching him elsewhere, Irving King Jordan, president of Gallaudet, is a regular at Bison basketball games. His usual companions are his wife, Linda, and Skip Williams, an old friend from the University of Tennessee and former colleague in the Gallaudet psychology department. Jordan makes the two-minute walk across campus and sits six rows up from the Gallaudet bench, directly behind Kitty Baldridge. For a couple of hours, King Jordan need not concern himself with congressional testimony or speechmaking or carrying the virtual banner of DeafNation. He shouts his support, raises his arms to cheer, and catches glimpses of Kitty's message to her players during time-outs and other stoppages. One of the advantages of being a Gallaudet fan is being able to visually eavesdrop. As Skip Williams said, "It's not like you have to sit close enough to hear." The players always notice when Jordan is there and seem to play a little harder when he is, a subconscious surge of energy taking hold, sort of like when you want to do well in front of your parents, only stronger.

"I always feel inspired when he comes and says things to me," Ronda Jo said. She still remembers the time she was body-slammed by a woman from Catholic University, a player Ronda Jo was sure was meant to play football, but got sidetracked along the way. Her picks were like cross-body blocks. She chased loose balls like a linebacker going after a fumble. Fighting for a rebound, the woman mashed into Ronda Jo, who twisted her knee and had to limp off to the trainer's room for treatment. On the table, feeling vulnerable and angry, Ronda Jo looked up to see King Jordan standing before her.

"How are you feeling?" he asked, then stayed and visited awhile.

"I don't really look at him as the president of Gallaudet. I look at him more as a friend," Ronda Jo said.

Jordan possesses the purest form of charisma: the kind that comes without trying. He's a lanky man with a narrow, likable face; sloping eyes; and a boyish thatch of silver-white hair. He greets visitors in his College Hall office with the warmth of an old friend, and though it is as splendid an office as any college president could have—a vast corner room with gleaming wood floors, antiques, arched leaded glass, and a fireplace—his manner makes it feel more comfortable than imperial. Jordan's friends have long been awed at his ability to be presidential without being remote, dignified without being stuffy, equal parts national leader and kid-next-door, even at age fifty-seven. He always seems to know what to say, and the best way to say it. Several years after he became president, he was profiled on "60 Minutes" and had this exchange with interviewer Meredith Vieira:

VIEIRA: If someone walked in this room with a pill that could give you back your hearing, would you take that pill?

JORDAN: Do you think that deaf people sit at home and worry about what we can do to cure deafness? (It) doesn't happen like that. Would you ever ask a black person, "Suppose you could take a pill and become white, would you take it?" Would you ever do that? You would never do that. Would you be offended if I asked you, "Suppose I could give you a pill, and it would make you a man, would you be interested in taking that pill, to become a man?"

VIEIRA: Except you had (your hearing) and then lost it. As opposed to I never was a man and then became a woman.

JORDAN: But still, you see something missing that's not.

VIEIRA: Isn't there a significant absence when you can't hear?

JORDAN: No! That's my point, there's not!

In twenty seconds and three responses, he encapsulated the feelings of how most deaf people feel about being deaf.

"He can sit down for dinner with a group of sanitationmen one night and a group of congressmen the next night, and be just as comfortable with one as the other," Skip Williams said. "When he talks to you, he really talks to you, and you can see that he's interested in everything you have to say. He loves to connect with people, especially with students. If his schedule would allow it, he would be in the classroom tomorrow morning, teaching Introductory Psychology to a group of freshmen."

Most people around campus call him King, or Dr. J. He would never describe himself as the most influential, visible, and dynamic deaf person in the United States, and perhaps the world, though it is pretty much beyond debate. The closest he ever gets to self-congratulation is when he talks about his semiobsession with ultramarathons, one-hundred-mile torture tests for those who are not satisfied with the torture of running a regular, twenty-six-mile marathon. Jordan has entered twenty-seven ultramarathons.

"Not one DNF (Did Not Finish)," he said, voicing the letters for added emphasis.

It is not for his DNFs, of course, that Jordan is principally known, but his place in DPN (Deaf President Now), the uprising by Gallaudet students in March 1988. The protest was triggered by the election of Elizabeth Ann Zinser as Gallaudet's seventh president. A hearing woman who was regarded as a fund-raising dynamo, Zinser had neither a familiarity nor a connection to deafness. Despite its unquestioned standing as the preeminent academic institution for the deaf in the world, Gallaudet had never had a deaf president, never been led by a person who could fully understand what the deaf experience is like. Passions were beginning to run hot on the issue, students taking mighty exception to the condescension implicit in it. Didn't virtually every black college have a black college president? Didn't every women's college have a female college president? The choice of Zinser over two candidates who were deaf—including King Jordan—was the match that set student passions aflame.

Days before the Board of Trustees was scheduled to vote, three thousand students rallied to demand a deaf president for the university. The night before the vote, a candlelight vigil was held outside the board's lodging place. The board, chaired by Jane Bassett Spilman, was unbowed. Indeed, on Sunday, March 6, Spilman dismissed the notion of a non-hearing president, reportedly saying that "deaf people are not ready to function in a hearing world." Those eleven words became the greatest rallying cry Kendall Green had ever known. The university's own board chair was perpetuating the stereotype that the deaf were pitiable and inept. They were second-class citizens even on their own campus! A dog sighted outside the library wore a white cloth with the same message on each side: "I UNDERSTAND SIGN BETTER THAN SPILMAN."

On Monday, March 7, the silent revolt was on. Students shut down the campus, barricading the side entrances with parked cars; the administration building with steel bicycle locks; and the front entrance, at

Florida Avenue and Eighth Street NE, with their bodies, a sixties-style occupation in the late 1980s. The uprising was poised and peaceful, and full of tenacity. Student leader Greg Hlibok and other protesters demanded that Zinser step down and be replaced by either Jordan or Harvey Corson, the superintendent of the Louisiana School for the Deaf and the third finalist for the position. They wanted Spilman gone, a deaf majority on the board itself, and no reprisals for their campus takeover. They held press briefings in sign language, churned out press releases and advisories, skillfully projecting themselves as reasonable people being subjected to unreasonable oppression. They got statements of election-year support from union leaders, congressional representatives, and a number of presidential candidates, including George Bush, Jesse Jackson, Paul Simon, and Robert Dole.

Meanwhile, King Jordan was finding himself in an impossible spot. While he certainly supported the idea of deaf people having greater representation in the university, he was less certain this was the time or place for a revolution. As dean of Gallaudet's College of Arts and Sciences, he felt obliged to carry out his administrative duties. As a presidential candidate who had been passed over, he thought it unseemly to protest actively and campaign for the position. His predicament got worse when Spilman insisted that he publicly back the selection of Zinser.

Jordan did so and felt terrible about it. Not even twenty-four hours later, after the faculty resoundingly voted to align with the students, he recanted. The depth of the students' passion had convinced him that perhaps it *was* time. He changed allegiances, declaring: *"Yesterday, because I had been a candidate and wanted to be both responsible and fair, I gave a statement recognizing the legal authority of the board to name the president of Gallaudet. In fact, my personal reaction to the board's decision was—and is—anger at the continuing lack of confidence that they have shown in deaf people. . . . I must now publicly affirm my support for the point of view held by the Gallaudet community."*

In the days that followed, the school's embattled administration began to crumble. Spilman resigned and so did Zinser, after a three-day reign, calling Deaf President Now "an extraordinary social movement of deaf people" and "a civil rights moment in history for deaf people." Philip Bravin, an IBM executive who is deaf, was named chairman of the board. Irving King Jordan was selected as the eighth president of Gallaudet University. The signed joke all over campus was, *It took seven days to create the world, it took us seven days to change it."*

Later that week, Jordan, Bravin, and Hlibok met to chart a course for the school's new direction. It was the first time that a Gallaudet president, board chairman, and student-body president had ever had a conversation without an interpreter.

King Jordan was an enlightened choice by the board, for several reasons. He was a popular former teacher and administrator, someone whom many students and faculty already liked and respected. Moreover, with a clear and well-modulated speaking voice, with a hearing wife and children, he was able to move easily in both the deaf and hearing worlds. Jordan did not become deaf until he was twenty-one. He did not grow up with any exposure to Deaf culture. Some of the more militant members among the student leaders resisted his candidacy because they did not consider him truly deaf. Jordan himself has never argued otherwise.

"I am not a deaf person," he has said many times. "I am a deafened hearing person." Even now, he willingly recognizes that the constellation of events in March 1988 had more to do with his becoming president than his qualifications did.

"I sit here as a deaf president, but what happened during DPN was not about me," Jordan said. "They weren't talking about me early in the week. They weren't pushing for me to be president. They were pushing for a deaf president. The main focus was the right for deaf people to lead their own lives—to not be dictated to by the hearing majority. Suddenly the artificial cap wasn't there anymore. There was a sense of possibility and empowerment. That was the change from within, and from without. I think people began to see deaf people differently. To see them not as less intelligent, not less able, but simply different."

Jordan grew up in a small, steel-belt town in Pennsylvania, as unlikely a candidate for university leadership as you will find. His father was a mill worker and an elementary-school dropout. His mother didn't graduate from high school, either. Both of them preached the importance of education, a lesson heeded dutifully by Jordan's two older sisters—both academic stars and National Merit scholars—and all but ignored by King. He went through grade school and high school with negligible interest in his studies, which cut into the time he had to bounce on his trampoline or goof around with his friends. He graduated from high school with a C average and the title of "class clown." It was hard to say what was the highlight of his high-school career: being the only boy in a typing class that was full of pretty girls, or the contest he had with his pals to see who could go the longest without washing his gym clothes.

With the prospect of college holding little appeal to him, Jordan enlisted in the navy. He figured the discipline would do him good. He wound up using his typing skills at a desk job in the Pentagon, where he spent considerable time around various Department of Defense honchos, finally coming to realize he had as much ability as many of the people he was typing for, but that what he lacked was an education. Jordan wound up getting that education at Gallaudet, where he enrolled after the accident that changed his life.

During his time in Washington, D.C., Jordan had become a motorcycle aficionado, riding, helmetless, all over town. He loved the freedom, the feeling of the air rushing through his hair. He was out riding one night when an oncoming automobile crossed over and rammed into him, the impact catapulting him into the air, over the car. He crashed through the back windshield. His skull was fractured, his jaw broken, his prospects for recovery so bleak a neurosurgeon suggested to the Jordan family that they pray that twenty-one-year-old King die. Doctors were stunned when he regained consciousness and mental functioning. After about a year in the hospital, he walked out, a new life awaiting him.

The only thing King Jordan wound up losing in the accident was his hearing. He took up psychology at Gallaudet. He studied constantly and became a straight-A student. Socially, the transition was more difficult, for he felt adrift between his old world and his new one. Though he still had very good speech, he could not hear. Though he was deaf, he was just learning to sign. He stuck to himself and his books and went on to get a master's and Ph.D. at the University of Tennessee. He got through all the work without an interpreter. A couple of classmates took notes for him, and Jordan did the rest on his own, in the library.

"He arrived early and stayed late every day," Skip Williams said. "He showed an uncommon amount of dedication." Jordan went on to become a noted scholar in the area of psycholinguistics. It's been more than a decade since Jordan has been active in researching and teaching. One of his favorite ways to stay connected with students is sitting in the front rows of the Field House during basketball games. It was in that same Field House that he gave his inaugural address to an adoring crowd on October 21, 1988, a night when he talked about how the enduring magic of DPN was not simply that a deaf president was in charge, but that it was the strength and resolve of deaf students that got him there.

"I challenge you to take up this motivation, this enthusiasm, take up this new courage and to try and do anything under the sun," he said. "I challenge you to succeed." The Field House was overflowing with students, alumni, parents, faculty. "My feet didn't touch the ground the night I *was sworn in,"* Jordan said later. *"I am deaf, and there I was, a college president."*

The Gallaudet bus is on its way to York, Pennsylvania, Hillel Goldberg doling out the Bison's per diem money, Ben drifting off to the jazz on his Walkman, and Jenny Cooper deep in thought in the back left corner. She is looking out at frozen creeks, thinking random thoughts about how to motivate her teammates. She is concerned that the team is still caught in its season-long Bison two-step—one step forward, one step back. She decides it is time for some reverse psychology. After the team arrives at York College, Kitty tells the Bison to have fun, to remember that's why they play. It's the same theme she had the night before, when she invited Ronda Jo and Nanette over for dinner. *"A team has to be like a river—flowing, moving, never stopping,"* Kitty said. *"It's when you stop that you become stagnant."* When she's done, the team meets alone in a basement locker room with skinny brown lockers, rust-colored floor, and green and white walls. "This room looks like it was decorated by a jockey," somebody said. Ronda Jo talks about the York peppermint patty she saw when they stopped at 7-11 and pretends to throw one on the floor and squish it into a minty pulp.

"This is what I want to do to the York team," she said. She smiled, *"We don't really have to squish them. Let's just win."* Nanette's eyes are defiant and her knob of hair is shaking when she said, *"Who are we? Gallaudet! Who's going to win? We are."*

Jenny is taking it all in in street clothes. She had played magnificently in the previous game, a loss to Marymount, but reaggravated her hamstring injury in the process. She waits until it is her turn to talk and then moves back a step so that everyone can see her.

"I don't have a good feeling tonight. I am not confident." All activity in the room ceases. Her teammates are looking at her incredulously.

"No, I don't like what I'm picking up. I think we are going to lose."

Ronda Johnson gives her a whack with the back of her hand. Jenny glares back at her.

"Why are you saying that?" Ronda said.

"Prove me wrong," Jenny said.

The Bison play from behind for nearly all of the first half and well into the second. When York scores inside over Courtney, who does little to contest the shot, Kitty waves her hand and snaps to Courtney, *"Keep your hands up! Play defense! Get that defeated look off your face!"*

Down 55–50 with just over seven minutes left, Touria hits a drive and Ronda gets the ball on the break and scores off a turnover. The Bison are starting to move better than they have all game. They're stepping up their defense, hitting the backboards. They're even doing a good job of fighting through screens, one of the areas that has historically plagued them (it's tough to get through a screen when a player can't hear her teammate calling it out). Courtney puts in two offensive rebounds for baskets, Natalie makes a steal and hits a three-point play, and Ronda Jo, controlling the post on offense and defense, scores on a short jumper. Gallaudet is playing beautiful, intense basketball, and the result is a 14–0 run. In a span of five minutes, they have turned the entire flow of the game around. Ronda Jo gets whistled for a reach-in foul, her fifth, and is out of the game, but otherwise all the news is good for the Bison. With under two minutes to go, they hold a 64–55 lead.

York calls a time-out and is desperate now. When play resumes, York comes out pressing. The scouting reports show that Gallaudet has been bothered by presses all season; it's time to put the heat on. York scores from outside and quickly induces Touria to turn the ball over. York scores again, and Ronda gets called for throwing an elbow. Touria loses her dribble and then throws a one-handed pass—a dangerous habit Kitty has been trying all season to rid her of (it's impossible to pull back a pass you've started to throw when you have only one hand on it)—for another turnover. The Bison, incredibly, turn the ball over two more times. York closes within four, then two, then ties the score at 64. Kitty calls a time-out, then another. The home crowd is roaring, taking delight in the Bison collapse. Touria feels sick inside, throwing her hands down in disgust. She's panicking again, and she knows it. She had been the Bison's best player for most of the game, and now this. *"Why am I so up and down?"* she said plaintively in the huddle, her head down, sweat running down her face in rivulets. Before the huddle breaks, Kitty says, *"Don't get down on yourself! We need you to forget it and be yourself—the player who helped us get the lead to begin with!"*

With sixteen seconds left, Ronda drives hard to the basket and makes a leaning, balletic layup. York inbounds the ball, and Touria anticipates superbly, darts in, and makes a steal. She gets fouled. She walks to the line, trying to purge her mind of her mistakes. She slips into her routine, bending her knees, spinning the ball in her hands, finding reassurance in the pebbled feel of the grain on her fingers. She takes a deep breath and shoots. Good. The Bison are ahead 67–64, and though her second shot spins out, the lead is safe. The Bison have held on. They've proven Jenny wrong—barely.

The players are still reveling in their relief when the York public address asks for everyone's attention: "Ladies and gentlemen, the Gallaudet victory today is the three-hundredth victory of coach Kitty Baldridge's career. Congratulations, Coach Baldridge." The crowd applauds politely. Kitty appreciates the gesture but looks uncomfortable with the attention. Some coaches relish such moments and embrace the fanfare; Kitty looks as if she'd rather go right to her next game. She thinks about how this game was kind of like the whole year, careening all over the place, and then gathers the Bison in a circle in the center of the court, arm in arm. *"You played with heart and desire, and I thank you for that,"* Kitty said. *"This happened today because of all of you."* They all put their hands in. Kitty is crying. The Bison disperse and bolt happily down the stairs to the locker room. Ronda teases Jenny about being wrong. The Bison hastily hatch a plan, each player grabbing a metal stool and scurrying to a corner. When Kitty walks in, they let loose, pounding the stools on the cement floor, a clangy cacophony to accompany the words on the blackboard: "Kitty: Congratulations on your 300th win." Kitty and Ben cover their ears, smiling. The merriment continues on the ride home, entertainment provided by Ronda Johnson. She still feels estranged from Nanette and has been telling herself for a while that she needs to talk to Kitty. But for now, the thrill of victory overrides all. Up and down the aisle she goes, conducting a poll on a topic only she could think of: *"Which would be a worse place to be, a men's prison or a women's prison?"* When someone asks why she brings this up, her pink face suddenly turns cerebral, as if to say: *"I have long pondered this issue. Haven't you?"* Paulina Wlostowski, the manager, looks at Ronda's fingernails, short and a little rough at the edges, and tells her that they really are not very becoming. Ronda unzips her jacket and peels it back and shakes her torso suggestively, sashaying like a model on a runway.

"I am a basketball player now," she says. *"There is plenty of time to be beautiful later."*

Ernie stops at a parking lot that has a Taco Bell on one side, McDonald's on the other. Kitty celebrates her three hundred victories by standing at the counter, taking a dozen sign-language orders for Quarter Pounders and Chicken Burritos. She looks as happy as she has the whole season.

• • •

Winter in Washington has arrived for real, and nobody is calling it a wonderland. As in most big cities, the snow stays white in the nation's capital about as long as a time-out lasts and then morphs into a brown blanket of trouble, a road-clogging, back-aching, life-complicating mess. Two storms in five days have dumped about a foot and a half of snow. Washington is paralyzed. Schools and offices are closed, and so is the government. Shovels fly out of stores. Some neighborhoods, like Kitty's, don't get plowed out for days. In those that *are* plowed, cars are so buried they look as if they won't be liberated until April. On Kendall Green, students page their friends and gather in their rooms or the Abbey to watch the closed-captioned news reports of all the storm-related chaos. Undergraduates aren't obligated to shovel. Few have to commute anywhere. In the time-honored tradition of students everywhere, the Gallaudet take on the mayhem can be summed up with three words: *"Yippee, snow day!"*

Snowball fights are rampant. Stacy, Nanette, and Touria are full participants. When their arms get tired, they go to the baseball field behind Clerc Hall, where they spell out the initials of their sorority: Phi Kappa Zeta. Each letter is about six feet tall. They want to make sure everyone gets a good view of it from the dorm.

Touria seems fully recovered from her late-game trauma against York. It has been a bumpy couple of games for her. She's still getting a hard time from her teammates about the technical foul she got—and then didn't get—against Marymount. Infuriated about a call that fouled her out of the game, Touria was starting to walk off when she put her thumb and forefinger about a half-inch apart and held and twisted them next to her temple. It is the sign for *"idiot."* Another official saw it, blew his whistle, and called a technical foul

"I don't know what that meant, but I know it wasn't a compliment," the official said. Kitty, whose attention was focused elsewhere, had not seen Touria do anything but screw up her face in disgust, which she does after almost every call against her; she's one of those hypercompetitive players who believes she never commits a foul. When the official came over to the scorer's table, Kitty began an impassioned, and in her mind, totally justified, defense of her player. "She didn't do anything! She was just upset with herself!" They called off the technical. It was only after the game that Kitty found out that Touria *had* called the official an idiot. *"If I'd known that, I wouldn't have defended you,"* Kitty said.

The shortest trip of every season is to Catholic University, the conference rival located just fifteen minutes away. It is snapping cold, and the snow is as crunchy as toast; and thanks to a busted boiler, the temperature is not much warmer in the Catholic gym. The Bison walk in and can't believe it: They can see their breath. The game is delayed a half hour to give the heat time to kick in, but it never really does. Ronda Jo has missed the last few days of practice with stomach problems. Kitty's rule is that if a player isn't at practice, she doesn't start. Ronda Jo enters the game about four minutes in, and within moments, she goes high to swat away a Catholic shot, runs the court and gets a nice pass from Touria, and buries a turnaround jumper. The Bison go up by ten. Courtney is playing her best game yet, knocking down jumpers in the lane and rebounding aggressively. Catholic can't match the Bison in talent or skill, but it's a team that always plays with heart and never gives in.

Midway through the second half, it's a one-point game when Ronda Jo hits an off-balance bank shot and a leaning baseline jumper. On the next trip down, Touria takes the ball on the left wing, sees an opening, and fires up a three-pointer, doing her usual little hop-step before launching it. The ball sails through the net, but when Touria comes down, she lands on her defender's foot and rolls over her right ankle. She goes down hard, screaming in pain and and grabbing her leg, the terrifying throbs taking her right back to the night against George Mason two years ago, when she was ahead of the field going for a layup, planted her left leg, and had her anterior cruciate ligament explode. It ended her season, and very nearly her career. Now she is on the floor again, crying before a suddenly silent crowd. She stays down for several minutes as the trainer applies ice. The tears dry and make her face feel stiff. Touria, who is having a tremendous game on both ends of the floor, tells Kitty she will lace her sneakers tighter and continue. The Bison are up eight. Touria can't put much weight on her foot, wincing with each step. Kitty tries to talk her out of it but knows she's never going to win a battle of wills with this woman, even if she is the one in charge. Touria plays on one leg for a few trips up and down and finally realizes that it is foolish and dangerous. She limps off, puts her leg up at the end of the bench. Trainer Bret Weaver applies fresh ice. Touria pounds the bench with her first. She starts to cry again. She feels betrayed by her body, and fate. *"Why was the defender's foot there? Why did she have to land right on it? Why now?"*

Catholic keeps coming at the Bison hard and ties the game at 57 with a few minutes left. Natalie sinks a clutch three-pointer from the right corner, but Catholic answers with its own three, a couple of jumpers, and hard, swarming defense on Ronda Jo. Things started to go wrong the minute Touria went down, and they never really get righted, as Catholic celebrates a 65–63 upset and runs jubilantly off the court. Ronda briefly mocks the celebration by jumping up and down clapping and draws a stern rebuke from Kitty.

After she showers and changes and puts on a pressure wrap, Touria comes out on crutches and stretches out on the second row of the grandstand. Her right foot and ankle are wrapped in a thick sock. She keeps looking down at it in disgust. It isn't a knee, and that's a blessing, but Touria is having a hard time being grateful. The flashback to George Mason keeps gripping her. Kitty gently rubs Touria's ankle and doesn't stop until it's time for the Bison to board the bus for the short trip back home.

"I know," Kitty keeps telling her. *"I know."*

Two hours before the next game, a nonconference matchup with Western Maryland, Touria gets her ankle taped by Bret Weaver and tests it by running in the gym. It still hurts. She can't cut without feeling pain. She decides it's not worth the risk. A mass of arctic air has descended on the nation's capital, and Kendall Green has turned into a tundra off Florida Avenue. The wind chill is seven below, and the Bison ranks are as low as the temperature. Nanette is just getting over a stomach virus and is far from full strength. Kitty has decided to sit Ronda at the beginning of the game for her antics after the loss to Catholic. With her starting backcourt unavailable, Kitty pulls Ronda Jo into her office and says, *"Your wish is finally going to come true. How would you feel about playing the point?"*

Ronda Jo has been badgering Kitty for a couple of years to give her a chance at point guard. She loves the idea of being able to face the basket and have some room, and not spend forty minutes being jostled around underneath the basket. From a strategic standpoint, it wouldn't seem to make sense, taking an All-American center and parking her twenty-five feet from the basket. Except that Ronda Jo is the best ball handler on the team. She sees the court well. She can drive and throw passes over people. She can create openings when the defense moves in to stop her.

"Let's see what she can do," Kitty said.

It is a strange sight for Bison fans, seeing No. 23 away from the hoop, but Ronda Jo runs the offense with aplomb, eluding defenders with quick, strong drives, whipping passes to open Bison. She knifes inside for the game's first two baskets. She threads a pass to Nanette for an assist and another basket. Taking the ball on a drive, she spins past a defender in the lane and whips a pass to Courtney. The game isn't even four minutes old, and the Bison are up 10–1. At halftime, Ronda Jo already has what would be a full game's worth of numbers for most players: eighteen points, nine rebounds, four assists, and three blocks. Midway up the grandstand on the far side of the Field House, Renee Brown, director of player personnel for the Women's National Basketball Association, is jotting down notes. It is the first time she has seen Ronda Jo in person. She likes what she sees.

Western Maryland, with superb free throw shooting, narrows the gap, and it is a two-point game with ten minutes to play. Jenny powers inside, goes up and under a defender, and scores. She follows a Ronda Jo miss and gets two more. On the bench in civilian clothes, Touria catches Jenny's eyes, holds up her right hand and says, *"I Love You"*—her thumb, index and pinky fingers up, and ring and middle fingers folded down. By the time Jenny makes a great pass to Ronda Jo for a fast-break layup, the Bison are up 71–59 with four and a half minutes to play.

Western Maryland scores a three-pointer, and Ronda throws the ball away. Western scores again, blocks a Bison shot, and works the ball inside for another basket. Kitty calls a time-out, calmly trying to stop the panic she senses that is building. In the huddle, she wishes she could purge every drop of the here-we-go-again attitude she's picking up on. She also wishes the officials would be more balanced; it seems that every call is going against the Bison.

"Take care of the ball and play defense and we'll be fine," Kitty said.

But things are not fine. The visitors have sniffed the Bison's vulnerability and are playing with more confidence than they have the entire game. The lead slips to four, then two. With ninety seconds to play, a Western Maryland guard, Patty Russo, hits only her second basket of the game, but it is a three-pointer, and suddenly the Bison are behind. It just keeps getting uglier. There are fouls, turnovers, forced shots. Incredibly, Gallaudet does not score a field goal again after Ronda Jo's layup from Jenny. Western goes on an 18–1 run to end the game and wins, 80–74.

The Bison look dazed as they sit in the classroom. Ronda Jo is so upset she bolts downstairs to the locker room. Jenny peels tape off her ankle, wads it up, and fires it across the room. *"I'm very disappointed in your effort,"* Touria said to the group. *"You stopped playing. In the last four minutes you looked like you didn't care."*

"We keep doing the same thing over and over, because we don't listen," Nanette said.

In the corner of the room is a handsome crystal plaque that athletic director Rich Pelletier gave Kitty at halftime to commemorate her three hundred victories. "I feel like throwing it away," Kitty said. Before she leaves the room, she talks about how the panic spread throughout the team at the end. She talks about how little leadership there was and about how, no matter how many words are spoken, only the Bison themselves can change the way they're playing—and right this season.

"We're running out of games," Kitty said. "It's up to you decide what you want to do."

Three weeks remain in the regular season. The days are getting longer—you can tell by the way the sun hits the windows in Room 142—and time is getting short. Everybody feels a swelling sense of desperation. It doesn't even need to be discussed. Ronda Jo and Nanette get together at Ronda Jo's apartment for their favorite supper—taco salad— and speak in the special shorthand of old friends and cocaptains. The information is conveyed by look, by feeling:

We need to get it together now. . . . Plenty of teams have gone through ups and downs and gotten it together late in the season. . . . We must keep believing in ourselves.

In Bison conversations all over Kendall Green, it is no different. Ronda talks to Stacy and Jenny from two stories up in Hall Memorial Building, in the atrium. Natalie and Cassey pass each other, backpacks in tow, in the dorm lobby. Touria and Courtney share a snack, and urgency, in the lunch-hour bustle of the Ely Center. The upshot is the same in all locations: *We are much better than this. So when are we going to show it?*

Just in case anybody needed any extra reminders, Alexander Long, sports editor of the *Buff and Blue,* provides it in a column under the headline, "Schizophrenic Basketball on Campus:"

> Hey, ladies, you want to go down as the greatest .500 team ever to lace it up? Or would you prefer to be the team that overcame maddening inconsistency to win a conference title and take a ride into the NCAAs? . . . Know this: when you are on top of your game, no one can beat you. No one.
>
> Will the real team please stand up?

Nanette has lost count of how many times she and Kitty have met this season, trying to figure out how to get the team straightened out. It burns her that she hasn't been able to get the Bison to play more consistently.

"All last semester, and even some of this semester, this season has felt like an oil spill. It reminds me of those pictures you used to see after the Exxon Valdez oil tanker had that leak in Alaska, and the birds and everything else were coated in oil and sludge. They couldn't move or do anything. That's how I've felt about our team."

It's a Saturday in late January and Nanette and Ronda Jo decide to call a meeting for the next afternoon. The team is supposed to be off, but this is too important a time to be idle. The players assemble in Room 142 and ask the coaches if they can meet privately. Nanette calls it "a rap session." Others call it an air-clearing session. The clouds are thick and flurries are swirling around Kendall Green. All gripes and grudges are brought forth. It isn't easy. There are tears and wounded feelings. People take responsibility for their actions. Cassey tells everybody that there have been times she has felt unwelcome, as though the upperclass-women were trying to shut her out. Her feelings are a little extra tender because she didn't get in the Catholic game at all. She invited friends to the game and then never got her warm-ups off. Natalie tells Nanette and Ronda Jo that she feels they aren't approachable. Touria is angry that people keep talking about what they're going to do and don't follow through. Ronda is mad at Nanette about going off with Ronda Jo, and Nanette is mad at Ronda for being so possessive. There is a lot of dis-cussion about players putting their own agendas first, and the team sec-ond. It goes on for two hours, and as hard as it is to hear some of these things, most of the Bison say they feel a lot better when they are done. They wish they could go out and play a game.

Probably nobody feels more relieved than Ronda, who's glad that at least the issues aren't hidden anymore. Now she has more housekeep-ing to do and stops by to see Kitty and asks if she can come over to talk later. Kitty says sure, and it is some night. In the basement, not far from the Hoosier-red bathroom, Ronda bares her soul. She talks about how confused she feels, her disappointment in her play, her struggles to detach herself from Stacy, who's still frustrated by her playing time. She owns her part in the Hall of Fame fiasco in December, tells Kitty she is very sorry it happened. She hugs Kitty and they cry, and when she leaves Kitty's house and walks back across the street to campus, she is grateful that she has a coach she can talk to this way, even with the differences they have at times. She feels strong and unburdened, forti-fied by her catharsis. Campus is dark and quiet. Ronda walks by the scrap-iron Bison in front of the Field House and the winter schedule posted out front. There are eight games left before the playoffs.

HOT AND
10
UNBOTHERED

THE BISON HAVE a long-held custom of taking the court in size order, from smallest to largest. This means five-foot, four-inch Natalie Ludwig runs out first, since (as the Bison like to joke to Kitty) coaches don't count. Six-foot, two-inch Ronda Jo Miller is last. Amelia (before she left the team) and Courtney would sometimes try to usurp this spot, standing extra straight and going on tiptoes, but Ronda Jo has never been bumped from her place as the Bison caboose. And that's how she likes it. She's heard of other tall female athletes who have gone through life wishing they could be shorter and resorting to various tactics, all of them useless, to achieve that end. Slouching, leaning, head-hanging, and flat-wearing are the most frequent strategies. Ronda Jo takes pride in her elongated body, her strong, spidery limbs, and carries herself accordingly, shoulders square, chin up, ponytail swaying almost seventy-five inches off the ground. She looks at her height the way she looks at the butterfly tattoo on her stomach. She likes it, and it doesn't matter what anyone else thinks.

"There's no reason to be ashamed of who you are," Ronda Jo said. *"If anything, I would like to be taller."*

From Ludwig to Miller, the Bison run single-file onto the Field House floor for their next-to-last Saturday home game of the season, taking a lap around the blue line that rims the court and going right into their layup lines, directly beneath the Erector-Set ceiling, a grid of pipes and girders and ducts, all painted day-glo yellow. "A very happy ceiling," as one Bison supporter describes it. Just beneath the grid is a long string of rectangular banners, every one blue with white letters, trimmed in gold and white, a tidy row of athletic history forty feet off the floor. There are thirty banners in all. The latest entry, hanging over the Gallaudet bench, says:

CAC
Women's Basketball League Champions
NCAA Tournament—Sweet 16
1999

That's the one the Bison like best.

Sometimes in a long season, even an uneven one, before certain games the atmosphere in the locker room feels inexplicably light and confident. The players sense it's going to be a good day, that all the pieces of the team are going to interlock. This feels like one of those times. It's sunny and bright in Washington, and from the Kellogg Conference Center, the Capitol Building is majestic against a cobalt-blue sky. Even Linnae Gallano, the Gallaudet student who signs the national anthem, seems especially luminous. Linnae has only been fluent in ASL for a couple of years, but she's a quick study, and she pours so much emotion into "The Star Spangled Banner," it's impossible not to be drawn to her. Her favorite part is when she sings:

All-American Ronda Jo Miller readies herself at the free-throw line.

Touria Ouahid makes a point during a timeout.

Ronda Johnson drives baseline against Wheaton.

Coach Kitty Baldridge goes over some last minute instructions
with her team.

Co-captain Nanette Virnig leads a pregame meeting.

Freshman Cassey Ellis goes up strong as Natalie Ludwig boxes out during the home opener against Potsdam.

Touria holding court on the team bus with Ronda Jo and Amelia England.

Cassey Ellis, Natalie Ludwig, Cathy Stutzman, Stacy Nowak, Nanette Virnig, and Shanada Johnson are all smiles after some pregame sharpshooting at Salisbury.

At 6'1", transfer Courtney Westberg is a big mid-season pickup for the Bison.

Nanette charges on to the Field House floor during pre-game introductions.

Touria goes in for a layup against Delaware Valley en route to victory.

Illness sidelined Jenny Cooper until January but her intensity is a big part of the Bison turnaround.

Sometimes Kitty agrees with the officials' calls, sometimes she doesn't.

Ronda Johnson sweats out the difficult road loss to Mary Washington.

An unhappy Ronda Jo towels off after a rough first half.

The Bison have lots of young fans; here's Stacy with one of them.

The Bison pose after beating Capital. *Back row, left to right,* Assistant Coach Ben Baylor, Cassey Ellis, Natalie Ludwig, Ronda Jo Miller, Stacy Nowak, Amelia England, Touria Ouahid, and Cathy Stutzman. *Front row, left to right,* Shanada Johnson, Nanette Virnig, Ronda Johnson, and Coach Kitty Baldridge.

The Bison bond before a game. "We love each other so much we'd probably fall off a cliff for one another," Nanette Virnig said.

"And the rockets red glare, the bombs bursting in air, Gave proof through the night that our flag was still there."

The literal translation of Linnae's ASL signs is:

"Rocket red bright, cannon shoot bomb bright. Proof All Night Flag Continue."

Even for someone who knows no ASL, seeing the song performed visually is a powerful image. When Linnae puts one hand beneath her right elbow, and bends the elbow at a right angle and flaps her right hand to and fro, fans *know* that the flag is still there. "It's powerful for me, too, and I've seen it hundreds of times," said Chris Kaftan, the editor-in-chief of the *Buff and Blue,* himself a latecomer to ASL. Kaftan's favorite rendition of the national anthem came a few years ago at a Redskins game; eight Gallaudet students sang it on the field. It was a magical moment, seeing sixteen hands flowing through the air, not on Kendall Green, but in Robert F. Kennedy Stadium. There were fifty-five thousand people on hand, and millions more tuned in on television. For Kaftan, this kind of public acknowledgment of his culture, his language, was hard to beat.

The afternoon's opponent is Goucher College, a school that is renowned for having educated Mary Tyler Moore but not for producing good basketball teams. Still, the Bison know they have no right to be complacent against anyone and come out hard from the opening tip. Nanette hits a pull-up jumper on the fast break. Natalie sinks a three-pointer and follows with a steal and a layup. Ronda Jo scores inside and then outside and begins a one-woman tear, scoring fifteen of the Bison's eighteen points. The Gallaudet lead hits twenty and doesn't stop there. Early in the second half, after hitting a baseline turnaround, Ronda Jo snares a rebound, fires an outlet pass to Ronda, who delivers a perfect bounce-pass to Nanette for a layup. It is a fast break right out of a coaching manual. The crowd is rollicking now, the pregame vibes spreading everywhere. What Kitty and Ben like the most is that the Bison are playing great defense, having fun and running more than they have all year. The whole game is like a trip to a funhouse. Blowouts can be very therapeutic, and this one, with a final score of 88–43, is all of that. Ronda may be more energized than anyone. With Touria still limited by her ankle sprain, Ronda takes over as point guard and has her tightest game of the season. She passes the ball superbly, hitting open Bison, moving it around the perimeter, driving at judicious moments. Nanette makes some lovely assists, too. She's never done a hard study of it, but Nanette has always been sure that deaf people have better peripheral vision—better vision of all kinds—than hearing people, because they are so reliant on it. Deaf people have safer driving records (and lower insurance rates) for this reason, having the ability to detect potential trouble with their eyes, and then avoid it. The vision sure is good against Goucher. In the midst of a high-speed 12–0 Gallaudet run in the second half, Ronda hits Touria for a layup, Nanette finds Touria for another layup, and then Ronda squeezes into a sliver of an opening and drives for another score. She feels so deliriously free and easy that she flashes the "I Love You" sign on the way back upcourt, her face red and happy against her white headband. The basketball doesn't rest. It moves smartly from one set of Bison hands to the next, and Ronda is at the hub of it all. She even puts in a funky lefty layup with her legs bowed wide, as if she were doing the Charleston. Kitty isn't wild about it but lets it go. It's Ronda's night, and it makes her fall in love with basketball all over again.

"I felt like I was flying out there," Ronda said.

Everyone agrees: This was the most fun they've had all year.

"Nobody can stop us but ourselves," Kitty said. *"The key to our success is in our minds. It's how we approach the game. It's playing together and unselfishly, playing our game, not getting lost in anything else that's going on. You've played a great game today. Let's keep it up."* For months, Kitty had been writing her three C's—control, confidence, concentration—on blackboards all over the northeast, in Pennsylvania and Virginia and

800 Florida Avenue in Washington. She and Ben walk out of the gym delighted that all three were present in abundance.

For considerable stretches of the season, for reasons that are still unclear to them, the Bison have been a team of soloists cloaked in the same blue-and-gold uniforms, a team more in name than deed. They would take turns going on their individual riffs, and sometimes it would work out and sometimes it wouldn't, but rarely would their notes converge, their melodies mesh, producing the sort of sweet, rich sound that only comes when the whole ensemble is connecting. Good team basketball is a lovely thing to behold—and a difficult thing to sustain. The Bison savor the harmony of their day against Goucher. Is it a coincidence that it happens right after the rap session, when the Bison got everything out in the open?

Not to Ronda. *"It's hard to play your best when you're weighed down and holding onto stuff,"* she said.

The Bison huddle up, gushing and giddy, one player after another raving about the great team play. Room 142 feels like a cocoon. Nanette doesn't have to talk about her vision for the rest of the season. They all share it.

The Field House is a place that teems with activity, all day, every day, but now is eerily quiet. The floor is gleaming and empty and looks the size of an airplane hangar with nobody on it. It's early evening in northeast Washington, and the last pink shards of sunset are gone, vanished behind the nineteenth-century row of red-brick, slate-roof buildings on Gallaudet's western edge. Kitty is sending e-mails to a few recruits when she hears a knock on her open door. It's Stacy Nowak, her frizzy reddish-blonde hair wet, her face full and serious. Stacy is not happy. She hasn't been all season. She is the one holdout to the positive groundswell that seems to be catching on. Other players have had their struggles. Natalie Ludwig is in a shooting slump and Cassey's role has been reduced and Jenny's nagging muscle pull is playing games with her head. But Stacy's unrest is deeper, more troubling, not something to be fixed by an ice pack or the dawn of a new day. The whole season has been convoluted. A small part of her feels she has let the team and herself down, by not being in better shape and not contributing more. A big part of her is upset at Kitty for not giving her more of a chance. She is playing even fewer minutes than she did the year before. It doesn't seem fair to her, and there are times she feels like a scapegoat for everything that has gone wrong this season. Stacy was the one player who didn't participate heartily in the chair-rattling celebration for Kitty's three-hundredth victory in the York locker room; it wasn't a conscious, in-your-face snub, but sometimes a hurt is hard to hide. Even after rousing victories like the one over Goucher, Stacy has been a little aloof. She had a great season in volleyball in the fall and feels as though she's spent almost the whole basketball season in quicksand, never sure where to step, always searching for a rope to pull herself out. Every time she is on the floor, she feels she can't make a single mistake, or else she'll be back on the bench. *"I never went through so much emotion in a season before. In my whole life I've never ridden the bench like this. I love the team, but it's very hard."*

It's been hard on Stacy's parents, too. Brent and Marcia Nowak are Gallaudet graduates, class of '68 and '69, respectively. Deafness goes back four generations in Marcia's family, one in Brent's. They are deep into Deaf culture, and sports. Marcia was a volleyball player for the United States in the Deaf Olympics in Malmo, Sweden, in 1973. Brent has been an avid basketball and softball player for decades. Their sporting passions now are achieved vicariously, through Stacy and her younger sister, Kristy. The Nowaks haven't missed one of their kids' home games in any sport—volleyball, basketball, or softball—since the girls were in middle school. They make a lot of the road games, too; it's never difficult to spot their arrival, with Brent's floppy, blue-and-gold Gallaudet hat, a conical piece of felt that looks like something a pilgrim might wear.

Brent is the president of the Model Secondary School for the Deaf's fan club; Marcia is the secretary. They are one of those couples who you never see apart, whose entire lives seem to move in lockstep. They both grew up in Brooklyn, New York, and attended the Lexington School for the Deaf in New York City. One of them starts a sentence, and often the other one finishes it.

"We love . . ." Brent begins.

". . . going to our girls' games," Marcia finishes.

"We use two languages at home," Marcia begins.

"ASL and English," Brent finishes. What do they miss most about Brooklyn? They turn to each other and smile knowingly, as though they'd rehearsed it ten thousand times, and then simultaneously finger-spell the name of the famous New York hot dog place: "N-A-T-H-A-N'S."

The Nowaks are united in their belief that the best thing parents can do when raising deaf children is to start teaching them English early. Marcia is an English teacher by profession and gladly brought her work home. The Nowak girls grew up reading and reading some more. Books spilled everywhere. Marcia would drill her daughters on English syntax, on plurals and tenses and articles, areas that are a huge problem for most deaf people, the Bison included. Hearing children pick up the rhythm and cadence of English by ear. It takes root even before they're out of diapers. The Nowaks were determined that English would not be a foreign language to their girls; theirs is a fully bilingual household. Stacy's writing is succinct and polished, her reading appetite voracious. Her teammates tease her because she's the only Bison whose sign language has tense and subject-predicate agreement built into it.

The Nowaks do almost everything together. They've gone through five Ford vans, crisscrossing the country summer after summer, camping across America. Stacy loves being outside, going barefoot, seeing the freckles pop out on her face from the sun. She'd wear shorts all year if she could. Sometimes she'll put them on in winter, as if to will the spring to arrive already. Stacy is impatient. She wants to get there yesterday. That was probably what was the hardest thing about her car accident in the fall of her freshman year. Everything went on hold. Life changed, big-time. It still isn't the same; Brett and Marcia are in total sync about that, too.

Stacy borrowed her parents' minivan that day and was driving on an interstate with a carful of friends. Suddenly there were brakelights in front of her, a four-car pileup, but Stacy couldn't stop in time. Her friends got pretty banged up, including Ronda, who hurt her back. *"I would never have forgiven myself if she did not heal,"* Stacy said. *"Thank God she did."*

Stacy suffered a compound fracture of her wrist in the crash. Her volleyball season ended that day. So did her freshman basketball season, before it even started. Three years later, her wrist still hurts when it's cold and damp. Stacy wonders what would've happened if she'd been able to stop sooner and the accident hadn't happened. Would she be a starter alongside Ronda Jo? Could she have supplied the extra strength and inside production the team has badly needed the last few years? Would she be fulfilled right now, instead of feeling kind of like a scrub, which when you think about it really is a waste for someone with a lot of natural strength and agility?

The problems started during her recuperation. Stacy was down, and for the first time in her life she wasn't playing a sport. She started partying more than she should've and picked up weight. She'd make progress taking it off, and then she'd slip back. She's seen those reports where medical experts talk about how of every one hundred pounds dieters in America lose, ninety-five are gained back. Nobody needs to tell her how true that is. The extra weight hurt her stamina and made it harder to maneuver in the low post. She knows that

Kitty, Ben, and everybody in the stands have never seen the real Stacy Nowak play.

Still, the accident hasn't taken away any of her boldness. Stacy is a big, strong personality in a big, strong body. She likes to make grand proclamations: *"I want to travel to all seven continents before I die." "One of my goals is to own a bookstore, and to have read every single book on the shelves."* Her goal before the season was to work out so hard that she'd drop forty pounds and get all the way back. It hasn't happened the way she wanted it to. The night she stops by Kitty's office, she talks to Kitty about her role for at least the sixth time this year. Kitty knows Stacy feels that she hasn't been treated fairly. Kitty has compassion for Stacy, but what good would it do a player to give her something Kitty feels she hadn't earned? Kitty has kicked Ronda Jo out of practice and yanked her out of games. She has done the same to Ronda, Touria, and Jenny Cooper, if she felt they were not concentrating or trying their best. To Kitty, the equation is simple: Stacy hasn't played well enough to warrant more playing time. It's nothing personal; it's about performance, what you've done and haven't done. Stacy's take is one hundred eighty degrees away. How can a player produce when she feels that she has zero margin for error? Doesn't a player deserve a chance to get in the flow and show what she can do?

Stacy and Kitty talk for about ten minutes, three feet apart in her office, a million miles in their view of things. Stacy walks out the blue Field House doors. The clouds hang low and dark. She turns right and heads past Hotchkiss Field toward Clerc Hall, her step more trudge than walk. The season will be over soon. That's one thing that is good.

This is the time of a basketball season when almost everybody's body is in some form of revolt. The Bison have been playing or practicing almost every day for more than three months, pounding on hardwood, pounding their bodies. Trainer Bret Weaver, who's got to look after the men's *and* women's teams, needs six sets of hands. Forty-five minutes before one of the last regular-season games, the training-room residents include Jenny, who's getting treatment for her hamstring; Natalie and Touria, who are getting their sprained ankles treated and taped; Ronda, whose back and shins have been acting up; and Ronda Jo and Courtney, who have miscellaneous aches and are getting both ankles taped as a precaution. On the only available table left, an opponent who's recovering from anterior cruciate ligament surgery is icing down her knee. Touria can tell another member of the ACL club without a second look. An interpreter is nearby, which gives Touria a chance to offer the woman encouragement.

"It's a long haul, but I'm sure you will make it all the way back. I did."

Sheets of sleet and freezing rain have turned Kendall Green into a rink. Maintenance crews have dumped so much orange-brown sand around that the campus walkways look like basepaths, a gritty coating underfoot as students walk into the Ely Center, the Merrill Learning Center, across the path that bisects the main quad. It's the same up the hill, in the back of campus, home of the Model Secondary School for the Deaf, and down below, behind Clerc Hall, home of the Kendall Demonstration Elementary School for deaf children. There's no demarcation, no tangible notice that you have left the grounds of Gallaudet University. They figure the playground is notice enough.

The grim grip of winter is back as Salisbury State comes to the Field House on the last day of January, for a makeup of a snowed-out game from the week before. The pessimist in Kitty questions whether the team will sustain the crispness and intensity it showed against Goucher. The coach in her prays it will.

"We Control Our Own Destiny," she writes on the blackboard before the game. Jenny's legs are jiggling constantly as Kitty talks, a good nervous energy that seems to infuse the whole room. Nanette, Ronda, and Stacy have an impromptu shouting contest, each one taking turns making the loudest scream she can. It's not clear who wins. The Bison start impressively again, bursting to a 12–2 lead after Ronda drives and flicks the ball to Courtney for a graceful baseline jumper. They are swarming on defense, connecting on offense. Late in the first half, Stacy line-drives the first of two free throws, barely bending her legs. Kitty tries to get her attention, wanting to tell her to bend the legs and use more arc. Neither her waves nor her stomps draw anyone's attention. Kitty sits down, momentarily exasperated. Stacy makes the second free throw, anyway. Maybe it means the night's karma is good, Kitty thinks. Salisbury State makes a strong run at Gallaudet early in the second half and cuts a fourteen-point deficit to three, but the Bison answer. Moments after Ronda hits a spectacular lefthanded layup on a feed from Touria, Jenny puts in a follow, Ronda hits two free throws and a three-pointer, and the margin is back up to ten. In the closing minutes, Salisbury State makes the Bison hit pressure free throws, and Ronda Jo and Ronda do exactly that. For once at the end, the Bison are crisp and composed, playing with faith in themselves. Ronda Jo hauls down twenty rebounds to go with her nineteen points, and Courtney has another strong game off the bench, and Ronda continues her renaissance. She hits three of her four three-pointers, scores twenty-three points, and doesn't have a single turnover.

With the revised schedule, the Bison have only two days to wait before a game they have been looking forward to for two months: a rematch with Mary Washington. This is the opponent that started the early-season derailment. Every Bison player knows it.

"Let's pay them back," Nanette said in the players' huddle.

"We need to play defense and play in control," Touria said.

"I want to score more than five points," Ronda Jo said, a droll reference to the worst game of her career.

Something is going on with her team, and Kitty loves it. It takes the Mary Washington players about two trips up and down the floor to understand that this is a different Gallaudet team from the one they beat in December. The Bison defense is suffocating. The rebounding is relentless. Gallaudet holds Mary Washington to seven field goals in the first half and is even better in the second half, when the Bison play with a speed and efficiency they've rarely achieved all year. They score fifty-three points in the final twenty minutes, and they come from all over: Touria's hard drives, Courtney's touch around the basket, Ronda's outside shot. And then there is Ronda Jo, who demolishes whoever tries to stop her with her cuts and hangers and jumpers. In just over a half-game, Ronda Jo scores twenty-nine points and has ten rebounds. She finishes off the most dazzling sequence of the night, Touria bolting down the lane, drawing the defense to her, then shoveling a wraparound pass to Ronda Jo for a layup. The Field House crowd goes wild.

On the bench, Kitty stands up and claps. *"I love watching good basketball,"* she said to no one in particular. When Kitty takes Ronda Jo out in the final minutes, her star's face betrays neither emotion nor satisfaction. Somebody says to her, *"I think you had more than five points."* Ronda Jo smiles and asks for a towel.

After payback is complete and an 89–61 triumph is registered, the Bison make their way out of the gym. The first person to congratulate them in the corridor is King Jordan.

"This is the Gallaudet team I remember," he said.

In Room 142, Jenny gets teased for fouling out in eighteen minutes. The room is alive with hope and good feeling.

"We live in the present. We work for the future. We forget the past," Kitty said.

In the *Buff and Blue,* under a front-page headline, "The Great Awakening," Alexander Long wrote:

> On Wednesday night in the Field House, in recognition of Ground Hog Day, the Bison squad arose from its deep hole in the ground, took a good look at the terrain and—much to the glee of Bison fans—saw their shadows looming large across the hardwood. The forecast? The winter season still has a long ways to go. All that's left to do is make sure that black hole remains a place of the past.

Gallaudet has won three games in five days. It stretches the winning streak to four by going to Marymount and beating one of the best teams in the conference on its home court. It's the game in which Kitty plays the box-and-one defense on Marymount guard Rachel Taylor and Nanette responds with an effort of almost maniacal intensity. It seems that in every contest now, there is a fresh hero. The Bison are suddenly 7–3 in the conference, in second place. They are not just talking about urgency; they are playing with it. Ronda Jo is playing better on both ends than she has all season, and the other Bison are not just waiting for her to bail them out. Ronda is playing with consummate skill and just the right amount of flair for her and Kitty to live with. Touria's drives and defense are an immense factor in just about every game. Jenny is getting healthier, and she and Nanette bring passion and egolessness to the whole unit, and so does Cassey. Natalie's perimeter game is a dangerous weapon. Stacy has had three of her best games in the last few weeks. Courtney, who was practically a mannequin when she first put on the Gallaudet uniform, is someone being counted on more each time out.

The great part of being on a campus with just two thousand students is that when the team does well, the news is everywhere, instantaneously. For the first time all year, the Bison feel as if they've dug out from the expectations that had been sitting on them like two feet of wet snow. The Bison were flattered by the expectations, and then flattened by them. Burdened by the task of providing a helium-balloon lift to all of deaf culture. It is wonderful to not have to answer questions about what's wrong or endure loaded looks of disappointment. They are back on their game.

To Kitty and Ben, it is one of the magical qualities about sports. There is always a chance for redemption, to get it right, up until the last game of the season. That hope is what drives a team to keep working, to fight through its frustration. Kitty and Ben often talk about how basketball games really amount to a forty-minute test of yourself, no matter what the opponent brings to it. The Bison are maximizing their talent and playing as a unit. Kitty at last isn't waking up and having her first thoughts turn to what she should do to shake up the team. It's a lovely switch.

Alumni Weekend has arrived, and campus is full of Gallaudet graduates. Upstairs in Ole Jim, the school's original gymnasium, a classic clapboard rectangle with sturdy nineteenth-century charm, a huge breakfast buffet is on for the alums and their families. Kitty is sitting at a table with her mother, Peggy, and brother, Tom. The smell of bacon, waffles, and syrup fills the old plaster walls. It is a bittersweet morning for Kitty. As happy as she is to have her mom in town, her dad couldn't make it and is back home in Indianapolis. It is the first time that he has missed Home-coming Weekend in twenty-five years—and the first season he has never made it to see Kitty's Bison play. The breakfast is held on the gym floor where Paul Baldridge was one of the Five Ironmen.

"I miss him a lot," Kitty said.

After breakfast, Kitty and Peggy walk across campus to the Field House, the Bison a few hours away from their Homecoming game against Catholic. The players begin to stream in and get ready. Nanette and Ronda decide to break from their routine and warm up for the game by playing racquetball. They get a full lather of sweat going, whacking a blue ball over four walls. Kitty finds out and is incensed.

Racquetball? Before a basketball game? Why not throw in a few sets of tennis, too? Racquetball is way too vigorous, way too hard on the ankles, to use as a pregame sweat-breaker.

"Did you ever think of just getting on a treadmill?" Kitty asked.

"We like racquetball," Ronda replied, more in innocence than impudence.

"I need a Valium," Kitty said.

Catholic is one more team the Bison believe they owe. As she comes out for regular warm-ups, Ronda sees Shanada up in the stands with a sign that reads, "That's my sister—Ronda 22," and is touched. Ronda Jo carries the whole team in a tightly contested first half. Catholic goes up by three early in the second half, and Ronda Jo responds with an off-balance bank shot. Touria hits a three-pointer from the top of the key, Ronda Jo gets a feed from Touria and hits a pull-up jumper, and then it's Jenny who takes over, fighting underneath, getting a gorgeous look from Ronda for a layup. Jenny is everywhere, hauling down boards, powering in follows. She scores ten straight points, and with each bucket, the energized Bison defense clamps down harder on Catholic. Cassey throws a perfectly placed home-run pass to Ronda for a layup. Stacy pumps in a few shots around the key. The Bison go on a 34–4 rampage, their most explosive burst of the year. Catholic makes six baskets the entire second half. It is another rout, 82–50, another display of speed and skill, and of Bison rejuvenation.

Before heading for the locker room, Nanette taps Kitty on the arm.

"Maybe we need to play racquetball before every game." Kitty rolls her eyes.

The Field House lobby is jammed after the game, random knots of fans and parents and alumni. You can always tell when it is Homecoming, one

195

player notes, *"because a lot of the people at the game are old."* The crowd lingers in the lobby even more than usual. When the players come upstairs from the locker room with their damp hair and gym bags, some fans throw up their arms and flutter their fingers in applause. The players are received like heroes, people clustering around them and hugging them and telling them how great it is that they are playing so well. It feels good to them to be fussed over. It feels good to be in this lobby, under the warming lights, everyone together.

Standing near the Physical Education office, Peggy Baldridge is savoring the energy, and the freedom, even with her conflicting emotions. She feels strange and sad to return to Gallaudet, the place where she fell in love with Paul, without him. But she also admits to relief to have a few days away. For eight months, she's been his primary caregiver, gone through all the ups and downs of Paul's stroke and his rehabilitation. There have been so many meetings and medications and decisions. Life has become heavy and unreliable, like a cranky old machine. Peggy has the same trim physique and youthful vigor that all Baldridges seem to have, but even she has her limits. She and Paul are coming up on fifty-five years of marriage. The toughest part has been his depression. It comes and goes, a tide moving on its own weighty whim, leaving both of them at times beached in hopelessness. The depression has been deeper since Paul's fall on New Year's Day.

Peggy is uplifted to see Kitty's players again. They are like grandchildren who live far away; she misses them a lot, but when she does get to see them, it's almost as if no time has passed at all. Kitty introduces Peggy to the new players on the team. In blue overalls and her orange hat, Cassey gives Peggy a strong hug. Sherry Ellis, Cassey's mother, has just gotten out of the hospital. Seeing Peggy reminds Cassey how much she loves her mother. Suddenly her mind leaves the Field House lobby and goes to Roxbury, Massachusetts. Cassey can't wait to go home for Spring Break.

Ronda Jo comes over, and Peggy embraces her, six feet from the display case honoring the Ironmen. Ronda, Jenny, and Nanette arrive in a group, and they all share more hugs and ask for Paul and tell Peggy that they sure hope he's doing better. Kitty appreciates her players' warmth toward her mom. The coach disappears briefly, into the copying room in the Physical Education office. She runs off the box score of the game and slips it into the fax machine. It is on the way to Paul Baldridge. She knows he would've loved the way the Bison played in the second half.

Senior Night is one of those occasions Nanette believes is never going to arrive. It's something that happens to other people, a nice tradition she has observed each year, without computing that one night she would be the one out there holding the flowers. On Wednesday, February 16, the day comes. All over Kendall Green, there is an outbreak of shorts and T-shirts, a ceremonial shedding of the woolens of winter. It is the last regular-season home game, against York, and Gallaudet honors its three senior players: Ronda Jo Miller, Nanette Virnig, and Jenny Cooper. Their names and numbers are put up on the Field House wall. Athletic director Rich Pelletier calls them out one by one before the game and hands each of them a bouquet, a mixed arrangement that stirs mixed feelings. The crowd cheers and raises its arms appreciatively and, standing near center court, Ronda Jo, Nanette, and Jenny wave graciously. None of them in the moment is prone to reflection or nostalgia. They are way too involved in the season's challenges to see the arc of their careers. Nanette, as the cocaptain, is focused on keeping the Bison revival going. Between her student teaching and the joyous news she got the day before—the birth of her niece, Abigail Louise Virnig—she just can't find room for more emotional energy.

She lets her teammates know about the baby moments before they go out on the court, waving her hand to get everyone's attention and motioning them forward, toward the chalkboard. Nanette has a small, conspiratorial smile on her face. She writes down Abigail's full name in huge block letters, inside a heart. She's a hearing baby, and Nanette loves her before she's even met her. *"My goal is to play my best for Abigail Louise."* Stacy and Ronda voice a loud noise, and everyone cheers.

"This makes me want to cry," Ronda said. Nanette hugs Ronda and Jenny and everybody. By the time Rich Pelletier gives her the flowers, Nanette almost feels as if someone else is standing out there. She looks over at Ronda Jo and thinks about the ten years they've played together, about an era passing. The first time they met was sixth grade, when Ronda Jo showed up at Minnesota State Academy for the Deaf, with spiky hair and hoop earrings.

"What do you expect? She came from a hearing school," Nanette said.

For Jenny, the whole year has been weird, with the mono and the late start and the chronic injuries, pulls, and strains that have not let her play, in her own mind, with full ferocity. She could've just scratched the season and retained a year of eligibility and returned to the team in the fall of 2000 to play a full year. She decided to play now and help this team, her friends. To be saluted for her last regular-season game seems way premature. She doesn't really want to be reminded. Ceremonies are not really her thing, anyway. And they're not Ronda Jo's, either.

Ronda Jo should be used to it by now; nobody in Gallaudet history has been honored more frequently. Each day on the way into the Field House, she goes by a display case with her pictures, plaques, and All-American awards. Announcements about her latest milestone—one thousandth point, two thousandth point, twenty-fifth hundred point—seem to come as often as the chimes in Chapel Hall. When Ronda Jo is introduced on Senior Night, so is her curriculum vitae: Leading scorer, rebounder, and shotblocker in school history . . . Top scorer in the nation in 1997–98 . . . NCAA recordholder for kills in volleyball . . . Three-time Capital Athletic Conference player of the year . . . Only All-American Gallaudet has ever had . . .

Ronda Jo has always had strangely ambivalent feelings about her superstar status. She's proud of her accomplishments, proud to be acclaimed as the greatest player in one hundred years of Gallaudet basketball. But she's never been comfortable getting singled out for mention. In interviews, she unfailingly credits her teammates and deflects glory. She is reluctant to take over games sometimes, not wanting to act as if she's better than everybody else, even though everybody knows she is. *"I love her humility,"* Nanette said. *"She has not changed at all. She never talks about what she has done or acts like she's the only reason we're any good."* Even without their shared history, Nanette said she'd be a huge fan of Ronda Jo's. How can you not love someone who is awesome at what she does but never lords it over anyone? Nanette was in bed with a 104-degree fever the night Ronda Jo passed the two-thousand-point mark. She ignored doctor's orders and went to the game. Nanette and Ronda Jo already have a pact: If Ronda Jo makes the WNBA, Nanette is going to be there.

The attention on Ronda Jo continues to build. The calls and visits from the WNBA keep coming. A few days before Senior Night, Nancy Darsch, coach of the Washington Mystics, sits across the gym from the Gallaudet bench and watches Ronda Jo pile up twenty-five points, twelve rebounds, four blocks, and seven steals and then slips out. Professional talent evaluators are a clandestine bunch, preferring to come and go unannounced, guarding their findings jealously. Ronda Jo doesn't know where she stands as the league prepares for its annual April draft. She just knows that the one career goal she's clear about is that she *"definitely wants to play professional basketball."*

"I'll go to the WNBA or overseas or wherever I need to do that. I just want to keep playing basketball."

Early in the season, Ronda Jo said she didn't feel the need to surpass herself, but that's changed, subtly, subconsciously. It's not about wanting to show off for the scouts; it's wanting to lead by example. Before games, she's going off by herself more than ever, doing her visualizing. A drop step on the baseline, a spin move in the lane, a double-pump hanger on the fast break, she summons the images of her signature plays, a mental dress rehearsal before tip-off. Sometimes it's helped, but other times it hasn't. Ronda Jo is still among the top scorers and rebounders in the country, but she isn't doing either as prolifically as in years past. Kitty is still convinced the problem is that she's trying too hard. The constant double- and triple-teams have not helped either. Ronda Jo seems out of sorts toward the end of the year. Frustrated by the way teams are bumping her and collapsing on her, she longs for space and freedom, having a chance to face the basket and create a scoring opportunity. She expects herself to dominate, no matter what the defense is doing. She's always been the self-reliant type.

This Senior Night game against York doesn't have huge implications for the Bison's Capital Athletic Conference playoff schedule; they have just about locked up second place, behind St. Mary's. Kitty wants to keep the high level of play going anyway, to build momentum for next week's playoffs.

"It's in your hands," Kitty said before the game. Ronda looks down and stares at her hands. The teammates who catch her doing it laugh.

The Bison come out oddly flat. Touria is attacking the basket and playing smothering defense, but just about everyone else looks lethargic.

The Bison are behind by six at intermission. They're shooting poorly from the field and abysmally from the free throw line, and as often happens, the bad shooting is contagious. Ronda Jo is in foul trouble, and Ronda's newfound efficiency seems to be taking the night off.

Gallaudet rallies to tie the score at 62. York pushes the lead back to six, and Touria answers with a three-pointer. Ronda Jo still hasn't really gotten going, and Kitty pulls her out to let her rest and clear her head. She's been getting roughed up underneath most of the game. As she sits down next to Kitty, Ronda Jo tells her that she wants to play small forward when she goes back in. She is adamant about it. She says if she can't, maybe she shouldn't go back in the game.

Kitty cannot fathom what she has just heard. On Senior Night, in one of the final games of her career, the greatest player she's ever had is laying attitude on her.

"What's wrong with you?" Kitty asked, before turning away sharply.

Ronda Jo looks down. She is instantly remorseful. It was her frustration talking, not that that's any excuse. She thinks, *"I can't believe I just said that to Kitty. Even if I think it's a good idea to put me somewhere else, that's not how I say it."*

Ronda Jo backs off and tells Kitty she's ready to go in, wherever Kitty wants her. She hits a big turnaround to make it a one-point game in the closing minutes, but the Bison are still flat, and wild, shooting twenty-nine free throws, making only fourteen. They wind up losing by three, and even though the defeat doesn't mean much in the standings, Kitty is disturbed that the players lapsed back into habits Kitty thought they had finally broken.

Mostly, though, she's disturbed at Ronda Jo. *"She says she wants to play in the WNBA, and she plays like this,"* Kitty said. Kitty purposely doesn't talk to Ronda Jo right after the game. She wants her anger to settle first. When Kitty arrives in the office the next morning, there's an e-mail waiting for her from Ronda Jo.

"You didn't deserve that. I can't imagine I said that. I'm sorry," Ronda Jo wrote. They meet later in Kitty's office, and Ronda Jo reiterates her regret, Kitty's anger dissolving on the spot. Kitty and Ronda Jo are standing face to face in Kitty's doorway. The Bison are about to practice, the postseason just days away. Ronda Jo still has no idea where her insubordination came from, but she resolves that it will never happen again. She and Kitty end the meeting the way they always end their meetings: with a hug.

FIELD HOUSE
11
FAREWELL

THE BISON SEE themselves as ambassadors of Gallaudet University, and Deaf culture. It's not a role they ever discuss or achieve a consensus about; there's no need to. Like their uniforms and their ASL, it's simply part of who they are.

At most games on the road, a group of deaf fans comes out to support the Bison. When they're playing anywhere near a deaf school, such as the National Technical Institute for the Deaf in Rochester, the group gets much larger. No matter what happens in the game, the players stay around and visit with the fans. A community is formed, right there on the hard planks of pullout bleachers. Young deaf girls, especially, are drawn to the team, their faces a study of awe and wonder when they get to see the players up close.

As the Bison prepare for what they hope is a long postseason run, they are invited to a party at the home of one of their Bison Backers, an informal, but intensely loyal, booster club. In big-time, Division I college basketball circles, boosters tend to be shadowy figures working the back corridors of arenas and locker rooms, people known for setting players up with no-show jobs or SUVs, anything to help "the program," as it is euphemistically known. At Gallaudet, the boostering is much more benign: They bake brownies and cheer. The hosts have a hot tub, and once Ronda Jo, Stacy, and Ronda go in, a trail of young girls, deaf and hearing, follows them. It's hard to beat sharing a hot tub with your heroes. Amy and Kristin McGregor are ten-year-old twins who attend almost every game; their mother, Daphne Cox McGregor, works in Gallaudet's alumni office. When Kristin had to choose a role model for a fourth-grade project, she chose Ronda Jo. She wrote a poem and drew a picture and presented them to Ronda Jo before the Bison went off to play The College of New Jersey in the 1999 NCAA tournament. Ronda Jo had thirty-eight points. Kristin likes to think her gifts had something to do with it. Kristin and Amy only missed one game the entire 1999–2000 season. It was the day their family moved to a new house in Virginia. Amy's favorite Bison are Courtney and Touria. She tracks their performances and keeps their statistics. The twins see female athletes like Sheryl Swoopes of the Houston Comets and Mia Hamm of the U.S. women's national soccer team on television and in the newspaper. Celebrity typically has deep cachet among girls of this age, luring them like a shiny locket. But Ronda Jo, Jenny, and the rest of the Bison have something much more important than fame going for them. They are deaf.

A class of hearing children from a local elementary school are guests at the Senior Night game. They watch from the Field House bleachers and file into a classroom afterward and wait to meet the Bison. The team has just lost a disheartening contest, but a half-dozen players show up uncomplainingly. They know these kids made a special trip to see them and to learn about deafness and ASL. When the players enter the room, the children's faces are upturned and curious. A little girl in pigtails whispers to the grown-up next to her, "I don't see anything wrong with their ears." Through an interpreter, the Bison introduce themselves and tell the kids where they are from and where they went to high school. It is a free-floating exchange, relaxed and random. The kids ask the players how they started playing, whether being deaf ever makes it hard for them on the court. The players ask the kids about their school and what sports they play. One of the teachers wants to know what advice the players would give to someone who wants to start playing a sport.

"*You've got to play with your heart,*" Touria said. "*Have fun, but make sure you always play with your heart.*" On the side of the room, the teachers and parents nod in concurrence, a lineup of yes women. Cassey said, "*You like to play? Is that your dream? Well, do it. Don't let anybody talk you out of it. Don't cheat yourself. My dream was to play basketball at Gallaudet, and it wasn't easy, but here I am. Go after what you want—and stick with it until you get there.*" The players thank the kids for coming. The kids thank the players for having them and for spending some time with them after a game.

"*I think you have some new fans,*" one of the teachers said as they all spilled out in the hallway, the college students and the grade-school students, the hearing and the deaf, the tall and the short, sharing a corridor and inspiration.

Change is hard to predict sometimes. There are times you make elaborate plans for it, as detailed as an architect's drawings, with all the cornices and moldings of your life predetermined. Other times, it just happens. In the middle of her spring term and the end of her first basketball season, without much forethought, Natalie stops using her voice when she signs. She had used her voice her whole life. She'd use it by itself at home, because nobody in her family except her mother could sign. She'd use it along with her signs in most other places—simultaneous communication, as it's known. Now she's all sign. It's one of things that Gallaudet does to people. And it's fine with her. Six months after her arrival, Natalie is as happy as she was the first day not to be reliant on her parents or an interpreter. Self-sufficiency is right below straight A's on her priority list, and she's there: *"If an emergency or anything else comes up, I can take care of it myself."*

Whether or not to use one's voice is a highly personal decision. Even for the Bison who haven't had a traumatic event associated with their voice, the way Ronda did when she was mocked by her old coach, it's often a hard choice. Ronda Jo uses her voice at home on the farm, but no place else. Cassey will voice a little bit around the team, more to convey powerful emotions than anything, but really will not use it with anyone but her mother. Stacy, whose parents were schooled in the oral method but are also fluent in ASL, is loud and emphatic. She enjoys trying to make herself heard, but she's one of the few. Years of getting strange looks—of pity, disapproval, and sometimes even revulsion—has convinced most of the players to voice only in the safest of places. It's that old preconception at work again, the world equating intelligence with the ability to speak.

"You get tired of people looking at you like you're mentally retarded," Nanette said.

During one of the last regular-season practices, Jenny and Ronda have a big blowup. They are close friends, sorority sisters, and soulmates, but they've been going through one of those patches when a few grains of sand have worked their way into the gears of the relationship. Ronda is playing point guard, directing the offense as the Bison run through plays. Jenny goes to the wrong place on the court, then does it again. Ronda chides Jenny for not knowing where to go. *"If you keep screwing up, we're going to have to run suicides."*

Jenny: *"You're playing the point. You're supposed to set everything up. Why don't you just do your own job?"* Ronda comes back again, and Jenny answers with a middle finger, then barrels out the back door of the Field House. Some coaches will tell you that when their team gets ornery, it means they're ready to play. Kitty isn't so sure. She's been through enough chemistry issues this season—from The Incident to the undeclared gulfs between newcomers and veterans to the ongoing realignment of friendships—that she can't laugh it off. Nobody expects it'll get as messy as it did a couple of years ago, when Ronda was fooling around with a ball in the Bison locker room and accidentally whacked Jenny in the nose with it. Jenny got angry, her nose got bloody, and soon punches started to fly, wild-fisted flurries that mostly missed. It was over almost as fast as it started, the friendship utterly unscarred. And that's how it is this time. On the bus ride to Goucher on the final road trip of the season, Jenny stands up, waves her hand to get everyone's attention.

"Everything is fine between Ronda and I. I was wrong to walk out and do what I did." In her right front seat, Kitty smiles and thinks: *"Wouldn't it be great if every problem were so easily solved?"*

"We're going to surprise a lot of people," Touria said. One of the good things about having an up and down season is that other teams sort of forget about you. In the beginning of the year, Gallaudet was the Capital Athletic Conference school everybody worried about. Now they're just one in the mix, and that's fine. The late-season resurgence has

almost everyone feeling loose. When the Bison crush Goucher in the last game before the playoffs, their conference record improves to 9–5. The whole team is meshing. The ball moves crisply. The Bison play aggressive, gambling defense, cutting off passes, going for steals. Their movements are assured, not tentative. Instead of building her pregame talk around the three C's, Kitty fills the board with a quote from Paul Valéry: "The best way to make your dream come true is to wake up!"

Beneath it is this:

B—Brave
E—Energy
L—Love
I—Inside
E—Elevate
V—Vigorous
E—Enjoy

Sometimes Kitty feels as though the players purge their brains of everything she tells them before a game. This time, it seems to stick. Winning the game isn't as important as coming into the playoffs with a positive frame of mind. That's what Kitty is after more than anything. The only glitch she sees against Goucher comes from Touria. She has a strong game, but when she has a couple of wide-open shots and doesn't take them, Kitty pulls her out. Touria's outside shooting has been erratic most of the season. Shots she would've attempted in the past without thinking about it, she finds herself hesitating on, her mind gummed up with doubt: *"Should I take this? Somebody else is probably open. Wouldn't it be better to pass than to probably miss another shot?"* When Touria comes to the bench, Kitty gets on her haunches, like a baseball catcher, directly in front of her. *"You had good, open shots and you didn't take them. If you are not going to shoot that shot, then you're going to sit, understand? You have got to believe in yourself."* Touria twirls her hair and nods. All season, she has been weighted down with too much mental clutter. She has done too much thinking and not enough intuitive playing. It is her harsh self-evaluation *(How can I be playing so badly?)* that is the germ of the trouble, the thing that sends her spiraling into Clutterville. Self-criticism is like a virus. It is voracious. It attacks all healthy cells in the neighborhood. In no time, Touria can go from "I am not a good shooter" to "I am a horrible human being." Kitty has been trying to help Touria give herself credit for the fine player she is. When she allows herself to believe that, each mistake is not an attack on her self-esteem. Self-confidence can be an anchor through the nastiest currents. Touria is fighting hard to get there. "She's a survivor," Kitty said. Touria believes that, too: *"I know I can do it if I set my mind to it. And that's what I plan to do."*

Postseason basketball is totally different from the game that's played from November to mid-February. The hoops are still ten feet high and the court is still ninety-four feet long, but everything else is changed. Schools with a record of 24–1 and schools with a record of 1–24 find themselves in the same place, the competitive slate wiped clean. The good news is that all teams get a fresh start. The bad news is that the fresh start—and the season—end the moment you lose. The season shifts from a full-length movie into a short, each scene, each sequence, suddenly shot up with urgency. *"Our record is 0–0,"* Kitty tells the Bison. *"Every game we play is potentially our last game. How do you want to remember the season? Do you want it to be fun? Do you want it to be memorable? It's up to you to decide. You're the ones who can do something about it, nobody else. It's up to you."*

The whole campus feels different, truthfully. The thermometer goes into the fifties on February 22, and you can smell the impending botanical outburst. The main green in the center of campus isn't just an expanse to tromp through, buttoned-up and gray-faced; it's a place to linger in again. Benches that have been vacant for months are peopled. Behind the Field House, the nets are up on the tennis courts, and yellow-green balls are being thwacked, and once again there is an outbreak of bare skulls in northeast Washington. Each year at this time, Gallaudet freshmen shave their heads. Not all of them, but enough so that campus has the nubby look of boot camp, minus the push-ups and thick-necked sergeants. Before the ritual shaving, many freshmen dye their hair aqua and pumpkin and purple for an added dollop of outrageousness. There are no long-term consequences, since it's all coming off, anyway. Ronda Jo, Nanette, Stacy, and Jenny all shaved their heads as freshmen; Touria was about to but backed out at the last second. This year, Cathy Stutzman shaved her head, but the change wasn't so dramatic; her hair is not much more than crew-cut length to begin with. The other freshman, Cassey Ellis, didn't even think about it. There was no chance her braids were going to wind up on somebody's floor.

A coach seeks a delicate emotional balance this time of year. Kitty wants the Bison fired up to play. She doesn't want them so fired up that they're overcharged, because then they won't play naturally. She wants them confident, but not so confident they think they're up ten just by lacing their sneakers. After a series of spirited practices, Kitty thinks the Bison are ready. It helps that the first playoff game is in the Field House, and that the opponent is Catholic. The Bison beat them easily just ten days before. The Bison also remember how wildly the Catholic players and crowd celebrated when it beat Gallaudet by two in the game in which Touria sprained her ankle. The memory isn't pleasant. The Bison don't mind using any perceived slight or misbehavior and milking it without shame. Players and coaches look for extra motivation wherever they can this time of year, even to the point of inventing it. Catholic is a D.C. neighbor, a school that had been drubbed by the

Bison in its last few meetings. Its players did nothing unsportsmanlike in celebrating; still, some Bison players have convinced themselves the jubilation was excessive. Kitty's approach in such matters is thoroughly practical: Hey, whatever works.

Kitty writes on the blackboard of Room 142, "There is no reason to overpower them when you can outsmart them." The Bison pass through a minigauntlet as they come into the room, Kitty, Ben, and Hillel waiting with hands up to high-five every player. Ronda is the last to enter, staying on the Field House floor until she made her last three-pointer, in her new playoff hairdo: two little pigtails in the front of her head, sticking up devil-like.

"What's up with Ronda's hair?" King Jordan asked when he walked in the Field House.

Kitty finishes her talk, about believing and about the choice being theirs what kind of season this will be, and the Bison all begin clapping furiously and huddling up, ten women and three coaches putting hands in, a tight circle of white uniforms and raised arms, a symbolic coming together before the actual venturing forth. The coaches leave and the players remain in the circle, classroom chairs strewn all around them. Jenny Cooper is sick with a stomach virus and is back in Clerc Hall, in bed, but she's there in an e-mail, which she sent to Kitty:

> I'm not ready to finish basketball. I want more of it this Thursday and Saturday, but it's up to our team. Will you please tell my team to play with their HEART and play as ONE PIECE OF TEAM and LOVE EACH OTHER?!!
> Thanks.
> I love you all . . . good luck
> JENNY

"I don't want this to be over for Jenny," Ronda says. Ronda Jo says, *"I want to wear out our sneakers by Saturday night* (the day of the CAC

championship game)." Courtney says, *"Don't pay any attention to the officials or the calls. Let's not get distracted. Ignore everything else and just play."* When it's Cassey's turn, she does a pantomime of lighting a match and setting something afire, something big, and then she starts voicing, piercing, powerful sounds, and the whole circle of Bison feels ready to combust. ASL poetry readings are a popular campus event; Cassey's performance is unscheduled, but moving.

Seven seconds into the game, Ronda pushes the ball hard to the basket, pulls up, and hits a ten-foot jumper. Courtney connects on a turnaround bank shot. Touria drives to the basket and scores. On both ends of the court, the Bison are honoring Cassey's pantomime; they're making heat. Their zone defense is stout, their feet moving, their seams tight. The Bison are up by nine at the half (35–26), and the best thing about it is that it's not one of those games that's The Ronda Jo Show and little more. Natalie Ludwig hits a couple of timely threes. Touria's drives are effective. Courtney takes advantage of Catholic's swarm of defenders on Ronda Jo and scores early, and Ronda and her devil horns are all over. Midway through the second half, Ronda extends the Bison lead to twenty when she hits a baseline fallaway that she almost shoots from out of bounds. The Bison fans go wild, and Kitty leads the cheering. It is not a shot she's ever diagrammed, but when it goes in, how do you argue?

With their propensity for blowing late leads, the Bison know—and Kitty keeps reminding them—that they have to play smart and can't let up. The pieces are all interlocking, like a puzzle, and nothing can pull them apart. Kitty and Ben can't get Courtney's attention at one point, their waving and stomping for nought. Normally it would make Kitty crazy with irritation, but the feeling passes. An official hands Ronda Jo the ball at the free throw line and, oblivious to her deafness, says a few things to her; that might bug the Bison players and coaches, too, but not here, not now. With Catholic making one last desperate charge, Natalie hits a three-pointer, on a sharp pass from Ronda. When the players had their rap session the month before, one of the things Natalie brought up was that she didn't think Ronda trusted her, nor did she think Ronda liked to pass her the ball. It was a serious charge, and not from Natalie's imagination. It took courage for Natalie to bring it up, and fairmindedness of Ronda to take it in and not bury it beneath an avalanche of defensiveness. They are as different as people can be, in temperament and background: hard-driving, serious-minded Natalie, from a hearing family and a mainstream school in Texas; and whimsical, extroverted Ronda, from a deaf family and a deaf school in Minnesota. But they worked through it. And now here was Ronda, in the playoffs, finding Natalie in a big moment, for a big basket.

"I love it when we play as a team," Kitty said.

The Field House is full of Bison family members: the Millers, the Westbergs, the Nowaks, Ronald Johnson, and Touria's brother, Abdallah, who just arrived from Sweden. They see the Bison play one of their cleanest games of the season, led by Ronda Jo, who comes on in the second half and winds up with twenty-nine points and fourteen rebounds. The final score is 77–61.

The afterglow is bright in the lobby. The Bison greet their Backers and families and friends, reveling in how good it feels to move forward and keep the season alive and be a team. A season that seemed headed for the Dumpster three weeks ago is pulsing with life. The Bison have made their choice. They've done exactly what Touria talked to those elementary school kids about: played with heart.

Gallaudet is in the conference semifinals, against Salisbury State, and the Bison are just two more victories away from a return trip to the NCAAs and the chance they want more than anything: to expunge both the memory of the Salem State game and the self-fulfilling doubts that poisoned it.

All over Kendall Green that night, the air feels good and clear. The earth smells rich. Freshmen hang out in the Abbey with their shaved heads. The Bison like where they are going.

As soon as Ronald Johnson hits town after the sixteen-hour drive from Minnesota, he starts nursing Jenny back to health. He has his Green Life herbal powder with him—when doesn't he?—and Jenny begins taking it. He has her soak in a special salt bath, at a temperature of one hundred degrees, not a degree more or less. *That's the temperature that allows for maximum absorption,* Ronald Johnson said. He hands her other virus-purging supplements, too, a mobile medicine man dispensing care with a folksy confidence. Jenny doesn't know what he's going to pull out of his bag next, but he's the father of one of her best friends. She's going with the program.

Kitty's coaching style stays inclusive, even in the playoffs. If the players are surrogate daughters, their parents are aunts and uncles and cousins. Practices are open, meetings are open, sometimes even the locker room is open. There is one day of practice to get ready for the third meeting of the year with Salisbury State, and Kitty lets Ronald Johnson and John Miller get in on the run for a while when she's working the offense against the zone. After practice, Ronald visits with his former players at the Minnesota State Academy for the Deaf, Nanette and Ronda Jo. The coach in him steps up: *"You owe it to yourselves not to hold anything back in this game. People all over the country are wondering about how Gallaudet is going to do in the playoffs. It's up to you to show them. Twenty years from now, you can come back and look at that display case or the record book and see that oh, yes, 1999–2000 season was a nice year for the Gallaudet women's basketball team. Or you can see a trophy sitting in that case, and have people rating it as one of the greatest teams in school history."* Ronda Jo and Nanette are as rapt as schoolgirls. They give him a grateful embrace before Ronald Johnson runs back to the dorm to check on Jenny.

Day breaks warm and golden on Thursday, February 24, the sunlight rising hopefully over the row houses to the east, the Capitol backlit like an amber beacon. It is one of those days that comes once every couple of winters in the northeast, the kind where you don't just feel thawed; you feel like your whole body is under a heat lamp. When the sun gets high over Kendall Green, the temperature reaches seventy, and the campus feels as though it has one foot in Margaritaville. The usual commotion of students and professors getting to class, interpreters reporting for jobs, administrators and staff tending to their duties is gone, replaced by a pace that is more languid. Even the sign language seems slower.

It's not a normal day, and it doesn't feel normal to the Bison. It's the day of the Capital Athletic Conference semifinals, one more one-game season. Courtney Westberg heads to her morning English class with Professor Karie Palmer and thinks about the game. Stacy Nowak takes the elevator down to the Clerc Hall lobby and thinks about the game. Ronda Jo Miller goes to Skip Williams's Psychology class, Crime and Punishment, and collects a pile of the handouts he's always distributing, because he knows it's impossible for students to look up at his signing and take notes at the same time. *"Even the best students haven't figured that one out yet,"* Williams said. Ronda Jo's mind isn't into Crime and Punishment, though; it's into Salisbury State. Natalie Ludwig stops by the Computer Room in the Hall Memorial Building, and Touria has lunch with her brother, and for all the Bison, the Lady Gulls of Salisbury State come with them everywhere.

At noontime, Ronda Jo heads to the Field House. She is in her every-day uniform—jeans, T-shirt, sneakers. She gets a ball and goes out on the floor and shoots by herself for forty-five minutes, jumpers and turn-arounds and reverses. Ronda Jo has never done this before, having a midday shootaround on game day. She felt tugged to the Field House. She swishes a jumper, a runner in the lane, the sound of the bouncing ball echoing off the walls, her mind bouncing with it, with reflection and nostalgia, the four greatest years of her life reeling through her head like a movie. She posts up an imaginary defender and thinks: *"This could be my last game for Gallaudet."* She does not like the thought at all.

"Desire creates the power," Kitty Baldridge writes on the blackboard, kneeling on the table as she goes. Seven guys with bare torsos each have a letter painted on their chest, and they're racing around the Field House in formation, spelling GO BISON. Kitty is working on her own letters:

B—Bold—Be brave, have no fear, confident
E—Execute—Right techniques
L—Learned—Basketball sense
I—Intensity—Aggressive, desire
E—Ensemble—Play as a team
V—Value—Cherish the moment and the opportunity
E—Exuberance—Unrestrained joy

The Bison are sitting in classroom desks, their white home uniforms with blue-and-gold trim almost blinding beneath the fluorescent brightness. Jenny Cooper is out of bed and back in commission *("I believe in Green Life!")*, her knees bouncing about hundred times a minute, the way they always do before a game. Ronda Jo is biting her nails and Touria is twirling her hair and Ben is in the corner with a clip-board beneath a wall-mounted television, waiting to give his you've-got-to-play-defense pep talk. On the other side of the partition, Salisbury

State is going over its own preparation, Coach Bridget Benschalter's words punctuated with claps and cheers. It's fully audible to a hearing person. Some coaches might stake out someone by the wall, ear against the opening, hoping to find out how they plan to defend Ronda Jo; Kitty has never done it. *You don't use deafness as a weapon.* It is no different from scores of other pregame routines, but the Bison insides tell a different story, churning relentlessly, edgy anticipation fused with nervous energy. Kitty is wearing pressed black slacks, black shirt, and black vest, looking neat and ready. She has no props or elaborate speeches planned. She is calm, low-key, her signs direct and understated. She issues the same challenge she has been, putting the responsibility squarely on the Bison shoulders in front of her: *"When we play our game and we play with passion, nobody can beat us. It's up to you: How much do you want to keep playing?"* She praises the Bison for their resurgence and invokes the memory of the season's highlights—the victory over Capital, beating St. Mary's when it was undefeated, rolling over Mary Washington earlier in the month. She cautions them against overconfidence, for this is a much improved Salisbury State team from the one they've already beaten two times. Kitty said, *"I know you can do it, because you have done it. I know how good you can be, because you've shown it. This moment is all we have. I hope we can seize it and have fun with it."*

Kitty walks forward, and the Bison bound from their chairs. She is a tiny figure in black swallowed up by a circle of white, and they put hands in and exhort one another one more time, and then the Bison take the court, the crowd cheering, the bare-chested letter boys flapping their arms like birds.

When warm-ups are done, Nanette and Ronda Jo join Kitty at center court to meet the other captains and the officials. They go over the usual material: Gallaudet is white, Salisbury State red. Stop on the whistle. Watch the hand-checking. If anyone steps in the lane early on free throws, we're going to call it. Good luck to both teams. Kitty interprets it all, and the captains shake hands. The starters are introduced, Touria and Ronda and Courtney, and the two starting seniors: *"At forward, No. 25 from Mendota Heights, Minnesota, Nanette Virnig . . . At center, No. 23 from Little Falls, Minnesota, Ronda Jo Miller . . ."* As Kitty watches them run out on her visual cue, it's sad to think that soon she will do this for the last time, sign the names of these young women who have meant so much to her for four years. Linnae Gallano performs a rousing rendition of "The Star Spangled Banner." The Field House crowd has that big-game feel, the charged current that seems to flow right out of the floor on nights when an entire season's work is at stake. The ball goes up.

Both teams start nervously. Courtney scores inside on a well-placed lob pass from Ronda Jo for the game's first basket, but the Bison go cold until Ronda hits a driving bank shot and Courtney hits a short baseline jumper. The Lady Gulls are pressing and throwing off the Bison rhythm. They are collapsing all over Ronda Jo, making it hard for her to get her shots, penetrating the Bison zone and beating Gallaudet on the backboards. Ronda Jo doesn't score until eleven minutes have elapsed. The Lady Gulls go on an 8–0 run, and then a 6–0 run, and suddenly the Bison are behind by fifteen points. Late in the first half, Ronda makes a cut and sprains an ankle, collapsing to the floor, crying. She limps off for the training room with Bret Weaver. Stacy puts in a short bank shot, Ronda Jo hits a jump shot, and Touria fires in a three-pointer and follows with a fast-break layup on a good outlet pass from Courtney. The deficit is only seven (32–25) at the half, but nobody is happy.

"We're playing like we're in a daze," Ronda Jo said.

"We're acting like they're outstanding and we're intimidated by them," Jenny said.

Kitty said: *"You're in panic mode. We couldn't get any shots to fall early, and then we lost composure."* Kitty urges the Bison to be aggressive, want the ball, take the risk of going all out. The Bison nod, hoping that their season is not down to its final twenty minutes.

Touria hits a weaving, scooping layup early in the second half, and the Bison are finally playing with fire. They get three offensive rebounds on one trip down, but they're giving up too many easy shots and getting sliced up by the Gulls' star center Lisa Neylan and freshman forward Amy Campion, her blonde braids flapping menacingly behind her, as she passes, rebounds, and steals. With her ankle iced and taped, Ronda returns and gives it her best, but the ankle is weak. It feels as if it might go at any time. Everything feels jerky for the Bison. Nobody's shots are falling, and the longer that goes on, the more the Bison look shell-shocked. Ronda Jo is taking pull-ups and turnarounds instead of driving. Jenny's fighting and winning the tugs-of-war underneath, but her putbacks keep rolling off. The Bison offense dissolves into: "I don't want the ball, you take it."

Ronda Jo has rarely been one to demand the ball, but with eight minutes to play and the deficit at sixteen, she turns manic. She pulls down an offensive rebound and scores. She follows with a hanging jumper in the lane and a muscled layup in traffic, and then with a three-point play on a fast-break layup. She scores eleven points in a row. She almost single-handedly narrows the gap to nine. The Field House crowd is making more noise than it has all night. People are standing and arms are waving. The Go-Bison crew is running around with renewed vigor.

Sometimes teams use so much energy to get back into a game that there's nothing left at the end. Kitty and Ben don't want to even think if that's going to be the case here. The Gulls' Lisa Neylan connects on a jumper, then another. The deficit is back to thirteen, and with just four minutes to play, the Bison know that more than ever in the whole season, the time is now. They are desperate. After a time-out, Ronda Jo gets the ball and fires up a fallaway. It glances off the iron. The Bison are playing intense defense now but lose the ball on their next two possessions. Just over two minutes remain. Two free throws have extended the Salisbury margin to fifteen, 69–54. The Bison get the ball back but do nothing with it. The hole is too deep; there can be no miracle

comeback. There are games when a player feels as though she's playing uphill, when the court's a ramp and she's at the foot of it. Everything is hard. The hoop looks to be the size of a Lifesaver. It is one of
those nights for the Bison. It isn't just all the missed shots; it's a reprise
of many of the problems the Bison had earlier in the year, the sloppy
ballhandling, the spotty defense. Kitty and Ben and the players thought
those lapses were in the past. On the last night of the season, they
make an untimely reappearance. The clock shows two minutes to play,
but the season is over.

It is time for Kitty to go the bench. She makes substitutions, and
Nanette and Jenny come off, getting a warm ovation, the fans raising
their arms and extending their hands, a thank-you for four years of
hard work and fine play. With forty-nine seconds to play, the buzzer
sounds again. At the scorer's table, Stacy walks on the court and points
to Ronda Jo. Ronda Jo figured she would be next but still isn't ready for
it. Stacy comes on and Ronda Jo comes off, a slow, sad trot, ponytail
swinging, head down, angular face as impassive as ever. She finishes
the game with nineteen points, twelve rebounds, six steals, and four
blocks, great numbers for someone else, maybe.

But definitely not for Ronda Jo.

Many in the Field House crowd are standing, arms raised once
more, fingers wagging, others stomping, all hailing. *"We just said good-
bye to the greatest athlete Gallaudet has ever had,"* one fan said. John and
Dolly Miller are among the standing, proud and sad all at once, but
mostly proud. Their daughter drapes a towel over her head on the
bench. Dolly Miller thinks about the day she knew for sure that her
baby girl couldn't hear, how she yelled Ronda Jo's name and woke up
her son and how her daughter didn't stir. Dolly cried hard that night, a
torrent of self-pity and heartsickness flooding over her. *How could my
baby be deaf? How is she supposed to have any kind of life? How am I supposed to deal with this?* Twenty-one years later, in the Field House stands
of Gallaudet University, the world's only liberal-arts college for the deaf

and the hard-of-hearing, Dolly Miller is looking at her grown-up, six-foot, two-inch baby, No. 23 with the towel on her head, the torrent now of love and gratitude. Her daughter is wonderful just the way she is.

The buzzer sounds at last, a horrible final sound. The scoreboard shows Salisbury State 72, Gallaudet 56. The teams line up and engage in the perfunctory postgame handshake, one set of hands heading to the finals, the other to the off-season. The Bison are walking out of the gym when Lisa Neylan, the Gulls' center, catches up to Ronda Jo and asks Kitty if she would mind interpreting. Lisa Neylan has competed against Ronda Jo for three years, battling her and admiring her and wondering privately what her world, what every Bison's world, is like. She had heard all about Ronda Jo from teammates before she'd ever played against her. She didn't get what all the fuss was about. "Then I stepped on the court against her, and it was like, 'Wow! Now I understand.'" In all that time, Lisa Neylan has never exchanged a word with Ronda Jo Miller, the gulf of culture and sound never once getting crossed. It just does not feel right to let Ronda Jo walk off, to have exchanged shoves and elbows and hard competition, but no thoughts or feelings. This isn't about the twenty-six hundred points and eighteen hundred rebounds and four hundred blocks Ronda Jo compiled in her career. It's about the sisterhood of sweat, one fine player wanting to pay tribute to another—the greatest player she's ever faced.

"I just want to tell you that it's been an honor to play against you," Lisa Neylan said. "You motivated me and you made me a better player. I hope you make the WNBA. I wish you all the best in whatever you do."

Ronda Jo runs a hand over her damp ponytail and forces a smile. Emotions are starting to spill out. She doesn't like not being in control. She doesn't like to hear about her career in the past tense, standing there in her Gallaudet uniform still wet with the last drops of four years of perspiration. Ronda Jo composes herself and she starts to sign and Kitty begins voicing almost simultaneously. "Thank you. That means a lot to me. I enjoyed playing against you, too. Good luck in the rest of the playoffs."

For Lisa Neylan, the games with Gallaudet have been one of the best things about her college career. She liked watching the crowd wave its arms, hearing the fans stomp instead of cheer, and loved seeing Linnae Gallano sign the national anthem. "I couldn't take my eyes off her. It was so amazing to watch." She still can't imagine how the Bison play without being able to hear. "I think basketball depends more on communication than any other sport. To play without hearing the whistle or horn or their coach is just awesome."

Elisabeth Barfuss, a Salisbury State guard, comes up next and offers kind words of her own to Ronda Jo, and then she and Neylan go to find their celebrating teammates, grateful to have crossed the gulf, to have finally connected with Ronda Jo Miller, even if it was just to say good-bye.

The door is closed to Room 142. The room has never sounded like this, the quiet broken by sobs and heaves, deep, fitful spasms of hurt. From the front of the room to the back, Bison faces are twisted in anguish and disappointment, bodies slumped and spent. Ronda Johnson has her team T-shirt on her head, her face red and tears flowing hard. Jenny Cooper takes off her sneakers and picks at the laces, her eyes wet. Now it's not her legs shaking; it's her face. Natalie Ludwig is hunkered down in her chair, inconsolable and angry at what she considers a massive letdown. Touria looks straight toward the blackboard, blank with disgust. The towel is still hanging over Ronda Jo's face, a drape against lights that seem way too bright, and against the finality. Kitty's manner is quiet and soft. She asks for comments, and Touria says that maybe

Salisbury State wanted it more. Kitty asks the players if they thought this game would be easy, since they had already beaten the Lady Gulls twice. Nobody thinks so, but Kitty wonders.

"I hate to end a year with a game when we didn't maximize our talent," Kitty said. *"I'd feel better if it was a game where we did that, and just got beat. There was a fearful attitude out there, instead of just going out there and thinking, 'I'm the best player on the floor.'"*

Suddenly Jenny is out of her seat. She is charging forward, gasping for air. Her cries sound like blasts. She rushes to the blackboard and scrawls out the words, "I'm sick of this shit," and fires the chalk to the floor and stomps out, down the hall, down the stairs, into the locker room, where she beats up a few lockers with her fist. She doesn't want any more comments. Doesn't want anything. She's sick the way she was sick the year before, knowing now as she did then that the Bison were capable of so much more, which means absolutely nothing now. She knows Ronda Jo is a player with few equals and knows how dominant Ronda can be and how explosive Touria can be, how much she and Courtney can do underneath and how Nanette keeps it all together, so why is there this horrible hollow feeling in her gut right now, instead of joy? *"We're not serious basketball players like some players are, I guess. We are more like family and friends,"* Jenny said later. She knows she could've done much more tonight and blames herself for that. So many Bison could've done more. She doesn't know what the trouble is. Are the players too easily satisfied? Too easily distracted? Do they not have the competitive toughness to grind out a victory with so much at stake, to ignore their misses and just dig in on defense and the backboards and tell themselves, "We are not going to let ourselves lose"? Or is the issue the same hideous one from last year—that somehow the Bison don't feel entitled to be champions because they're a bunch of deaf girls? Theories spin through Jenny's head. She wishes they would stop, but they don't.

"We aren't robots. We have feelings. In our hearts we know if we perform our best we can be the best, but up and down seems to be our way," Jenny said. She decides that maybe the lesson in all of this is how much it hurts to know you could've done better. Maybe, Jenny decided, she had it right that day at halftime after she'd just rejoined the team and told everyone: *"Please don't take this for granted."* Maybe that's it right there: *Don't take anything for granted. Life is not a dress rehearsal. Don't make excuses and don't be negative and don't think about what other people think you should or shouldn't be capable of. Just go out and honor yourself by doing the best you can, all the time.*

A yellow half-moon hangs over the Field House. The night is warm and inviting. Sitting in the lobby against the blue door to the gym, legs stretched out in front of her, hair still wet from the shower, Ronda Jo's gaze is almost trancelike. She is wearing her blue Kodak All-American parka. *"I feel like life is over,"* she said.

That night and beyond, Bison thoughts are a gnarled web of what-if's and if-only's. All thoughts about the season seem to lead right back to a question: What could we have done differently? In 309 Peet Hall, Courtney lies down beneath her wooden cross and feels emptier than she ever has after a season. She isn't comfortable showing emotion in front of everyone, but she got broadsided by it once she returned to her dorm room. *This is the last time this team will be together. That's it. No more season.* Courtney is a first-basewoman on the softball team and doesn't have long to wait for more competition. She still feels beseiged by hollowness. Six stories up in Clerc Hall, Touria is surrounded by photos of the twins, Jamila and Amina, and the four tapestries she's pinned up to cover the walls: purple, green, red, and yellow. Regular, dorm white was too boring, she decided, and she didn't want to have the blue and gold that you see all over campus. Her mind speeds, a fast, free association of disgust and disappointment: *I think this was my worst year and that makes me so mad. I was expecting so much more of myself and this team. I put so much pressure on that every little mistake was magnified. I have one year left, and I want to make it my best one yet, and just go out there and not think and not worry and let myself play.*

Next door, next to her tidy dresser and organized closet, every hanger going in the same direction, Nanette feels a surge of homesickness for her parents and brothers, her baby niece Abigail, and her Boston terriers, Holly and Nana. Nanette has had nine dogs, every one a Boston terrier. That's how much she likes order and familiarity. The disorder of the season is what really bothers her, as she thinks: *It seems like we were always having trouble getting our footing this year. It was as if we were on rocks. Even after we beat Capital and St. Mary's and had that stretch of really good games at the end, we would lose it again. We weren't as together as we needed to be. We didn't communicate well. We tried to take care of it by talking. It seemed to go away, but maybe it didn't completely. I know I have leadership skills, and I'm disappointed in myself that I didn't use them better, that I didn't stick up for my beliefs when I disagreed with people. If you aren't true to yourself, then where are you?*

Outside in their suite, surrounded by her spices, hot plate, and makeshift kitchen, Ronda talks with her father and sprawls on the couch, feeling betrayed by her ankle sprain, by the game she loves, by everything: *I feel like I never got started this year. How many more things can go wrong? Shanada quits and Stacy isn't happy. There are poor games and great games. I have differences with Kitty and then I feel much better and we're winning, and then we have this ending. I don't know what to think. I know we have the talent to be one of the best teams in the country, but we don't do it. I'm tired of deaf people not doing more and not proving themselves, and then we do the same thing.*

In her apartment on West Virginia Avenue, right across the street from Gallaudet and the hill that rises up to the Field House, Ronda Jo pulls up the comforter her mother made of all of her basketball T-shirts and wants to cry, but she can't. Her head is too full, her wants too many. She thinks of things possible and impossible: *I wish we could go back to the beginning of the season and be more serious and be a team. Not let anything bother us—just stick to our dream and go after it. I tried to give all I could tonight. You can only do so much on the court, but where I wish I had done more was off the court. Sometimes I hate that I am a good listener and I don't confront people. I could've been the one who pulled everyone together, who told them to QUIT doing that. I could've been tough on them or encouraged and helped us be a team. It just happened too fast. I know my life really isn't over. I have my WNBA dream and I want to give that everything I've got. I know I will learn from this. You never assume anything. You have to keep your goal alive, and keep pushing for it even when you feel like stopping. Being deaf is not going to stop me; it has nothing to do with anything I want to do. I would not change anything about myself. I am proud to be deaf.*

Shortly after the season, Alex Long wrote a column in the *Buff and Blue*. The headline was "A Love Letter." He begins:

Dear Ronda Jo,

We are writing to you while the disappointment of last week's loss probably still grips your mind. It might be easy for you to believe that you somehow let us, the community, down. I'm here to tell you how wrong that is. To thank you for bringing us pride and admiration the likes of which we likely won't be experiencing again anytime soon.

It isn't very often our obscure world known as Gallaudet gets the chance to showcase a legend in action. One of our very own, humbling opponents day in and day out. The type of special athlete with a warm, humble persona that betrays the level of her stardom. Someone who transcends the barrier of deafness which we all struggle with throughout our lifetimes into hearing world consciousness. Simply put, you, if nothing else, brought our school and your people much-needed respect . . ."

He ends:

It was an honor to be here with you. You may not want to show us pride, but when you're in private and thinking about these days, remember them as your glory years. The years when you were simply one of a kind. Unlike any other before and, no doubt, after you. Next year, it'll feel like we're watching volleyball and women's basketball for the first time again.

We'll miss you something terrible. Thank you.

Sincerely,

The Deaf World

It's noontime in the Gallaudet library, and a maintenance worker is near the back of the stacks, running a vacuum cleaner. The vacuum runs regularly during the school day at the Merrill Learning Center, not bothering anybody. At the reference desk, a librarian is assisting two students who are working on a research paper, the conversation in ASL, the paper *on* ASL. They depart with a small pile of books and walk across the green to the Ely Center, which is in full midday swing, the open-air space full of diners and signers, fingers moving, hands flashing, faces gesturing.

For the Bison, the disappointment of the season's end gradually recedes, and the rhythms of their lives on Kendall Green return. There are papers to write, parties to go to, summer plans to make. Nanette arranges a trip to Oklahoma and maybe Texas. Touria will go to Greece for a training camp with the Sweden's national women's deaf team and go home to see her parents and the twins. Ronda Jo gets a letter from Renee Brown of the WNBA, inviting her to the league's predraft camp in Chicago in late April of 2000. She is the only Division III player in the country invited. Natalie will go to a work/study program at Duke University, and Kitty will begin preparations and hold tryouts for the U.S. national team that she will coach in the Deaf Olympics in 2001 in Rome. It will keep her three-decade record intact; she still won't need a whistle. Kitty's already dreading the impossible emotional conflict of coaching against Touria, who will be competing in the Deaf Olympics for Sweden for the third time. "It's going to be a lose-lose proposition," Kitty said. "If I try something I think will work against her and it *does* works, I'll feel guilty. If I don't try anything against her and she beats us, I'll feel lousy."

The distaste for the way the season ended stays with Kitty longer than anybody else. She is reminded of her own cautionary words to the players before the season began: The only constant in life is change. We're all different from how we were six months ago. We have to start fresh with this season and construct another season game by game, the same way we'd put together a building, brick by brick.

Kitty was right: There are no guarantees.

Kitty rarely stopped worrying about her dad, fighting to reclaim his body and his language. She was stung by The Incident. She never quite found a way to close the gap between Bison words and Bison deeds. When she got home on the last night of the season, she found Dale, her thirteen-year-old dog, gravely ill. Dale never recovered and had to be put to sleep. "Sometimes it felt like it was one disaster after another," Kitty said. It was a while before she was in a place to sit at home in front of a candle and take in the good parts, because there were a lot of them, too. The players showed a ton of guts rescuing the season the way they did. There were the stirring performances against Capital and

St. Mary's, and many others in the late-season run. There was Cassey's spirit and Touria's courage, Courtney's progress and gentle manner, Natalie's passionate pursuit of perfection, in everything. Ronda made her laugh, as always, and if she frustrated Kitty, she also showed her a whole lot by coming to her house that night and owning her mistakes the way she did. Stacy didn't get the minutes she wanted, but she was proud and strong and cared deeply. There were sweet times on warm buses, funny times in too many fast-food places. There was also the gift of her three lovely seniors, Jenny and Nanette and Ronda Jo, who have brought so much richness and joy into her life over four years, to say nothing of victories. Jenny is as passionate and honest a player as Gallaudet has had in a long time. Nanette is as overachieving a player as Gallaudet has had in a long time. Ronda Jo? Well, how often is the greatest player you've ever coached also the most humble player you've ever coached? Kitty loves Ronda Jo for that, for so many things, for never changing, for doing Gallaudet proud, for being so magnificently reliable, the same way Nanette and Jenny were, each in her own way.

When they arrived four years earlier, nobody knew that Gallaudet women's basketball was beginning its greatest era and that people far beyond Kendall Green would begin to find out about the only deaf women's college team in the world and its laconic star, Ronda Jo Miller. "I remember the first day I saw her at practice," Ben Baylor said. "I could see she was an athlete and that she had skills, but I was thinking, 'Can this skinny kid really help us?'" Ronda Jo dominated from the start. "I never underestimated her again," Ben said.

It is another springlike day on Kendall Green, forsythia blooming yellow and bright, grass awakening green from its brown winter slumber. The air is warm, the wind soft. The semester is winding down, and campus tours are heating up, knots of prospective students and their parents crossing Florida Avenue and passing through the iron fence and heading up the little hill, into the only university in the world where students listen with their eyes and speak with their hands; where you enter a room not with a knock, but a flash of a light; where pagers rule and deafness is an alternate hearing style, but not a disability.

The visitors take in the Victorian splendor of Chapel Hall and an exhibit commemorating Deaf President Now, and they might even get to meet I. King Jordan, Gallaudet's first deaf president. They see the goateed visage of the school's founder, Edward Miner Gallaudet, and pass the majestic buildings behind him, with slate roofs and spires, and the prosaic ones ahead of him, brick boxes that look as if they came out of a kit. They pass the rambling corridors of the Ely Center and see the quietest lunchroom in America and maybe catch the view of the Capitol and the Washington Monument from the upper floors of Hall Memorial Building. They are surrounded by two thousand students and ten Bison women who, like any other group of college students, have good days and bad days, but mostly feel blessed to be in their bilingual haven in northeast Washington, where they are together and empowered, not on the murky margins of hearing culture, but in the center of their own.

The players on the Gallaudet women's basketball team have no desire to hear, and no use for people who want to fix them. They aren't in denial about the pain they've experienced because of their deafness. They don't dispute that there are issues related to being closed out of the world of sound, gaps in their knowledge and development that are as inevitable as lobbying in Washington; that's how it is when you can't overhear anything, can't hear sirens or standing ovations, can't pick up a thousand little pieces of aural information from the world around you. They move forward with their lives anyway.

The tour continues over to the library and the dorms and the Field House. Downstairs, three guys are taking turns grunting beneath a loaded bench-press bar in the fitness room. Upstairs, music is blasting from a dance studio, the bass deep and pounding, an aerobics class dancing to the feeling of the beat. About fifty yards away, in the gymnasium, a solitary, ponytailed woman is dribbling the length of the court, full of vertical grace. The guide explains that it is Ronda Jo Miller, All-American, who is getting ready for the WNBA predraft camp in Chicago. The visitors are led to the west, past the front entrance of campus, and the gatehouse, until they find themselves standing before a statue. It is Daniel Chester French's one-hundred-thirteen-year-old work of Thomas Hopkins Gallaudet, the itinerant preacher turned educator of the deaf, and Alice Cogswell, the nine-year-old Connecticut girl who was his first pupil. This is the part of the tour where Stacy Nowak, the former guide, used to say, "Without them, none of us would be here."

The visitors look intently at Alice. She is beginning her education with the first letter of her name, Thomas Hopkins Gallaudet showing her the manual letter A, and Alice replicating it. Her little girl's face is rich with hope and possibility, with the wonder of a world opening up before her. It is opening up still on Kendall Green, where the Bison of Gallaudet University call themselves deaf and wouldn't want it any other way.

EPILOGUE

GALLAUDET UNIVERSITY WAS chartered by President Abraham Lincoln in 1864 and has been serving students who are deaf and hard-of-hearing ever since. It has never endured a more painful period than the 2000–2001 school year. Students, professors, and administrators were accustomed to, and proud of, the university's position as a mecca of deaf culture and education. Nobody was prepared for Kendall Green to be a crime scene, or for the daily campus dialogue to include a strange and horrible question: Anything new on the murders?

On the night of September 28, 2000, freshman Eric Plunkett, 19, was found bludgeoned to death in his room on the first floor of a dormitory named for Alice Cogswell. Four months passed, and the fear that rampaged through campus in the immediate aftermath of the crime slowly abated, despite the fact that no suspects had been apprehended. Then, in the predawn hours of February 3, 2001, Gallaudet's two thousand students were rocked anew. Another 19-year-old freshman, Benjamin Varner, had been stabbed to death in his room. It happened in the same wing of Cogswell Hall. Pagers began vibrating all over campus and in deaf communities around the country, the news grisly and fast-spreading.

"I felt like it couldn't happen at Gallaudet," Amelia England said. *"Maybe at another college. Not at Gallaudet."*

Ten days after the second murder, in the university auditorium police interpreters disclosed that Joseph Mesa, a fellow freshman and Cogswell Hall resident from Guam, had confessed to the crimes. There was a palpable sense of relief around campus that the alleged murderer was no longer at large. Students were eager to go back to thinking of Gallaudet as an oasis of inclusion and open communication. Still, it was jarring to think that a deaf person could murder another deaf person. Nobody has ever claimed the deaf have moral superiority over hearing people—indeed, many students abhor the stereotypical depiction of deaf people as benign, helpless souls—but this cut deeply just the same.

Nanette Virnig says the murders left her more scared than she has been in her life. *"I couldn't sleep in my bedroom (for a while),"* she said. *"I had to stay with a friend. I was just imagining too much. When I finally went back to my room, I walked around the suite and all the rooms twice before I went to bed, and I still couldn't sleep."*

By the close of the school year, much of the grief and the sense of violation had been processed. The memories of Eric Plunkett and Ben Varner were tastefully invoked at commencement. There were posters and tributes to them, and sensitive words from President King Jordan. More closure came a full year later, in the spring of 2002, when a jury in Washington D.C., Superior Court found Mesa guilty of premeditated murder. On July 10, 2002, Mesa, 22, was sentenced to two life-without-parole terms.

As for the Bison of 1999–2000, they moved on in a variety of directions:

Courtney Westberg played her first full year with the team, earning a starting role and a spot on the U.S. national team, which competed in the Deaflympics in Rome in the summer of 2001, coached by Kitty Baldridge. Cassey Ellis completed her sophomore season and also played for Kitty in Rome. Ronda Johnson and Stacy Nowak came back for their final year of basketball in 2000, but both had lingering differences with Kitty and wound up quitting the team in December. Ronda returned to play for Kitty in Rome and, after graduating with honors, Stacy played for the U.S. volleyball team in Rome, with fellow graduate Shanada Johnson. The U.S. women's volleyball team won the silver medal.

Natalie Ludwig made the Deaflympics in track and field. To train for the games and improve her aerobic conditioning, she chose to compete for the Gallaudet swim team rather than the basketball team in her sophomore year. Still a bit short of completing her degree, Jenny Cooper was another U.S. basketball player in Rome. Amelia England had a busy year in the nets as the goalkeeper for the Gallaudet women's soccer team, her goal to be the first person in her family with a college degree.

Nanette Virnig worked as assistant coach on the Bison softball team, earned her B.A. in Elementary Education, and then returned to her old school, Minnesota State Academy for the Deaf, to teach middle-school math and coach the girls' basketball team. Nanette had a great group of girls and completed the 2001–2002 season with an 11–10 record and the stunning self-realization of how little patience she has for poor officiating: *"I never use my voice, and I actually screamed at the referees with my very high-pitched voice at one of our games,"* she said. *"I tried to control myself, but I couldn't because they kept on making bad calls."*

When Touria Ouahid graduated in May, 2001, she pumped her arms as she strode across the commencement stage in the Field House, hugging King Jordan so hard she almost snapped him in two. *"I didn't mean to hurt him. I was just so happy,"* she said.

Touria returned home to Stockholm and competed in her third Deaf-lympics for Sweden. In the gold-medal game against her old coach and a roster full of her friends, Touria and her teammates lost a hard-fought contest, 60–58. Touria had a chance to tie it in the closing seconds, but her layup rolled off. The gold medal was one of the highlights of Kitty's coaching career, but impossibly bittersweet; the spectacle of Touria crying after the defeat was more than she could take.

"It broke my heart," Kitty said. "I knew it was going to be hard coaching against her. It turned out to be much worse than I thought it would be."

Touria returned to the Washington, D.C., area later that summer and embarked on a coaching career of her own in the fall of 2002, having been hired to be the girls' varsity coach for the Model Secondary School for the Deaf on the Gallaudet campus. Stacy Nowak, back at Gallaudet as a graduate student, was considering being Touria's assistant coach.

Six weeks after her final college game against Salisbury State, Ronda Jo Miller went to Chicago for the WNBA pre-draft camp. Kitty accompanied her as an interpreter. The lone Division III player among the one-hundred-plus players there, she performed creditably, but when draft day came, her name was not called. For one of the first times in her basketball life, Ronda Jo felt that her deafness had worked against her. She thought her performance warranted an invitation to an individual team camp to try out.

"I don't think they took me seriously," she said.

"She was more down about that than anything that has happened to her in a long time," Dolly Miller said.

Ronda Jo wound up joining a startup league, the Women's National Basketball League, playing with the Kansas City franchise. After competing as a volleyball player in Rome, she was contacted by a pro-basketball team in Denmark—and reported there immediately after the Games. She had no interpreter, no friends, and not even a vague familiarity with the country.

"I wasn't worried about that. I just wanted to play basketball," Ronda Jo said.

Starting as forward for Alliancen Herlev, a team based near Copenhagen, Ronda Jo scored 34 points and had 8 rebounds in her professional debut, and hardly let up thereafter. Averaging better than 20 points and 12 rebounds per game, Ronda Jo led her team to the league championship. Her coach, Claus Stroh, initially had deep reservations about having a deaf player on the team. He feared that Ronda Jo would require so much special attention that it would be disruptive to practices and team unity. By the end of the season, Stroh was delighted to report how wrong he had been. The team provided an interpreter, and Ronda Jo's teammates were quick to pick up a few basic signs. Between that and her ample lip-reading skills, Ronda Jo had few difficulties, communication or otherwise.

"Ronda Jo is one of the finest players I have ever coached," Stroh said.

In April 2002, toward the end of her Danish season, Ronda Jo took a few days off and flew to Vancouver, Washington, for the Northwest International Exposure Camp—a chance to be seen by about a dozen WNBA teams. Ronda Jo played superbly—and was rewarded by an invitation to try out for the Washington Mystics from the team's new coach, Marianne Stanley. She would have been ecstatic about interest from any team, but getting it from one that plays about two miles from the Gallaudet Field House was almost too much to ask for.

Ronda Jo reported to training camp in late April, undaunted by the prospect of playing against the premier women players in the world. She played with unstinting energy and enthusiasm, and more polish and fundamental soundness than ever before, the hard-earned residue of a full year of pro ball. Physically stronger and more confident, she moved with an assurance she did not have in the pre-draft camp twelve months prior.

"She's improved a lot in the last calendar year," Stanley said, standing on the edge of the MCI Center court while Ronda Jo engaged Chamique Holdsclaw, the Mystics' star forward, in an impromptu sign-language lesson during a preseason shoot-around. "I think what she's doing is pretty remarkable. For her to get to a place where she's on the bubble for making the league says an awful lot about her strength of character. You need that warrior mentality to make it in this league, and she's got it."

Midway through training camp, the Mystics played a home game against the New York Liberty. An estimated 500 people from Gallaudet turned out, including King Jordan in the first-row courtside, and Kitty Baldridge not far beind. When she was introduced and ran onto the court before the game, Ronda Jo saw deaf people in every direction, standing and stomping, holding up signs, raising their arms and waggling their fingers.

"It meant so much to see so many people from Gallaudet," she said later.

Ronda Jo was with the Mystics until the last round of cuts. Marianne Stanley called Ronda Jo and her interpreter in and said they were going to go with more experienced inside players. The coach thanked her, and urged her to go back overseas and to keep on working on her game.

"I was surprised they let me go," Ronda Jo said. *"I really thought I had a good chance to make the team."* She felt adrift, sad, and confused. It was strange to wake up the next day and not have a practice or game to go to. Still, there was no denying the positive side of the experience. Stanley, who would coach the Mystics to the WNBA's Eastern Conference finals, was tremendously impressed by Ronda Jo and believes she can make the league if she stays with it.

Ronda Jo had three offers to play overseas, but as the fall of 2002 arrived, she was still in the United States, teaching American Sign Language at Metropolitan State College in Denver, Colorado, and living in nearby Lakewood with a friend. She also agreed to be an assistant coach to a hearing high school team. She was playing regularly, finding the best competition possible, and wasn't ruling out the possibility of going back overseas early in 2003.

The training camps for the 2003 WNBA season open in May. Ronda Jo Miller is confident she will be with a team somewhere.

"I know I can't give up," she said. *"I just have to keep pushing. I really believe I have the ability to make it and I know if I do that it will make a huge impact, not just on my life, but in the way people look at deaf people. I really want to make sure that dream comes true, and I believe it will."*

ACKNOWLEDGMENTS

I N THE SPRING of 1999, I descended on the lives of the Gallaudet University women's basketball team and remained there for close to two years. Coach Kitty Baldridge and her staff and players were kind and welcoming from the start, and stayed that way till the end. Their warmth, cooperation and good humor were without limit. They made me feel part of the team. Without their trust and patience, this book never would have happened. To merely say thank you here doesn't seem nearly enough.

Mary Thumann, my interpreter for the entire project, was no less patient and hospitable. They told me I was getting the best, and they were right. Sue Tyler, of Gallaudet Interpreting Services, accommodated my needs and made sure Mary was available.

Many others in the Gallaudet community extended help, support, and expertise, and they have my profound gratitude as well. President King

Jordan offered his time and encouragement. Athletic director Richard Pelletier said he would assist in any way he could, and he did. Mercy Coogan, the university's director of public relations, was a major help throughout, and so was Robert (Skip) Williams, who was by turns a sounding board/basketball fan/seasoned observer/friend. Dwight Benedict and the staff of the Campus Life Office were always ready with a room and a key, even when I didn't provide adequate notice. Ben Baylor and Hillel Goldberg generously gave assistance and companionship, and made room in the front of the bus. Donalda Ammons, John Vickrey Van Cleve, M. J. Bienvenu, Jay Lucker, Mary Anne Pugin, Nancy Carroll, and Carrie Palmer all shared their expertise, their offices, their classrooms. Sue Hotto and Robert Johnson of Gallaudet Research Institute were armed with all sorts of valuable information, and offered it freely. Bob Johnson skillfully explained the nuances of American Sign Language to a manual neophyte. In Clerc Hall, my home away from home, Thomas Koch and Karl Ewan kept me in sheets and towels, just as Chris Kaftan and Alex Long of the *Buff and Blue,* the Gallaudet student paper, kept me current with clips, insights, and suggestions. Ernie Young behind the wheel and Maria Danso behind the desk in the Phys Ed department were gracious mainstays through the season, as were Paulina Wlostowski, Chuck Rubisch, Ronnie Zuchegno, and Jean Buchanan.

Madeleine Blais, writer, journalism professor at the University of Massachusetts, and author of the wonderful *In These Girls Hope Is A Muscle* and *Uphill Walkers,* generously shared her wisdom as I was getting started. Leon Carter, Adam Berkowitz, Teri Thompson, and Peter Barzilai, estimable front office of the New York *Daily News* sports section, were hugely supportive, but one reason they are such good people to work for.

The families of the Bison players were as helpful and delightful as their daughters; special thanks to John and Dolly Miller; Brent and Marcia Nowak; Wayne and Dottie Westberg; Sherry Ellis and Ronald Johnson. Andrew Stuart, full-service literary agent, helped conceptualize the book before he sold it. Charles Euchner always saw the possibilities and did what dear friends do, lending encouragement and unsparing honesty. Ed Dowling accentuated the positive for a lot of years. Reverend Paul De Hoff and my friends at Union Church of Pocantico Hills provided spiritual nourishment and a wonderful cubbyhole in the basement. I wrote to the sound of bells. It was a blessing.

Pete Fornatale wasn't just a skillful editor; he was a kindred spirit, a big believer, and a pleasure to work with. His namesake and father is a giant in New York City radio history, the disk jockey of my youth. Pete the younger is no less a talent. Thanks also to the entire team at Crown, especially Dorianne Steele and Susan Westendorf.

My bride, Denise Willi, put up with an absentee husband and father, an Amtraking nomad, and never stopped encouraging the whole process. She knew when the author needed a boot in the pants before the author did. Alexandra, Sean, and Samantha are the three greatest gifts from God a man could ever have. You are my team, and my inspiration.

ABOUT THE AUTHOR

WAYNE COFFEY is a sportswriter with the *Daily News* (New York) whose work, across nearly two decades, has made him among the premier sports feature writers in the nation. A former girls high school basketball coach, he has been honored by the Associated Press Sports Editors and the U.S. Basketball Writers Association, as well as by the American Library Association and the New York Public Library, both of which hailed one of his previous nonfiction titles, *When Your Parent Drinks Too Much,* as one of the best young-adult books of the year. He lives in the Hudson Valley with his wife and three children.